STAUBACH ON . . .

TOM LANDRY: "To me he was, is and always will be special—a man apart from other men."

CLINT LONGLEY: "The most unpleasant chapter of my NFL career."

THOMAS HENDERSON: "His failure with the Cowboys was a simple case of self-destruction."

WINNING: "At the professional level, there is no substitute for winning."

CHILDREN: "It's easy to tell children the ideal way to do things, but I always remember if I don't try to live that way and do those things, they won't either."

FAITH: "Faith is the *only* answer to things we can't understand about God's eternal plan."

TIME ENOUGH TO WIN

ROGER STAUBACH
with Frank Luksa

WARNER BOOKS

A Warner Communications Company

WARNER BOOKS EDITION

Copyright © 1980 by Word, Incorporated, Waco, Texas
All rights reserved.

This Warner Books Edition is published by arrangement
with Word, Incorporated, 4800 West Waco Drive, Waco, Texas 76703.

Cover photo by Frank Munson

Warner Books, Inc., 75 Rockefeller Plaza, New York, N.Y. 10019

W A Warner Communications Company

Printed in the United States of America

First Printing: September, 1981

10 9 8 7 6 5 4 3 2 1

Acknowledgments

To my teammates, coaches, and good friends throughout my career on and off the field, I offer my thanks and gratitude. Life has been comforting, fulfilling and satisfying because of the people I have played with and shared with.

Contents

Prologue

He said it during postgame interviews and reporters thought it was a priceless quote. How typical of him to gloss the sting of the moment with a dry one-liner. He was kidding, of course.

He repeated the words to a cluster of friends as he exited the player's gate at Texas Stadium. All of them laughed. It broke the tension. It made sympathizing with him easier. Like the reporters, they knew he wasn't serious.

Moments later, he said it one more time. Somewhere along the homeward-bound drive he turned to his wife, Marianne, and their three oldest daughters. "Can you believe after all these years I completed my last pass to Herb Scott?" he asked.

This was no joke to Roger Staubach. Marianne knew

it, but to what degree her husband was serious she remained uncertain. The girls—Jennifer, Michelle and Stephanie, ages 10 to 13—were startled. They realized their father enjoyed his put-on moments. But words like "last pass" sounded serious and, well, sort of final.

"Are you kidding, Dad?" they asked, because they'd never heard him talk like this before.

"I've thought a lot about retirement," he told them. "There is a chance I'm going to retire this year."

Thus, a twin pall enveloped Staubach on the evening of December 30, 1979. The bitter aftertaste of defeat mingled with sad, resigned knowledge that there would be no next time or next year. And for a final memory, something of a career epitaph, he had left them laughing, of all things. On the Cowboys' last series he'd tried to ground a pass but instead sailed it directly into the bellybutton of Scott, a guard and a quite ineligible receiver. Guffaws and titters filled the stadium as an official walked off the 15-yard penalty.

Fate saved its last trump card for Staubach. His became an incongruous, ironic farewell to the Dallas Cowboys and National Football League after 11 glorious seasons. Dallas lost to the Los Angeles Rams 21–19 as the Cowboys so often won with Staubach—on a 50-yard touchdown pass in the game's final two minutes. Vince Ferragamo's completion to Billy Waddy settled the National Conference playoff with lightning-bolt suddenness.

"It's like running into a brick wall," said Staubach, speaking for the stunned losers. "All of a sudden everything stops."

In his case it was game, set and match: game, season and career. And to think it had ended with such an O. Henry twist. The player who helped win two Super Bowls, the arm which just claimed its fourth League passing title,

10

the talent which placed him No. 1 among all-time NFL quarterbacks wrapped it up by slipping on a banana peel. To laugh or to cry, that was the question.

That Staubach would fail when faced with a brick wall shocked him as much as it did the spectators. Just two weeks earlier on the same spot he'd worked a miraculous rally against Washington. Trailing 34–21 with four minutes left, he'd fashioned a 35–34 victory for the NFC East championship.

"He was super," Coach Tom Landry said afterward. "What can you say about a guy who's done it so many times?"

Those last-chance situations were Staubach's finest hour, or two minutes. He brought the Cowboys from behind to win 21 games in the fourth quarter, 14 of them in the last two minutes or overtime. No NFL quarterback, past or present, could match those figures. With Roger the Cowboys knew everything was possible. Especially the impossible.

The 1979 season had increased their belief. They'd seen him position Rafael Septien for a field goal that beat St. Louis 22–21 with 1:16 left to play. They watched him call Tony Hill off the sideline to catch a screen pass touchdown that clipped Chicago 24–20 with 1:57 on the clock. They whooped when he produced 10 points in less than two minutes for a 16–14 victory over the New York Giants that climaxed with 0:03 remaining. Then he capped everything with that preposterous rally against Washington on a pass to Hill with 0:39 to go.

Four times Staubach rescued the Cowboys and more than any single player influenced their 11–5 finish. His teammates felt that the game wasn't over until Roger said so. If Dallas was behind at the final gun, tight end Billy Joe DuPree remembered that he never gave the word.

11

"The one thing that will always stand out in my mind about Roger is that he never knew when it was over," Dupree said. "At the end of a game, even if we're down by 20 points, he'll be standing there by himself trying to figure out a way we can win it."

The enemy knew those traits as well as the Cowboys. "There wasn't a player on the Cowboys, offensive or defensive, who didn't look to him and think, 'As long as we have Roger we have a chance to win this thing,'" said St. Louis coach Jim Hanifan. "That's a real tribute to him. I know this. The opposition thought that way, too."

It was through their secondaries that Staubach set all of the Cowboys' major passing records: most attempts (2,958), completions (1,685), yards (22,700), and touchdowns (153). His career completion percentage was a brilliant 57.0. Under its formula for ranking all-time passers, the NFL lists Staubach No. 1 with an 83.5 rating. Below him rank the gloried and storied names of the game: Jurgensen, Dawson, Tarkenton, Unitas, Graham, Starr, Van Brocklin, Luckman, Tittle.

"When you talk about great quarterbacks Roger has to stand alongside Graham and Unitas, all the ones I can recall," said Landry from a perspective of 30 years as player/coach in the NFL. "Mainly because he was such a consistent performer and one of the great, two-minute clutch players like Bobby Layne in his prime. I don't know of any quarterback I've played against or watched that I'd rather have than Roger."

Most of all Staubach was a winner. Through Purcell High School in Cincinnati, one year at New Mexico Military Institute, four at the Naval Academy and 11 with Dallas, he played for only one losing team. Almost as a harbinger of his NFL fade-out with the pass to Scott, the nonwinning season was his senior year at Navy in 1964.

He'd won the Heisman Trophy in '63 but hopes of becoming the first two-time honoree was dashed by an injury plague.

As a professional he won regular season games at a remarkable .746 (85–29) clip. The Cowboys never were shut out behind Staubach and only twice during his starting reign ever lost more than two consecutive games. In playoffs his record was 11–6, the most significant victories those in Super Bowls VI and XII. He always lost grudgingly, but more so in postseason. Four of those six defeats were by a combined margin of 12 points: to Los Angeles at the divisional level, 14–12 ('76) and 21–19 ('79); to Pittsburgh in tingling Super Bowls X and XIII, 21–17 and 35–31.

Largely because of Staubach the Cowboys became the NFL's winningest team during the 1970s. He finished eight of those years as their No. 1 quarterback beginning in 1971 when he wrested control from Craig Morton at midseason. The exceptions were in 1970 when he still understudied Morton and in 1972, a regular season lost via a shoulder injury following a stubborn collision with a Rams linebacker during an exhibition game.

His eight-year legacy is virtually pure championship. Dallas captured its division title six times, the last four in succession. Only once, in 1974, did Staubach fail to qualify the Cowboys for the playoffs. But he followed that 8–6 season with a year that Landry still considers Roger's greatest. Infused by the enthusiasm of 12 rookies and armed by a daring return to the shotgun formation, the Cowboys of '75 became the only wild card team ever to become a Super Bowl finalist.

Facts and figures carry only so much impact. Then the numbers begin to blur and lose their meaning. One measure of Staubach is to underline that at the end of the eight full seasons he played, his teams competed for the world championship four times. To hit .500 as a Super Bowl contestant over a career may be the most telling statistic of all.

Along the way he earned multiple individual honors, among them an unprecedented triple of Heisman Trophy (1963) and Maxwell Trophy (1964) in college, and the Bert Bell Award (1971) at the NFL level. Each is symbolic of player-of-the-year status. In 1971 he also was named Most Valuable Player in Super Bowl VI and winner of the Vince Lombardi Award, the only trophy on which the late Green Bay coach authorized use of his name. Four times Staubach was chosen to the All-National Conference team by writers and broadcasters. Five times voting by players and coaches sent him to the Pro Bowl.

Yet one curiosity overhangs his NFL deeds. Staubach never was named All-Pro. The closest he came was second-team mention by the Pro Football Writers in '71. When his five-year mandatory wait has expired and he is announced as a Pro Football Hall of Fame enshrinee, the invitation may be extended with an overdue apology.

Fellow players recognized his ability better than did the writers and announcers. Prior to the 1978 season five All-Pro defenders, among them long-time Staubach opponents Bill Bergey of Philadelphia and Ken Houston of Washington, selected Roger as the NFL's best quarterback.

What the nation's teenagers knew about Staubach they also liked— better than anyone. He was No.1 with them, the country's favorite sports personality among boys and girls 13–18 years old, according to an early 1980 Gallup Poll. In Dallas his popularity was beyond measure. However, one yardstick was an annual Favorite Cowboys Contest sponsored by a local dairy. Staubach won it six times.

If the quarterback was aware of these honors, oddi-ties and accolades as he fluffed a post-Rams game pillow that night, they didn't ease his mind. He passed a fitful night. He awoke next morning with the same thought churning internally: "I don't think I'll play again."

Marianne Staubach would hear those words repeated around their sprawling, contemporary home in north Dallas for the next three months. Privately she wondered if he would be able to withstand the pressures that would con-spire to alter his decision. It wasn't that she didn't know her man. Not at all.

This was the man she first remembered as a boy when they were fourth-grade classmates in a Catholic school in Cincinnati. The one who was squawking, "Polly want a cracker?" and getting in trouble with the teacher. The same kid who lived about a half-mile up the street.

This was the husband she married in September, 1965. The one freshly graduated as the Naval Academy's greatest athlete with seven varsity letters in football, bas-ketball and baseball. The fellow who proposed marriage just in time, because after two years of nursing in intensive care units at Good Samaritan Hospital she was thinking of leaving Cincinnati if he didn't.

This was the father of their five living children. To him she had borne Jennifer, Michelle, Stephanie, Jeffrey and Amy. There had been another child. Another girl. Another they called Amy and buried as Baby Girl Staubach in March, 1971. Inexplicably, she was stillborn.

So this man and Marianne had shared moments of supreme personal happiness. They also had cried together in times of grief. There had been more of those than the public knew. Roger's father, Robert, died in May, 1970, from diabetes and its complications. Less than a year later there were graveside rites for the baby. Then, after a long and painful battle against cancer, her final months spent in their home with Marianne at her bedside, Elizabeth (Betty) Staubach lost her fight for life in December, 1973.

Marianne knew him well, yet . . . he was a man who could still fool her with a tease. True, he'd told her as early as the previous October, "There's a chance I won't play anymore." But that had been when both were worried over what happened in Pittsburgh. Steelers defensive end L. C. Greenwood had hit Roger so hard that Sunday afternoon.

It was an accidental but fearful collision. Roger was back to pass and tried to run. Knocked off balance he was stumbling forward at the line of scrimmage. Coming from the side Greenwood drove the top of his helmet into the left earhole of Staubach's headgear. Roger went down with a concussion. It was one of five he suffered during the season. It was the sixth he'd experienced within a calendar year dating to the '78 playoff against Atlanta.

The aftereffects were scary. As Staubach fought his way out of sideline grogginess he drew upon enough consciousness to realize this knockout was different. His left arm and hand were numb. So was his face.

But on the subject of injury and how much it might bother him, Roger was capable of camouflage even to Marianne. He never complained of headache, nausea or even mild discomfort. His references to injury were purposely light and, in retrospect, hilarious. Such was his protective device which had been sharply honed against reporters sniffing out a topic he chose not to explore. He would mislead or deflect their questions with a put-away quip.

For instance, a few days before making retirement official, Staubach's secretary, Roz Cole, said she had a medical writer for the Washington *Post* on long-distance hold. The writer wished to confirm her story which was to read that repeated concussions were forcing the quarterback out of the game.

"Tell her I can't talk to her now," Staubach instructed. "Tell her I can't because my head is bothering me."

To a how-do-you-feel? inquiry after his knockouts, the typical Staubach reply was, "Oh, I'm OK, but the telephone keeps ringing."

Frankly, there were occasions when Marianne didn't fare much better.

"A long time ago, his first or second year with the Cowboys, he got knocked out," she recalled. "We were new to pro football, and driving home after the game I said to him, 'Well, did they check you really good before you left the locker room?' He said, 'No, they didn't do a thing.'

"I said, 'I think they should have checked you a little better.' I was thinking medically, it being a head injury. I can remember we were just getting off the expressway by our house and he said, 'Well, Marianne, if I die tonight, get a really good lawyer.'

"All night long I kept thinking, 'Is he breathing?' Head injuries worried me. They worried me a lot."

The night Roger returned from Pittsburgh she expressed deep concern. Normal wifely anxiety was magnified by her nursing background. Therefore, Marianne was ultrasensitive about head injuries in a sensible, straightforward manner.

"I really think you need to see a neurologist or neurosurgeon," she told her husband. "I don't know a lot about this type of thing. Just enough to know it's bad. How do we know the next time it happens you aren't going to be a vegetable?"

"Oh, which do you prefer . . . broccoli or asparagus?" asked Roger.

This time his attempted humor misfired. "That is *not* funny," Marianne snapped. "I didn't bargain to raise these five kids alone."

It was Marianne who wore the I-told-you-so look the next morning. Roger returned home from the practice field with a somber report. The Cowboys were sending him to a neurologist that afternoon for precautionary tests. He would be cleared to continue playing but neither would forget the episode.

Part of it, however, escaped Staubach's memory. He doesn't remember Marianne's "didn't bargain to raise five kids" remark. Informed of this memory lapse of her husband, Marianne was none too surprised.

"He doesn't remember, huh?" she smiled. "Well, that's how bad his head injury was."

In time Roger did ask Marianne's opinion as to whether he should play on. A pert and pretty 5–3 blonde, she was out front with her views. She would advise on the subject but issue no ultimatums. Only he could consent not to play.

"I really wanted him to retire. I was ready for him to retire," she admits when looking back. "The head injuries bothered me although in all honesty I know he would not have retired if that had been the only reason. I told him that. But I never told him to quit.

"I also said if he wanted to play another year that was fine. I know it sounds wishy-washy. Yet I knew if I really pressured him to retire and he wasn't comfortable with the decision, if he did it 'because Marianne is upset about the head injuries,' and 'Marianne is tired of the pressures of football,' he wouldn't be happy. Then it would be a terrible burden to live with."

Coach Landry and Cowboys president-general manager Tex Schramm were next to know that Staubach's retirement plan was serious. The quarterback told them prior to leaving for Hawaii and the January 27 Pro Bowl game there.

"I want you to know this didn't have anything to do with the last game," said Staubach. "Nor is it an emotional thing. I'm thinking seriously about retiring. There is a 90 percent chance I will. You need to know about it now so you can make your plans accordingly for next season."

Neither tried to argue with Staubach. Each knew of his stubborn streak. Once Staubach's mind was fixed on an objective he could be intractable. Schramm and Landry saw this characteristic on the playing field in the way he quested for victory and resisted defeat. To dispute what they hoped would only be a flirtation with retirement might have lost him on the spot.

But gentle persuasion? That avenue was open. Each in his own way would attempt this oblique approach. Landry would tell him he was too good to quit. Schramm would tell him he was too young. They wouldn't fail through lack of an attempt.

Staubach had one last football formality on his playing card, the Pro Bowl. He started for the National Conference which was coached by Landry. It would be their last game together and a forgettable one for Roger. Mentally distracted, he played poorly, completing only three of 10 passes for nine yards.

"They elected me team captain and I couldn't even win the coin toss," he capsuled at game's end.

Back in Dallas Staubach sought counsel to remove that last 10 percent of doubt in his mind. A visit from Father Joseph Ryan was the near-clincher. Father Ryan and Staubach first met during Roger's Plebe Summer at the Naval Academy. Recently retired as a Navy captain, the priest had remained close to the player for the next 20 years. Their relationship eventually deepened into almost father-son richness.

When Staubach mentioned his slight indecision, Father Ryan proposed a possible solution. They would list the positive aspects of playing in one column of a sheet of paper and the negatives in another. Then they would compare and see which way the scales tipped.

Among the negative factors were, of course, the head injuries. But there were many, many more. As Staubach talked Father Ryan made notes from his conversation.

"I like the idea of being able to live a life where you aren't always in a bubble with people looking at you constantly," said Roger. "The game creates that attention which is good to a certain degree. It shows people are concerned about you. But it still creates kind of a monster as far as the demands.

"With five children it comes to the point where they need their own identity. They don't need to be Roger Staubach's children. And I don't need to be somebody who is constantly in demand. I just can't do it anymore. I have a hard time saying no, so I get put into situations where I'm not around my children as much as I should be. All of that has increased with the success of our team.

"I wouldn't be thinking about this if I were 32 years old unless we'd won eight Super Bowls in a row or something like that. As a matter of fact, I'd be playing at 38. Is it worth it to play just one more year?"

Before Father Ryan could reply, Staubach answered his own question. He admitted feeling the first flicker in what always had been a blowtorch competitive spirit. The backstage tedium of pro football— offseason workouts, quarterback school and training camp—had become just that for him. He couldn't gear up mentally to participate in the all-consuming way that set him apart.

"When that mundane routine gets to you, it's not a good sign," he admitted. "The routine of football is something veteran players are fighting all the time. I've started to fight it. The idea of the offseason program and knowing I'd have to rush to the practice field at 3:30 every afternoon starting in April. . . . And then going away from home for five weeks to camp in the summer. I dread it. I couldn't stand being away again for five weeks.

"At the beginning of your career, training camps are a bit easier because you're fighting for a job. You're headed toward new ventures in football. It's such an important time, too, getting ready for the regular season. But there's that routine. And after a long time I guess you just get tired of it."

Father Ryan's list of negatives was complete: 1) a desire for more time with family, less for football and the public; 2) diminished zest for the rigors of preparing to play; 3) the potential health risk.

On the positive side there was a single entry. Staubach's skills showed no signs of deterioration. At age 37 he'd become only the fourth quarterback in NFL history to win consecutive passing titles. So opposite the negatives Father Ryan wrote, "Can still pass better than all the young 'uns."

Then the priest observed, "Roger, the negatives seem to outweigh the positives."

The session with Father Ryan convinced Staubach he was thinking in the right direction. In only one other area did he feel a remaining nag. He needed to consult brain specialists to determine whether a series of football knockouts dating back to high school had resulted in discernible damage. The question had to be resolved for two reasons.

21

First, there was the matter of his general health. Second, just in case he about-faced at the last minute, it was necessary to know if it was safe to continue playing.

In mid-February he was examined by Dr. Fred Plum, a neurologist in New York City who had been recommended by a friend. Because brain scan machines were in use, most of their appointment was spent compiling the history of Staubach's concussions. He accounted for 20.

The worst were the ones in Pittsburgh and in Texas Stadium during a '78 playoff against Atlanta. In the Falcons game Staubach had dumped a short pass when an Atlanta linebacker struck him high in the chest. The momentum and weight of the 220-pound defender threw Staubach backward with nothing to cushion his fall. The back of his head was the first thing to strike Texas Stadium's hard artificial turf.

The tackle occurred late in the second quarter. Staubach did not regain command of his senses until almost 30 minutes later. He awoke to a game in progress in the third quarter. He did not remember anything in between—walking off and on the field or being in the locker room. This was his longest kayo and something else was different about it. He was nauseated to the point of vomiting.

Dr. Plum could not make a diagnosis or offer a recommendation on whether Staubach should play again without specific tests. Arrangements were made for these to be taken at Presbyterian Hospital in Dallas. Dr. Phil Williams, a local neurosurgeon, also would examine Staubach and render a separate opinion.

The tests included a computerized head scan, known medically as a CAT scan (from computerized axial tomography); an electroencephalogram (EEG), which measures electrical impulses in the brain; others that examine reflexes.

Dr. Williams analyzed the x-rays and data. Text results also were forwarded to Dr. Plum.

The Cowboys also volunteered a suggestion through Schramm. He wanted Staubach to check into a clinic for days of the most stringent testing. Staubach declined.

"If I got any negative feedback from *one* doctor . . . it didn't matter if I had five that were for playing and one against . . . it would affect my decision," he was thinking. "I'd be wondering, 'That one doctor who is against . . . *why* is he against?' After all, they're messing around with my head."

The specialists soon reported and made their recommendations. Dr. Williams was less concerned about the injury factor than his New York colleague. The way Staubach remembers it, his opinion "wasn't specifically that I retire. I think the way he put it was, 'If you retired it wouldn't be a decision you would regret.' "

Dr. Plum was forthright in expressing a negative opinion on Staubach's playing again. He detected neurological changes on Staubach's left side. They were extremely minor. Yet they were there.

"He felt it *could* be related to the concussions and his personal recommendation was that I should seriously think about retirement," Staubach said. "He felt there was a gray area on the number of concussions, that having some change he could see—even though very minor—it could be cumulative. The next one *could* be worse than the previous one.

"This could be a factor in later life if you have too many. You could develop the syndrome of a punch-drunk boxer. Again, it was a gray area. But the history of my concussions was enough to concern him.

"He did recommend that probably I should retire at

my age. But it wasn't anything adamant like, 'If you don't retire you are going to have brain damage.' Yet it was enough that I had to weigh what he said seriously.''

The findings were that the reflexes in Staubach's left foot were a shade less responsive than the right. This *might* indicate scar tissue formation on the brain. Marianne pondered the results without undue alarm. In her pragmatic way she wondered to herself . . .

Maybe he'd always been like that but nobody looked this closely before. His reflexes could have been just that hair different from the age of 10. But who checks your reflexes that closely until there's a problem?

Even if there were no internal problem, even if Roger's left-side reflexes were entirely normal, Marianne had had enough.

''I don't think I ever said this to Roger. But I thought to myself, if he plays another year I probably would have panicked the first time he went down with a head injury,'' she confessed. ''I really do not become unglued in the stands. I'm not a yeller or screamer over anything. I sit there very calm. But had we gone through another season. . . . ''

There were too many stark memories of what *might* happen. The reminders often intruded in unexpected ways. For instance, during the 1978 season the Staubachs were watching a home video replay of the Los Angeles–Minnesota game. They broke off for the 10 P.M. TV news and were puzzled by a sports item that Tommy Kramer, the Vikings quarterback, was reported to be in no danger.

''We go back to the game and both of us are watching to see what happens,'' Marianne remembered. ''When he got hit [by a blitzing linebacker] neither of us thought it was going to be that bad. It just didn't look that bad. But then he lay there and went into convulsions.

"I told Roger then, 'If that ever happens to you I'd be down over that concrete wall.' I'm afraid if he played another season it would have been very hard because there would have been gnawing fear. I've never had that before. Honestly. People say, 'How can you stand watching your husband get hurt?' It's something you live with. If you become consumed with worry and fear of it, it's bad for both of you."

For Roger the wondering was almost over. It was early March and the odds on retiring had risen to 98 percent. He said as much to No. 2 quarterback Danny White when they met accidentally. Despite four years of competition theirs was a harmonious kinship. Each was an accomplished put-down artist, which helped.

Staubach referred to White as "America's Punter," a take-off on the Cowboys' label as America's Team. In turn White twitted Staubach about his age. When Roger missed a practice-field pass Danny was in his ear whispering, "I understand the arm is the first thing that goes."

During this period Staubach walked into the locker room and found a message taped to his dressing stall for all to see. It read: "Roger, please clear out your locker and turn in your equipment. (Signed) T.L." Somewhere Danny White was laughing.

On the occasion of their by-chance meeting White realized Staubach's retirement intentions were earnest. But in parting he couldn't help half-kidding, "I'll believe it when I see it."

White was more than a fringe factor in why and when Staubach quit. Had Roger felt his absence would leave the position ill-manned, thereby jeopardizing the team, he says he would have suited up again. But he felt comfortable about passing the quarterback torch to the 28-year-old understudy and his challenger, the promising Glenn Carano.

To make the transition clean he purposely set a public announcement March 31 to coincide with the opening of the club's off-season program. White would take over without Staubach's shadow hanging over him.

Staubach firmed the retirement date with Cowboys public relations director Doug Todd. It was his intention to speak privately to teammates at the practice field, then step into another room and inform the small cadre of beat reporters. Todd knew that wasn't possible because Staubach's exit would be an enormous media event. Over Roger's objection he set a noon press conference in the Stadium Club at Texas Stadium. Staubach made one last counterplea.

"I don't want to go out to the stadium and give another talk," he said. "They know I'm retiring anyway. The best way to do it is have everyone sitting in the Stadium Club. We'll have the cheerleaders lined up at the goal posts and start playing 'Red Neck Mother' over the public address. The team will line up on one side of the field. My office staff will line up on the other side. I'll come running through the cheerleaders. But I'll have on my business suit and be carrying a briefcase. I'll run over to my office staff, hop into a car and we'll take off. Everyone would know which decision I'd made. I wouldn't have to say a word."

Staubach now had gone too far to retract. Or had he? No one outside the Cowboys family knew of his commitment to retire, although a strongly speculative story had appeared in the *Dallas Times Herald* as early as mid-January. And there were periods when he wavered. Teammates showed up to play basketball on Staubach's backyard court and urged him to reconsider. These would give him a momentary itch to try one more season.

Then there was Schramm and his telephone calls. "What can we do to get you to play?" he kept asking. A better contract? Not one which had been renegotiated since that was against club policy, even for Roger. But a healthier financial deal could be arranged. If not, perhaps this? Or that?

Mostly, Schramm left no psychological ploy untried. He felt Staubach had been psyched out by the calendar, that simply because Roger was 38 years old he felt compelled to quit. So when Billy Jean King, age 36 and fresh from a tournament victory in Houston, came to Dallas with the women's pro tennis tour Schramm dialed Staubach.

"How are things going?" Schramm opened, innocently enough. "Just wondering if you saw the newspaper story about Billy Jean King. It's the one where she said age wasn't really a factor. How she was coming into her prime. Interesting, don't you think?"

Only one prominent hurdle remained before Staubach crossed the point of no return. He must confirm the decision to Landry. Landry had to be told that the 90 percent odds Staubach quoted in January were 100 percent in March. A week prior to the press conference date they met in the coach's office.

"Once I was able to tell him, there was nothing that could have changed my mind," Staubach said afterward. "That was the key time. Ever since January I knew I'd have to do it again and tell him for sure. Once I went in there and did it and didn't feel any regrets I knew that was it."

Landry's reaction was calm and philosophical. Accustomed to command, Landry does not plead or cajole. He analyzes and speaks to the resulting facts. His persuasive powers are contained in statements that sound dry but are weighty with significance. In case of a player considering retirement Landry speaks to his performance level. Either he's still skillful enough to play or he's not.

"We've analyzed your play last year and you have not reached a point where I feel you should retire," Landry told Staubach. "I think you could play for us. You *should* play again. We want you to play. But if it's something that is strong in your mind then you have to make that decision."

Landry's emphasis on "you *should* play" was extremely meaningful to the quarterback. Earlier that spring the coach had told offensive tackle Rayfield Wright he should not, and waived him from the team after 13 years. That Landry felt Staubach was still in peak form pleased him. The flattery also confirmed this was the best time to go—while he was on top.

Last minute appeals continued. Offensive coordinator Dan Reeves telephoned with word that Landry wouldn't be calling plays at least during preseason. The head coach planned to concentrate on defense. He, Reeves, would be in charge of play selection and if Roger came back they would be an offensive team. Think of the wide-open possibilities, Reeves's words implied.

Of course, Schramm persisted. "What can we do to change your mind?" he repeated. By now it was evident. There was nothing.

At 9 A.M. Monday, March 31, with son Jeff in hand, Staubach walked into the Cowboys's locker room to address his teammates. No coaches would be present. The players were to be first to hear Staubach's decision although most already knew he was gone.

"I want to let all you guys know that I won't be calling plays for you next year," Staubach began. "Come to think of it I didn't call plays for you last year either, did I? I also want you to know I'll miss football a lot, especially training camp."

Players started chuckling. Staubach was notorious for his distaste of the annual summer pilgrimage to Thousand Oaks, California. They also began to sense how he would carry off this emotional moment.

"Yes, I'll miss training camp tremendously," Staubach said. "I'll miss the booze and the broads. Breaking curfew. The nude beaches."

The room exploded with laughter. Teammates knew Roger's idea of a racy evening in California was playing ping-pong. The last few years he'd even taken to wearing a robe and slippers around the dorm at night, earning the nickname of "Pop."

"I've been fortunate to be a part of this team," he continued. "I've been surrounded by great players through the years. Especially as a quarterback I've been blessed with great receivers like Drew Pearson, Tony Hill, Billy Joe . . . and, of course, Herb Scott."

Everybody whooped again. Here was their leader. This was the guy they always looked to in the clutch. Facing his last pressure situation he was putting on another grand show.

"When the season starts there will be things I'll remember about games that will stick with me forever," Staubach went on. "Such as Drew barfing in the huddle in the fourth quarter. Tony Hill telling me he's open *all* the time. And Tony Dorsett chasing a fumble all over the field."

At this point Staubach wanted to turn serious. But he felt himself beginning to crack inside. He'd planned to say things like, "I wanted you guys to know first about what I decided because too often when players retire, you read about it in the paper and never see them again. I wanted to say how much I appreciated your support over the years. It may sound like baloney but it's true. I wanted you to know it was you who made me.''

The words stuck in a lump that had formed in his throat. He never got them out. ''Hey, I just want to thank you guys,'' he mumbled. As players rose to respond, Staubach bolted through the door. The goodbye lasted six minutes.

Another gamut awaited Staubach in the parking lot. A dozen reporters and cameramen surrounded the locker room door. He must face them, too. He fetched Jeff who'd been left to eat doughnuts with team trainers Don Cochran and Ken Locker. This was a children's tradition at the practice field on Saturday mornings when workouts were no more than limbering up. While their fathers romped the kids ravaged trays of doughnuts.

Staubach brought Jeff for a reason other than free breakfast. His son was an emotional stabilizer, a tousle-haired blond tyke off whom Roger could joke to maintain composure when he faced newsmen. Jeff served the purpose. When Staubach was asked what he told the team, his reply was, ''I said I'd retired. Jeff also wanted to announce his retirement. He won't be eating any more doughnuts at Saturday morning workouts.''

All that remained was the formality of the press conference at Texas Stadium. In a sense it was anti-climactic since words of Staubach's swan song to the team already echoed through Dallas like a thunderclap. Publicist Todd correctly judged the impact and ordered buffet lunch for 200. He didn't miss the turnout by much.

Staubach, this time flanked by Marianne, was flabbergasted at the scene. By Todd's official count 179 media reps were there. Some were writers from distant points such as Washington, New Jersey and Miami. The event was carried live on local radio and television. It would be the largest sports-related press conference in the city's history.

Staubach spoke extemporaneously. He reviewed two early, pivotal moments in his athletic career. First was the 1965 College All-Star game when NFL scouts showed interest in his pro career after he served a four-year Navy hitch. Then came the 1968 training camp with Dallas while he was on two-week leave, which convinced him to leave military service and go pro with the Cowboys the next year.

Twice it was obvious he came close to tears. Speaking of the Cowboys's system and the people who make it function so successfully, he said, "Of course, the nuts and bolts of the Cowboys is . . ." and paused. Swallowing hard, Staubach continued . . . "the man who wears the funny hat on the sideline, Tom Landry."

Seconds later he reached another emotional spot. "I appreciate my teammates," he was saying. "I'm just one who's been successful but there's been a lot of other good ones. There'll be many more good ones." Here he choked up before proceeding to say, at last, the words that would do it: "I thank the Cowboys and I'm retiring."

Then came the questions. Staubach repeated the reasons he was stepping out. They were the same as those Father Ryan helped list— family, diminished zest, the concussions, lack of privacy, age. Would he return if White were injured early in training camp? someone asked. "I'm not adverse to helping out because I have a good relationship with the team. But I don't look for that to happen," he said. "I would have to cross that bridge as it developed. It would depend on circumstances . . . how I feel."

Driving home from Texas Stadium, the Staubachs felt almost light-headed. En route to the press conference their conversation had been funereal. The return trip was giddy by comparison. "Gosh, Marianne," said Roger, "the way we were talking going out I didn't think either one of us was going to make it."

Staubach's farewell to football was done. But parting from the game was not that sweet or swift. His athletic eulogies began. The *Times Herald* published a special section reviewing career highlights. TV stations showed specials. "The Today Show" and "Good Morning, America!" leaped in with interview requests. All of it made Staubach most uneasy. "It was like I had died," he said.

By an accident of timing, in conjunction with the retirement the commercial real estate firm of Holloway-Staubach was launching its most ambitious project. A $12.5 million office complex in north Dallas reached completion. Suddenly everything was different. Staubach wasn't practicing football anymore. He was reporting to a new office in so-far strange surroundings.

His uneasiness subsided after a few days but was replaced by something worse. To this day Staubach doesn't know what it was. Perhaps an anxiety attack. Whatever, his pulse felt like it was racing. His heart thumped. Even sitting down the adrenalin pumped. Staubach feared a heart attack although he'd recently checked out super during a thorough physical exam.

Within a week Staubach reported these sensations to Dr. Kenneth Cooper, nationally known fitness expert in Dallas. Dr. Cooper ran tests and assured Staubach his problem was psychological rather than physical. It's the retirement syndrome, Roger was told.

As mysteriously as it appeared, the anxiety vanished

within 48 hours. Roger Staubach returned to normal. He relaxed. He is at ease again. Now the quarterback famous for his two-minute rallies finds he has the rest of his life to win—and that's time enough.

Frank Luksa
June, 1980

I

The Man in the Funny Hat

"We'll miss Roger tremendously. But I'm not so sure the National Football League and the sport won't miss him as much or more. His was the type of image you wanted in the game for young people. You can't afford to lose that type of person."

—*Cowboys Coach Tom Landry*

There was nothing left to say except goodbye, and Coach Tom Landry and I got that out of the way in 10 to 11 minutes. I didn't think it was unusual that my departure amounted to about one minute per year I had spent as a quarterback for the Dallas Cowboys. When you talk football with Landry—even about your own retirement—never expect idle chatter.

We met on a late March morning in his office, at his

request. Before leaving town the next day Landry wanted to know whether my intention regarding a press conference the next week had changed. If I went through with it the purpose would be to announce my National Football League career was over.

We had covered the same ground in January. I thought it the honest and fair thing to forewarn Tom I was 90 percent convinced I wouldn't play anymore. He could make personnel plans in the offseason accordingly. Now we had returned to the same subject—for the last time.

Landry never directly tried to argue me out of retirement. He mentioned that based on my performance level in 1979 I could play, *should* play at least one more season. I repeated the reasons that convinced me it was time to leave the game. All the pros and cons were covered. In a switch from his no-small-talk manner he inquired about a real estate project the Holloway-Staubach company was completing. I told him we were in good shape.

We stood. There was no handshake, but none was necessary. I know both of us felt what was happening. I had kept my distance from Tom on a personal basis and he had kept his. Yet we had come together to form an extremely strong athlete-coach bond which now was breaking.

So much mutual respect had been built over the years. At this moment we felt that relationship slipping away. Neither of us reacted visibly, but that was normal for both of us. Although Tom has the reputation for being stoic in times of emotional stress, I, too, often disguise what my heart is telling me.

That neither of us felt compelled to make this a dramatic goodbye by word or touch simply underlined the depth of our bond. As far as how we felt about each other, a word or handshake was insignificant.

We *knew.*

So I walked toward the door. There was nothing left to say, except...

"Coach, what if I come back this year? Will you let me call the plays?"

Even as a tease, the words surprised me. They weren't preplanned or rehearsed. They just tumbled out. I must have looked like I was trying to suppress a grin because Landry caught the humorous intent. He replied in a light vein.

"Oh, sure. You can call some from the press box."

"Seriously, what if I come back? If I played again could I call plays?"

What was going on here? Play-calling was a subject Tom and I sometimes joked about but that last question was earnestly put. We clashed philosophically on the subject and at times even argued over it on the sidelines. He called plays through a messenger shuttle. I always believed this was the quarterback's business, and still do.

Why pursue this question, especially since I'd just settled the retirement issue with him? To tempt Landry? To tempt myself? Curiosity over his reaction? What *would* he say?

Tom's mood remained airy. He smiled and with a soft chuckle said, "No, we have a system going here."

As well as anyone, probably better than most, I knew that. Long ago I learned that the Dallas Cowboys' system is Tom Landry and vice versa. Our goodbyes said and done, our strange conversation ended, I closed a door that never would open to me again as an active quarterback.

That meant a special relationship had been severed. Someday Tom and I may relive the good times but our perspective toward each other will have changed. We won't be *together* anymore in that unique way in which athletics emotionally binds people. He'll be my former coach. I'll be his ex-quarterback. There'll be a distance between us. We won't ever be as we once were.

I used to sit by my home telephone the night before every Cowboys game at Texas Stadium, game plan spread at the desk. At 8 P.M. the phone would ring, and it would be Landry, calling to make a final review of offensive strategy. Funny, the way he'd do it. I'd pick up the phone and say, "Hello." The next thing I would hear was his voice saying, "Now, you know on that Slant 24, we are going to run it from. . . ." He wouldn't say, "Hello, Roger, this is Coach Landry," or anything else before starting right in on the game plan. It was as if I were in the room with him.

Next day when I got to the locker room Dan Reeves, our offensive coordinator who helped call plays from the press box, would sidle up and grin. "Make any changes last night?" he ask.

Everyone connected with play-calling knew this was the way Coach Landry operated. He's an amazing man. All week long he'd be involved with various areas of defense and offense so that he really didn't have a chance to study films in depth. We'd see him leaving the practice field on Friday with a load of film cans under his arm and think, "Oh, boy, here we go." He was taking them home to analyze.

During Saturday morning practice he might make some changes. He was good about not trying to change too much. He probably had a lot of things in mind to switch around but he knew he couldn't do it that late. Then he'd watch film again Saturday night and call me to correlate what he'd seen with what we planned to do.

He'd go over everything and ask my reaction to the plays. "On third down, how do you feel about these plays?'' he'd say. Or, ''What do you feel good with? Are there some you don't like? Which ones do you prefer? What play-action passes do you like best?'' I really appreciated that. Then he might make a minor adjustment. Sometimes it would be significant, such as adding a play. I would have all night to think about it, get it set in my mind. On Sunday before the game he would give it to the team as a last-second addition.

I won't sit by the telephone on Saturday night anymore. It's not going to ring. No one will call to ask my preference on the next day's play-action passes.

Nor will I see Tom exhibit pregame nervousness the way he sometimes would. No, he's not always unflappable. I'd see his jitters in the locker room when he'd walk around and talk to more players than usual. He would be tense, excited, but really have no way to work off his energy. That's when he'd get something in his mind about a certain play. He would come over to me and talk about a technical point. Then off he'd go, but soon he'd be back again. He's talked to me about the same point on the same play as many as *three* times.

After he would leave I'd tell the other quarterbacks, Danny White or Glenn Carano, ''Tom's going a mile a minute today. We've been over that play a bunch of times and probably won't even use it.'' It wasn't a big deal. It was Landry's way of biting his fingernails.

Some of what we'd go over *was* pertinent, but other times I could tell Tom was just going through the motions of trying to occupy himself. He'd try to cover every little point. To be honest, there were times when I tuned him out unless it was something that represented a definite change. But to keep going over something we'd covered all week . . . I didn't need that.

Now if he said, ''Instead of 83 Pass from a Red

Formation, run it from Red Flip,'' *that* was significant. The way our system worked was that he would send in the play and I would determine the formation, whether we'd use a man in motion and, of course, the snap count. If he sent that play in and I called Red instead of Red Flip he would brace me and say, ''What were you doing in the locker room when we went over this?''

I'll not share those jumpy pre-kickoff moments with Landry again, nor feel the vibrations of his growing excitement as the team built toward what for him were special games—against Washington, any time and any place; against the New York Giants in New York.

Tom always had a feeling for going back to New York. That trip brought back all the old memories because New York was where he played his NFL career and began coaching on the Giants staff which included Vince Lombardi. Landry was the defensive coordinator there when Cowboys owner Clint Murchison hired him for the Dallas job. New York was The Big Apple to Landry. He even gave us a talk in my early years that if you wanted to make All-Pro you had to do well in The Big Apple. New York was an emotional game for him, and still is even though the Giants haven't been division contenders for years. I could sense that going back was a special occasion for him and his vivacious wife, Alicia.

There was an extra dimension to the Redskins games because of the rivalry. Washington was a consistent reference point to Tom as early as training camp. We started working against Washington-type defenses that soon. When Landry put examples on the blackboard they would always be of the Redskins. ''The Redskins play like so, therefore this play has to work in this type situation against them,'' he'd say. There was no reason to refer to a particular team. He could just diagram a defense. But the references to Washington would come out. I hear it's the same in Washington, that the Redskins are always referring to the Cowboys and what we're doing.

Tom and George Allen, the former Redskins coach, had a thing going between them. You could never tell that about a coach of any other team we played. I'd say George got Tom's goat pretty good because sometimes he talked about Allen in less than the fondest terms. I understand they fell out in the late '60s when Allen coached at Los Angeles and the Cowboys accused the Rams of spying on their practices. Allen came back and said he discovered a Cowboys spy up a tree outside the LA practice field. He claimed it was then Dallas scout Bucko Kilroy, which was a laugh. Kilroy weighed about 300 pounds in those days and had enough trouble climbing into his shoes much less a tree.

Despite their differences I think Landry and Allen could sit down in the offseason and get along fine. They're both fierce competitors. I didn't like Allen when I was playing because he always seemed to start a psychological campaign against me before every game. I've come to understand Allen better and now think he did it because he respected me as a player. The guy's dedicated—football is his whole life—and he got the job done, which is what it's all about.

But he used to get under everybody's skin, mine and Tom's included. Landry didn't like the way the Redskins talked about us through the media. He's really big the other way. He doesn't believe in saying anything about the other team. Landry would get mad if someone on our team did.

"Keep your comments to yourself when you're talking

to the press," he'd tell us. "Teams are just going to use what you say against you. There's no point in mouthing off against anybody." Before a game against Washington Landry would say, "The Redskins are talking again," or "George has really got them talking this week."

One thing was different about what the Redskins said. It wound up on our bulletin board, something the Cowboys don't normally use. There are exceptions but Dallas is not a bulletin board team. There always was a lot of material available because teams liked to beat us and didn't mind saying so. Through the '70s Washington led the verbal attack by far.

There were a couple of years, around '74 and '75, when St. Louis got into the act. When those guys beat Dallas it seemed they held a press conference in the locker room to start mouthing off. Really incredible the way the Cardinals went at it.

Not only did Tom object to knocking the other team, he fairly sizzled when something said privately in a team meeting wound up in the next day's newspaper. I always talked to the press but never told anything confidential. Some players did leak things to the papers. If a confidential subject came up in a meeting, they'd leave the meeting and it was like Watergate all over again. Landry would just go crazy over that. He'd come to a meeting the next day and say, "When we're in this room we're like family. We are a team and what's said here is not supposed to leave this room." Sure enough, there it would be in the next day's paper. Someone would have a scoop.

Reporters who followed the Cowboys for years tell me that Tom is tops among NFL head coaches as a cooperative, accessible subject for interview. They say he's unfailingly polite, thoughtful of their job pressures and tolerant of even the dumbest question. But he also seems to view their work in curious fashion.

For instance, he would tell us not to worry about what we read. Then a few weeks later he was saying, "You know what they're writing about us. They say we're finished, that we're down." He'd use *that* to get us motivated. I suspect Coach reads every line of newspaper type relating to the Cowboys. Either he was reading it or somebody was telling him because he sure knew what had been written. Of course, he was on safe ground when he reminded the team we were being written off. The Cowboys in '70 and '71 were buried in the newspapers at midseason and wound up in Super Bowls. The '75 team got there, too, after being written off before the season even began.

It is this relationship with Tom—and more—I left behind. I'll miss the personal glimpses, those uncommon moments when the curtain lifted for a peek at the man behind the sideline mask. Thinking back I suppose the happiest I ever saw him—when he let it show— was after we beat Miami in Super Bowl VI. Players lifted him on their shoulders and carried him off the field. Tom wore a smile as wide as a rainbow that day. You could see the load lifted from his shoulders for all the past playoff disappointments.

To me, Landry's low point was after a playoff loss to Cleveland my rookie year in 1969. We were getting ready to board a flight to Miami for the Playoff Bowl. People were crying for his scalp and he looked like a beaten man that day. We had a meeting at Love Field before taking off and he was the lowest I've ever seen him. He was ashen. He'd had it and he was down.

I'll also remember his stubbornness or conviction,

whatever you want to call it. As an illustration, he still believes the ultimate play-calling system is to shuttle quarterbacks on alternate downs. Craig Morton and I were the last NFL quarterbacks to be used that way in a 1971 game against Chicago, which we lost 23–19. Statistically you couldn't entirely blame the system because we had more than 400 yards total offense.

Yet I believe Coach revealed much of himself that day, with his conviction that at least in theory a quarterback shuttle is the premier system. I think he used it with me and Morton because neither of us was the dominant quarterback at the time and he felt *he* was the dominant figure. We were just there to exercise his will. Deep down I feel he likes to be the quarterback on the sideline with the ability to tell the player everything he's supposed to do. He sends in a play and says, "We will run an 88 pass. Look to the post. Watch the weak safety. Keep your eye on this . . . ," and goes over the whole thing like we do in a meeting. Then we have it fresh on our minds as we walk on the field—like machines.

What that showed was he had more confidence in himself than his quarterbacks. Landry probably still does but he realizes the quarterback shuttle isn't practical. He still thinks of that concept mainly because he knows if you do it his way it's going to be the right way.

Like a lot of successful people Tom Landry has an ego. His isn't overbearing but it's large and strong. He believes in *his* system and *his* way. It doesn't always matter who the person might be to carry out the system's function—as long as you do it *his* way.

Back when Craig and I shuttled, I think he was saying to himself, "They are just two people. They can pass and hand off. The system is fine." He didn't consider that our styles were different, or that the team needed one player to look to, or how we felt about it. He just looked at it and said, "I have two human beings here and they can throw and do what I tell them and that's it. The job is done." And if you had two robots, yes, it *would* work.

Tom settled for a single quarterback and since then has used guards, tight ends, wide receivers and running backs as play messengers. This is what he feels better about than anything—knowing what the play will be so he and other coaches can concentrate on the point of attack. If the play fails then they determine whether the breakdown was our fault or the defense made a great play. As long as Landry coaches I doubt the play-calling system ever will change.

I retired with mixed emotions over not having called plays for the bulk of my career. I think it's something the quarterback should do, so in that respect I'll always feel unfulfilled. The last time I called plays was in 1973 against Miami, a game we lost 14–7. Our record fell to 7–4 and three of the defeats had been by margins of a touchdown or less. Upcoming were tough games in Denver and at home against Washington that would decide whether we qualified for the playoffs.

Statistically I was having an excellent season and won the NFL passing title. But personally it was a period of tragedy because my mother was bedridden in our home, terminally ill with cancer. The night before the Miami game she was in critical condition and had only a few more days to live.

After that game Landry called me in and said he would call plays from there on in. His reasoning was, "Roger, I'm going to take some of the pressure off. You have your mother's situation, we've lost some close games and our whole season rides on the next two. I'll call plays so you won't have to worry about that. Just concentrate on the passing game.''

We beat Denver, the Redskins and St. Louis to finish with a 10–4 record and won the NFC East title. You couldn't argue with the results—which raises a counterpoint to the play-calling question.

Regardless of who called plays, Tom or I, I don't believe it would have influenced the team's record much one way or the other. The most critical item in football is preparation—the game plan. The quality of the game plan is ultra-important and this is where I think the Cowboys have great strength. They are *very* prepared. The process begins with special assistant Ermal Allen who starts analyzing an opponent the week before we play them, and by Tuesday before the kickoff the game plan is ready. Once you have that in hand it's up to whoever is calling plays, either the coach or quarterback.

Had I been calling plays instead of Tom our style of attack would have differed in two areas. I would have passed more often on first down. I would have thrown deep more frequently than he prefers.

Otherwise, we were pretty much on the same page offensively because often the game plan dictates it. For instance, the game plan is set up with specific plays for certain situations such as first down, second-and-three, third-and-long, short yardage, on the goal line and so forth. We also have what the Cowboys term Plus Territory, which is inside an opponents' 20-yard line. Even that area is broken into five-yard increments—20 to 15, 15 to 10 and 10 on in. Maybe there are two plays in each area. So if we were on the 18-yard line I'd have a 50–50 chance of calling the same play Landry would because there are only two.

We had some sideline arguments over play selection, although if you look at it in the perspective of a season or career, there weren't that many. His calling a play-action pass on second-and-11 would lead to words. I'd throw it and later come to the sideline where he'd be waiting to say something beginning, "You shouldn't have. . . ." That's when I'd say, "That was ridiculous! Second-and-11 is not the time to call a play-action pass."

As I said, had I been calling plays we would have thrown deep more often even if it didn't work. Our passing game was built around the intermediate area of around 15 yards downfield. Going deep a lot would open up those areas more. We talked about it during every training camp but for Tom the long ball is not a percentage play. He is a percentage coach.

Teams look at the way we move and shift but say, "Dallas doesn't do that much different than anyone else." And it's true to a large extent. We just camouflage it. We will throw the flea-flicker pass and run reverses. But on first down we still go with the percentage-type play. *That* is when you want to go deep, not on third down when defenses are set against it.

Percentage-wise if we hit one of three deep passes, we're in great shape. Landry knows those figures as well as anyone. So he's thinking on first down, "Do I take a 33 percent chance of completing a touchdown pass or just go for the sure thing of three or four yards?" Almost without exception he takes the relatively sure thing because percentages pay off in the long run.

We often discussed letting me at least call plays from the shotgun formation. But he would say no, it would mess up the continuity. I'd have to worry about play selection instead of simply executing the play. Besides, the coaches are sending different people into the game.

In Dallas it would be more difficult for the quarterback to call his plays because of the way the Cowboys substitute. About half our running game uses two tight ends. If I wanted two tight ends and only one was in the game I'd have to be signaling to the bench to rush somebody to the huddle. Sometimes we would even use three—Billy Joe DuPree, Jay Saldi and Doug Cosbie. So that would get even more confusing trying to get players in and out of the game. It's confusing enough as it is and sometimes even Landry has forgotten who's supposed to be where when he calls a certain play.

I would have enjoyed play-calling. The advantage of a quarterback calling his own plays is that he has selected a play he personally believes in, especially in a key situation. He's going to have more confidence in it. Landry, in turn, knew what I did best. A lot of things in our passing game were geared around my strengths.

My view was that calling plays from the sideline reduced a sense of the quarterback being in control. It was always important to me that my team felt I had command and knew what I was doing. I believe the players still had confidence in me and that's where I had it over some quarterbacks in a similar system. But my point never wavered: if there is a quarterback who can call plays then he should do it.

The play-calling system started with Craig and Landry liked it. That was part of his ego as far as controlling the game. I don't think there's a great advantage to a coach calling plays. He might rationalize it because he doesn't want to offend the intelligence of his quarterback. Intelligence had nothing to do with why Landry called plays for me because in '73, the last time I was on my own, we finished high in every offensive category.

Of course, I wasn't stuck with every play Coach sent in if I saw it headed into a stacked defense. We had audibles whereby I changed the play at the line of scrimmage. There were other times when I improvised. If we had a sideline pass called to one side I might tell the receiver on the other side to run a post route. All he was supposed to do was clear an area, but maybe I'd seen the weak safety having a tendency to hang in the middle. Anyway, the receiver who wasn't supposed to be involved except as a decoy would run this deep route and frequently wind up open.

Later we'd be watching films and Landry would say, "I thought we called an 83 route." Somebody would start yelling at the poor receiver and I'd have to defend him by saying, "Oh, I told him to do that." Landry rarely said anything about these free-lance passes even when they didn't work. Maybe it was because he knew sometimes they clicked big, like the 45-yard touchdown catch Butch Johnson made against Denver in Super Bowl XII. That one was improvised just as I outlined.

I remember another time when the results—and Tom's reaction— were different. During an overtime game against St. Louis in 1978 Landry called a short pass to fullback Robert Newhouse on first-and-10 from the Cardinals' 36. I sent Drew on a post route and instead of dumping the ball to Newhouse tried to hit Pearson deep. Just as I let the pass go I got hit by a blitzing linebacker who cut my lip and knocked me so dizzy I had to leave the game. The pass was incomplete and Danny White took over.

We won on a field goal by Rafael Septien but I wasn't sure of that until one of their players congratulated me after the game ended. Since everything came out OK Tom told me after the game (and I swear he was almost smiling):

"Roger, every time you look in the mirror to shave you'll have a reminder [the cut lip] *not* to change my plays."

So why suggest changing Landry's entire system on that last visit? Was it a Freudian slip? Was I dangling one final play-again carrot in front of my own nose? Subconsciously, I think so.

One reason I retired was inability to gear up mentally for the tedium of *preparing* to play. I never tired of the thrill and challenge of the actual games. It was the preparation that was getting to me and I didn't want to be involved if I couldn't fully commit to the necessary training. The year before I began to notice in training camp that the repetition of plays and the same routine had become a drudgery to some degree.

That began to concern me. Once you start thinking you know everything because you've been through it so many times, you're in trouble. So I kept thinking maybe I needed a shot in the arm, something to stimulate this dwindling enthusiasm. If I found it *maybe* I would play again.

Reeves knew how I felt. That's why he phoned to say that Landry planned to concentrate on defense in 1980 and that Danny, not Coach Landry, would call plays, at least during preseason. "Things will be a little different this year," Reeves told me. "Would that make any difference to you as far as preparing for the season?"

It wouldn't. Neither would permission to call plays, even if Tom had given it. Things would have been the same as they are today. I'd still be Roger Staubach, quarterback (Ret.).

Sure it would have been a temptation if Landry had phoned me one night at home and said, "If you will come back you can call the plays." But that would not have been a make-or-break issue. When I was weighing all the pros and cons of playing again that factor would have gone in the plus column. But change my mind entirely? No.

How can I be sure? Simply because I didn't really confront Landry about play-calling. Had I wanted to create a showdown about it I would have sat down very seriously and discussed it with him. I would have gone to that last meeting with a specific position in mind and said, "There *is* one way I will come back . . ."

I didn't challenge him for several reasons. For one, it would have been unfair to put him in such a tough position which would eventually have become a big public flap. People would have taken sides. I could foresee a huge controversy, and no team needs that or functions well under such a distraction.

Had Tom decided I could call plays he would have set a precedent that he would regret in later years. After I was gone each succeeding quarterback could demand the same privilege by asking, "Why won't you do it for me when you did it for Roger?"

The Cowboys were successful under Landry's system as he operated it while I was playing. If there had been a losing season or the offense was off, then circumstances might warrant a change. But I'll bet our offense in the last three or four years, probably in all our years together, gained more yards and scored more points than anybody. I couldn't say that the system was hurting for a different approach. And had I, I would have been saying in effect that I could do better.

Third, last and most important. I knew the play-calling format was something that Tom believed in deeply. It had nothing to do with my ability to call plays. He *liked* it. I believe no matter what he said about strategy and everything else involved, he just liked to call them. If that's what he believed and preferred so strongly I didn't think it was right to put pressure on him to change.

It was ironic when Tom announced last spring he was surrendering play-calling duty to Reeves and would concentrate on coaching defense. Reeves is a brilliant assistant who someday will be an outstanding NFL head coach. He's Landry-trained over a seven-year playing career and this is his eighth season on the Cowboys' coaching staff. Therefore, I don't think you'll see a dramatic difference in play-calling between Dan and Tom.

My supposition is that Landry made the change for at least two obvious reasons. First, mostly because of injuries, our defense last year was not strong at season's end. Tom's major priority during training camp was putting this unit back into tip-top shape. His knowledge of defense is unparalleled and this area of the game always has been his first love. The way I see it, Tom's desire to call plays was superseded by the necessity of restoring our defense.

Since he hasn't time to work almost exclusively with defense *and* study enough offense to call plays, the second reason for the move emerges. He has utmost confidence in Reeves. Insofar as Tom's philosophy is concerned, nothing changes. Plays still will be shuttled to the quarterback.

Again, why mention play-calling on my way out of Tom's office? Consciously, I did it as a joke. One last little needle. I wanted to get a reaction out of him. After all, we did share a few laughs over play-calling and believe it or not he has dropped a clever line or two.

Such as the time he was interviewed on a radio program. As usual, the questions got around to play-calling, how much longer he thought I would play and how much longer he might coach.

As only he could do it. Tom gave a three-in-one

answer: "I plan to coach as long as Roger lets *me* call the plays."

Another time we attended a Fellowship of Christian Athletes fund-raising dinner. He was coach of one side and I coached the other. The audience followed the amount of money pledged by movement of two footballs. It was a contest to see which team would be first to move its ball to the end zone objective.

My side was about $25,000 short when I thought of a quick way for us to win. "If Coach Landry will let me call plays next year I will cover the rest of the contributions," I announced. Alicia was in the audience and that broke her up. After the dinner Tom came up to me and said, "I've never been so tempted in all my life."

On most other occasions when we discussed play-calling or play-selection, Coach did not think I was entertaining or amusing. In a meeting room, practice field or playing field, Landry believes football is as serious as the Dead Sea Scrolls. I think there's room for laughter in the game at certain times, although I knew he didn't.

I learned that lesson early. Because of an injury to Morton I wound up having to start against St. Louis as a rookie in 1969. I was tremendously excited but Landry wasn't. Rookie quarterbacks aren't his cup of tea. The night before the game the team met in our hotel and I noticed him sitting alone in a corner with a worried look on his face. I wanted to cheer him up so I walked over and said:

"Coach, do you realize that a year ago today I was the starting quarterback for the Pensacola Naval Air Station Goshawks? We were playing Middle Tennessee State. And here I am, ready to start against the Cardinals tomorrow."

Tom gave me a peculiar look and walked off without

saying a word. Incidentally, we won that game 24–3 with Landry calling all the plays for me.

I used to needle Landry from the banquet podium but whether he ever heard or read about it I never knew. I'd start out by saying when I learned Tom was going to call all the plays I didn't care because I was just happy to start.

"I didn't worry about it until one of Landry's neighbors called and told me Tom had been working out in his backyard—throwing the football," my story went on. "That was too much. I realized he didn't like rookie quarterbacks," I'd say and pause. "But a comeback?"

When we were together, however, I picked my spots carefully. I was never insubordinate. But there were what you might call maverick moments.

One of them took place during a sideline conference. A time out was called with only a few seconds left to play. We had the game won so there was no pressure.

As usual I trotted over and stood beside Landry to receive the next play. He was looking at the sky. I stood and waited. He kept looking upwards. On and on we went—me waiting, him transfixed with the heavens.

Finally, Tom turned his gaze on me. Before he could speak I told him, "I always wondered where you got those plays."

Ernie Stautner, our defensive coordinator, and some of the other coaches were there and started laughing like crazy. Tom just looked at me, gave me a play and off I went. He doesn't take to those little jokes out there on the field.

Another time we were on the practice field working on a new goal line play. I faked a handoff and rolled out to the right. The first time I ran it he said, "No, no, no. You have to fake longer." He normally doesn't do this but to emphasize the point Landry got under center like a quarterback. He took the snap, executed a fake to the halfback and rolled out—limping all the way. Coach has a hitch in his stride, a noticeable gimp from an old football knee injury.

Now it was time for me to run the play again. The whole team was watching as I got under center, made the fake and rolled out . . . limping, just like he did. Well, everybody cracked up on the spot. Landry smiled . . . sort of. As I said, he doesn't have a great sense of humor on the field.

Reminiscing about Tom gave me the only choke-up moment during the retirement press conference. I had to force out the words when I spoke of ''the nuts and bolts of the Cowboys . . . the man who wears the funny hat on the sideline.'' The ''funny hat'' reference wasn't planned and later I wondered whether he appreciated it. Landry *does* take great pride in his hats.

I understood why to the very last this man stirred my deepest emotion and made my voice wobble. Others didn't. Even a few teammates questioned whether it was coincidence or genuine feeling for the coach which almost caused me to lose composure. At first I found their reaction curious, even a bit discouraging in that Landry remained such a distant figure to them.

Then it came to me that Tom and I had been on unique terms. Ours was a relationship like no other on the team. By necessity of a system built around coach-who-calls-plays and quarterback-who-executes-plays, I had observed him close-up longer and more often than any other player. The system put us in almost daily contact, whereas most of my teammates had little personal contact with the head man.

With us it was different. Our dialogue was almost constant. I listened to him during quarterback meetings. He listened to me and other team captains during captains' meetings. We talked on the practice field . . . every Saturday night before home games when he called to review the game plan . . . in pregame locker rooms when he decided on a last-second play change . . . during timeouts as we selected the next play . . . on plane flights outward bound or returning to Dallas.

In this manner I listened to him and learned from him for 11 years. I never totally agreed with everything I heard or was told but still . . . Tom was *the* authority figure to me longer than anyone except my parents. Father, mother and wife aside, he was the person I was most emotionally involved with during my lifetime. As such he moved me through the entire range of human feeling over the years— anger, love, frustration, pride, disgust, awe, loyalty, respect.

In composite I remember him as a towering figure. To me he was, is and always will be special—a man apart from other men. What made him so beyond his brilliant technical grasp of football were two bedrock Landry characteristics: enormous self-discipline and consistency. Landry is the rock against which we all lean, often without realizing it, at some point during our careers.

What is he *really* like? I don't think any of us will every know or completely understand the man inside. Either purposely or through a naturally aloof personality he will remain hidden to insiders and outsiders alike.

Yet I think my insight of Landry is more balanced than Don Meredith's, who quarterbacked the Cowboys for nine years during the 1960s. Meredith has what I'd describe as a love-hate relationship with the coach. We've never gone into great psychological depth on the subject but this is what I gathered from conversations with Don recently.

One of those sessions took place during the 1979 season. Don and his wife Susan came to our home prior to an ABC-TV Monday night telecast which brought Meredith to Dallas. I believe that through the years Don has mellowed and come to appreciate Landry more. Meredith, who I thought was a great quarterback, went through a tough time building this team, taking unjustified abuse from the fans and feeling the dominance of Landry. All those things were harder to handle in the '60s because things were going wrong on the field. You might have a tendency to blame the system or Tom when it could have been team-mates who let Don down. Or maybe he was having a rough time. He just went through a lot building the team and was very close to the point where it was a success when he quit.

When Meredith talks about Landry it's not the same man I know. He has a different feeling about Tom. Some of those feelings I recognize, such as Landry being some-what aloof and dominant to the point of what he says goes, and what you have to say really doesn't mean much. I've felt that in passing but because I've seen the other sides of Tom I understand him better. The things you say *do* have meaning to him. He just doesn't let it show.

Landry has this sternness about him with everybody. It's not personal. It wasn't anything personal when he cut me short in a meeting. He's done that to his coaches. He doesn't even know he's doing it sometimes. I believe Don took a lot of those situations on a personal basis.

On the exterior Tom never changed from the first time I saw him. That was prior to the 1965 North-South game when he visited our practices. I'd been drafted by

Dallas as a junior but faced four years of military service which looked like an eternity at the time. Yet something inside told me that maybe one day I would play for this man. He didn't say much to me but there he was—young-looking and stern even then. My perceptions of Landry would form from reading about him and catching glimpses over television until the late '60s. I pigeonholed him as an exacting taskmaster. A man of no humor. Someone who never smiled. Something virtually chiseled from granite.

I was wrong, too.

Under certain conditions I did learn that Landry is inflexible, impenetrable and unsmiling. But not to the degree that Meredith once suggested: in a personality contest between Tom and the similarly composed Bud Grant of Minnesota there would be no winner. I know that Tom is not entirely what he appears on the sideline—cold and mechanical.

Physical appearance has much to do with Landry's image. He is a tough-looking guy. His jaw juts out like the bow of a ship. He has deep-set, crystal-blue eyes which can turn simply icy when he gets a good stare working. During games, Landry's concentration is so intense that his cheeks appear to sink and shadows form in their pockets. Hands on hips and glaring, he is an intimidating figure.

Strange as it sounds Landry is at the same time physically deceiving. He is a bigger man than most realize, about 6–1, 200 very solid pounds. The calves of his legs, arms and shoulders are sized like a weight-lifter. He pumps iron and runs after practices as much as that bad knee permits. He's not a smoker, takes alcohol sparingly if at all and as a result is extremely well-conditioned for a man who turned 56 last September. But when he's dressed in a sports coat, tie and hat on the sideline little of the person or personality is transmitted to spectators or through the TV camera. Tom comes off cool, composed and nerveless.

His self-control is amazing. I know he's been in moods or situations where he wanted to explode. But he wouldn't. His emotions stay inside. Tom controls himself better than any human being I've ever seen. He rarely lost his temper on the sideline although I've witnessed a few times when his composure snapped. Once he threw his headset to the ground in momentary fury. He also picked it up quicker than anyone else could have. Landry's hands always were quicker than the TV's eye.

Last season's great game against Washington proved the same point. We won 35–34 in a last-second thriller that decided the NFC East championship. Afterwards, television had one shot of Tom walking off the field. He wasn't smiling in any way, shape or form. But just before he'd been shouting and jumping into the air after Tony Hill caught the winning touchdown pass.

I watched a tape replay and was struck by this single shot of Landry. Somberly, he was leaving the field, looking neither right nor left. To Tom the game was over and already his excitement had become internal. The way he looked over TV you would have thought we lost when only moments earlier he'd been involved in all the celebration. I remember coming to the bench after throwing the pass to Hill and Tom was right in the middle of all the sideline commotion. He was walking around and hitting everyone in his own way, sort of giving them a nudge.

In a different manner and with a different purpose in mind Landry has touched every player who ever suited up for the Cowboys. Each can tell the story behind his mental bruise. No one ever forgets what happens on Monday when the meeting room lights go off, the camera rolls and Tom begins to critique Sunday's game film.

He has a low tolerance for mental errors. I would say those mistakes are his pet peeve. He has a difficult time with them probably because Landry believes he has *the* system and sometimes can't understand why we don't make it work.

He has his favorite phrases to emphasize displeasure. In pass blocking it's, "keeping your head on a swivel." He'll say that constantly if someone gets beat on pass protection. "You have to keep your head on a swivel." Or, "How many times have I said, 'You've got to move your feet'?" On defense it's, "You have to play your gap and *then* react." When Tom's in the mood he can go on and on.

Tom is not a screamer. He talks pretty much in a monotone but you can tell when he's upset. He'll begin to speak more emphatically and that's when players start to squirm. It can get pretty embarrassing for the guy he's talking about. Landry gets tough on those who keep making the same mistake. In such an instance he chose to make the most biting comment I ever heard from him. To a running back whose blocking was consistently poor, he snapped, "If you don't improve your techniques you aren't going to be around here much longer."

One thing Landry does *not* do in Monday meetings is criticize or praise the quarterback very much. He keeps the quarterback performance a private thing to be discussed in quarterback meetings. He never came down unreasonably hard on me during one of those sessions.

Nor would he criticize during a game very often. Sometimes I or someone else made a mistake, in a close, critical game. It's also happened that we've lost by a couple of touchdowns. He doesn't chew out people there.

He keeps that inside. On the sidelines or in the locker room when the game's over he won't show what he's feeling. But after he's thought about it that night and comes to a Monday morning meeting, that is when he lambasts people. That's really the only day he does it. We might have a seven-game winning streak but wind up thinking we'd lost after Monday morning.

Win or lose, preparation for the next game or next season goes on. That never stops. It has to be a consistent thing. This is where Landry is so important because consistency is one of his major qualities. Lose eight games in a row and his approach would be, we'll win the ninth. Win the Super Bowl and the next training camp, zap, we're back to fundamentals. Week in and week out, season after season, there is no letting down for Landry. While others straggle or waver he is always in a forward-march gear. When others criticize he sticks with what he believes. Over the years he has modified and refined his program but the basic philosophy remains virtually the same he brought to Dallas in 1960.

If the team loses or has a lousy season, Tom bounces back with a new attitude. In training camp he's back to fundamentals and preparation for the next season. If we lose on Sunday he bounces up as quickly as possible for the next game. There are times when doing so requires an iron will. When I lose on Sunday I don't want anybody talking to me for a couple of days. Landry can't afford that attitude, won't permit himself the luxury of self-pity. He has to look at film, get everybody else motivated, create an upbeat mood again.

When things go wrong some of us get down and discouraged. Either we want to change or we don't want to put our heart into what we're doing. He's not like that. He can get up off the floor after being knocked down. We can see that on Monday after a tough loss. He's in there criticizing and upset. By Tuesday he's into the next game plan. By Wednesday it's like nothing happened on Sunday, win or lose.

Quarterback meetings follow this same consistent, decisive pattern. He doesn't mince words and it's quite impressive. If you attended a quarterback meeting and didn't know anything about football you'd be in awe. He knows what he's doing and says, "This is the way to do it." He doesn't leave a lot of things hanging, like, "Well, this might work," or "Maybe we'll try this." If someone brought up a point he would say, "That *could* be good," and every once in a while he'd go along with it. But normally when someone suggests something he already has the answer to why we weren't going to use it. "This is the way it has to be done," he'd say, "because we've looked at the films and . . ." and this and that. That's the way he always handled those meetings. Very concise and *very* decisive.

Tom wasn't all rip and tear in meetings. He praised quite a bit. As we watched film he would critique offense, defense and specialty teams and single out top performances. He'd also talk about those who really had an awful day. It put guys on the spot to hear him say, "So and so, this was a terrible day. You graded out 60 percent, lowest we've had in the history of the franchise." The guy would be sitting there trying to crawl under his chair.

He's mentioned quarterbacks at times. He might say, "Roger had an outstanding day," but it would have to have been a *really* outstanding game. Handing out game balls on Monday gave Landry an opportunity for praise.

He'd talk about guys who got game balls for a few minutes. Say Benny Barnes, the left cornerback, had a super game. Landry would go over how many tackles

Benny made, or how they threw 12 passes in his area and only completed two, or point out he graded fantastically against the run. Tom would do that with five or six players.

In recent seasons I think Landry has tempered his criticism. He's more aware of people's feelings today than 10 years ago. Quite a few players used to complain about how harsh he was in those film sessions.

Tom has a feel for players and you can't get away from that. He has a sense for how far he can push certain guys, what their tolerance is and whether it's worthwhile to push them any further. If he feels he has to push them further and they don't like it, then he gets rid of them. Thomas Henderson, the linebacker he kicked off the team last season, fell into the latter category.

Only once did I hear a player talking back to Tom. Of all people it was Toni Fritsch, the place kicker from Austria. Toni came to practice one day and probably had had a couple of beers. He was out there kicking when Landry came up to him and started talking about techniques. Fritsch said, "You get away from me! Get away from me!" I don't know if he even realized it was Landry. But he looked around and it *was* Landry. Then Tom realized Toni had tipped a few, fined him $500 and almost kicked him off the team.

For reasons less obvious than Fritsch's indiscretion, I'm sure Tom has been displeased at some point with every player he's ever coached. But that never meant he didn't care about us. He does have a personal concern and I would point to the Bob Hayes narcotics trial as an example. Landry testified as a character witness for Hayes. He looked at that from every angle and went to the courthouse despite the case involving drugs, which he is very much against.

Players tell of the old days when he was less flexible

in relating to players. They said when George Andrie's wife was pregnant Tom wouldn't let him go home from training camp when the baby was born. Yet in recent years he's been receptive to personal situations like that. Last year a couple of players went home when their wives were having babies. I believe what most of us didn't realize is that we needed to go to him and explain the problem because he's so engrossed in what he's doing and there are so many players.

Landry wouldn't come around and say, "Hey, Roger, what's wrong today? Feeling OK? Everything all right at home?" But if I went to him and said, "Coach, I have a problem at home, something is wrong and I need some time off," he would know it's important to me. He also understood that problem would affect me on the field if it was left unresolved.

Landry doesn't go in for small talk but he can be a very warm person. He does a lot of things, particularly dealing with kids who are sick, very privately. He goes out of his way to help people. He gives his time, which shows the warmth of the man. Tom probably gets more done quietly behind that cold image than anybody.

Intentionally, though, I think he keeps a distance from players in order to be objective. You can't be buddy-buddy with 45 guys who change every year. As a coach he has to cut some from the team. He promotes and demotes. It's like the autograph thing. Everyone expects me to give them an autograph and there is just one of me and many of them. Well, there is just one head coach and all of us with our problems. One man can do only so much with those problems. Each year he can become just so close to so many players, handle their needs and still get the most out of them on the field.

The way the Cowboys have handled certain situations hasn't been good. Rayfield Wright's situation just killed Tom inside. After 13 seasons Rayfield wasn't asked to rejoin the team. Landry wanted him to retire but Rayfield thought he'd play another year at offensive tackle. That stalemate led to Wright's clearing waivers and being signed as a free agent by Philadelphia.

I saw Tom at a banquet before the season began and he was still bothered by what happened. The Cowboys haven't used the best judgment in handling some of their older players. The Jordans, the Edwardses, the Howleys were here today, suddenly gone tomorrow. Wright's case left everybody saying, "Well, the Cowboys got rid of another one."

Something different should have been done in all those situations. I don't know how you handle them, but the problems didn't all stem from Tom. They're a product of the business, and I don't have the answers. I just knew that Rayfield's departure disturbed Landry greatly. I'm not sure he even knew Lee Roy Jordan had a contract problem working with Tex Schramm, the general manager. Lee Roy didn't walk away the happiest guy in the world. Dave Edwards wasn't asked to come back, and he probably thought he could play another year. Those things bother Tom, but once a decision has been made he goes about his business. Whether it's a trade or a cut he doesn't look back. I admire him for that. As long as you have a feeling for people there is just so much you can do.

Landry really never came down heavy on me with criticism. Oh, I could tell when he was annoyed by the way I was playing. I had two low points during my career and, to his credit, each time Coach became a calming influence. Both instances were significant because the first, in 1974, resulted in the only time I was invited to Tom's home. The second, after the 1976 season ended, found me so upset I suggested he consider trading me.

The meeting at his house in '74 took place the weekend following our miraculous 24–23 victory over Washington on Thanksgiving Day. Clint Longley sparked the comeback after I was knocked out in the third quarter. I was happy about beating Washington but down about the season in general. Our record was 7–5, we were headed toward an 8–6 finish and the first nonplayoff season in Dallas since 1966.

Landry used that time to talk to me about the whole season. He sensed my despondency. Things had been rocky. I was taking the brunt of criticism and a lot of it was justified. Overall, I was just feeling terrible. But Tom said, "The season hasn't been your fault. It's been the team, the way we started out by losing four close games, and the things that happened to us in the offseason."

Just about everything had gone wrong. I had ankle surgery in the offseason which cut down my pretraining camp work and I suffered from it. There'd been a Players Association strike. The World Football League signed our leading rusher, Calvin Hill, and his lame duck status was a source of controversy. Early in the year we lost four straight games by a total margin of 16 points. Landry pointed out that all those things created an atmosphere which had been a problem from the beginning. The team, he said, just never came together.

He sensed that I was trying to overcome the problems single-handedly. In his view I was trying too hard because there was a stretch of games where I had about 10 interceptions. He saw the interceptions as my attempt to force a big play which wasn't there. I could see he wasn't happy with the way I was playing but the overall team situation had most of his attention.

When he got on me it was always, "You have to set up stronger." In other words he was thinking I jumped around in the pocket too much and was run-prone. "You've got to set up stronger," he'd repeat. When Tom said that to me I knew I had a problem.

In '76 I did. At midseason I cracked a bone in the little finger of my passing hand. The next week, against Washington, somebody stepped on the finger and messed it up for good that year. Our running backs, Robert Newhouse and Preston Pearson, were hurt much of that season so the passing game was carrying us.

Before the finger injury I was hitting 70 percent passing. Afterwards I completed less than 50 percent. I wound up adjusting my passing motion to the pain caused by gripping the ball and developed a sore forearm. We couldn't run and now the passing game failed. Things went to pot at the end of the year.

We lost the last regular season game to Washington at home 27–14. From our standpoint it was a meaningless outcome because we were in the playoffs. I completed some ridiculous number of passes, like 6 of 22, and the next week Tom was saying, "You're not setting up strong . . . you're not taking what you can get . . . you're not keying right."

I watched that film. We didn't try very hard and the Redskins did a great job against us. But I didn't think receivers were open like he did. I watched the same film he did, and he was telling me these guys were open. They didn't look open to me. Tom was just mad. He let that game upset him a great deal and it upset me, too. Losing that game, even though it didn't mean anything, hurt us.

Going into the playoffs against Los Angeles there was somewhat of a negative feeling because we weren't playing well offensively. We wound up losing to the Rams 14–12, and I got extremely emotional about it.

"Maybe it's best if you traded me," I told Landry a few days later. "I feel like I've let the team down. I don't know if I have them with me anymore."

Actually, no one had said anything like this. I overreacted because the LA playoff was such a disaster. The defense played great but the offense just couldn't get going. I was in a highly emotional state.

"That's crazy," sand Landry when I poured out my feelings. "The team had problems in the running game and you had the injury. You were playing well under the circumstances. We just didn't have support in other areas."

The Cowboys are pretty good about solving problems sometimes. Next year the running support materialized when a blockbuster trade with Seattle allowed Dallas to draft Tony Dorsett. A year after I thought about being traded we won Super Bowl XII.

Only one aspect of my association with Tom bothered me through the years—that people believed he and I were personally close because of our Christian faith. That always disturbed me because I've never been given anything in athletics. I always earned it. When I joined the Cowboys I didn't undergo a religious transformation. I'd heard that Landry was a very strong Christian, but I was, too. If I'd been transformed into a Christian after I came to Dallas that would have been a beauty.

I never wanted people to think I was trying to get close to him or to use religion to maintain my stability with the team. So actually I went the other way early in my career. I'd stay away from the functions he attended. In the last few years I've been more receptive to appearing with

Landry; in fact, one year we co-hosted a Fellowship of Christian Athletes dinner in Dallas.

Even that made me uneasy because I had no fore-knowledge that Landry was on the program. If it had happened when I was fighting with Craig for a job I would have been a basket case. I would have had them send out a retraction. I didn't want anyone to think I was using my Christian faith to be close to Tom.

Landry has said many times the priorities in his life are faith, family and football, in that order. He is a great Christian example. Tom not only talks about his faith but lives it. I can think of no better definition of a devout Christian. Despite this common ground between us I didn't pursue a close relationship and neither did he.

As I pointed out he invited me to his home once. He's never been to my house. Keeping our distance was the best way to maintain a respectful coach-quarterback dialogue. Socializing together wouldn't work because of the demands each of us faced. He had to tell me about my play, and sometimes what he had to say wasn't favorable. I had to be open with him, even if it meant saying I didn't think the last play he called was so hot.

It's obvious that when Tom quits coaching he will be hailed as one of the giants of his profession. Entering the 1980 season he was the fourth all-time winning coach in NFL history behind George Halas, Curly Lambeau and Don Shula. When his career is analyzed I'll bet most people will overlook one of his major assets, perhaps the greatest of all.

I mean his wife, Alicia. They are an ideal couple who truly love each other. I'm sure she's been a great outlet for him. She can handle his moods, the highs and lows. Alicia's personality complements his. He's not gregarious. She is more outspoken and outgoing at a public function. Tom's OK; he's not a stick in the mud. But he's there thinking about other things that might be more important than this particular cocktail party or dinner. She shows her enjoyment more. Alicia is a beautiful woman. I've always liked her. She's been a tremendously important asset in Tom's life, handling the family the way he wanted and adapting to the time-consuming pressures of his job. It's the same with me. If I didn't have Marianne, if our relationship weren't good physically, mentally and spiritually, it would be disastrous to try to quarterback a football team and come home to five children. You need someone like that, and Tom has been blessed to have Alicia.

The most persistent question I hear about Landry is: How much longer will he coach? Alicia figures in my answer. Admittedly it's all guesswork but I would say Tom will coach a couple of more years at the most. Who knows? He may coach another 20 years. But he has dropped some hints that long-term coaching might not be on his mind. He's been asked time and again about retiring. Just kidding, he has said, "I'm going to retire when Roger does." Although jesting, I think he was trying to say it might not be that long.

I think he's leaning toward getting into politics and I believe that would be a good move. One reason I think he could handle politics is because of Alicia. When he retires what she wants to do will be important, too. She would be great in a political atmosphere. She would like it and be a positive influence on any campaign.

Another reason I'm speculating Tom may decide on a political future is because he is a concerned citizen. I think he feels a responsibility to society and the country. It's not an outlandish possibility. His children are grown. He's still young enough. He wouldn't compromise his principles. He'd have people to support him financially who wouldn't demand repayment with favors. He's financially stable enough to handle much of the expense, which also would avoid compromise situations.

If Landry went into politics, again I would speculate it'd be on the national level, as a United States Senator. If he went into it state-wide I think it would be a position of significance, like governor.

Can't you see Tom giving one of his Monday morning critiques to Congress or the Texas Legislature? I can hear him saying, "Senator So-and-so, I've just graded the bill you proposed and it's the worst in the history of the country." Landry wouldn't mess around. He'd do a great job, as he has for the Cowboys.

Knowing what I know about him, I'd be on his bandwagon.

II
What if...?

"I tried to make it a joke. But I said, 'Craig, I'm glad it's you instead of me against this guy because anybody who takes a vacation and comes to two-a-days has got to be a little weird. He's gonna get your job.'"—Don Meredith to Craig Morton during training camp in 1968

Who among us hasn't paused to review his life and wonder... what if?

What if I hadn't been at a certain place at a certain time and done a certain thing? What if I'd decided this instead of that? What if I'd turned right instead of left? Where would I be today? *What* would I be?

Who or what decides the paths our lives follow? Is it us? Is it God? Or is it fate, chance and pure circumstance?

I've pondered those questions like everyone else. I

don't pretend to know the answers because in reflecting on my athletic life I find some unexplainable quirks. Without them the road I traveled from Purcell High School in Cincinnati, to junior college, the Naval Academy and the Dallas Cowboys would never have led me that way.

Some incidents were outright flukes, such as being allowed to enroll in the Naval Academy when actually I wasn't eligible. Over the years some equally strange and unrelated events influenced what happened to me . . . my faulty vision . . . recovery from the only sore shoulder I ever experienced . . . a Super Bowl fumble . . . an unsuccessful experiment with the quarterback shuttle.

People whose involvement provided career twists range from famous to enigmatic to anonymous . . . Lamar Hunt, Don Meredith, Craig Morton, Duane Thomas . . . a Pensacola, Florida doctor whose name I've forgotten . . . a lazy Navy seaman whose name I never knew. Each unknowingly played his part.

True, I made major decisions along the way. But sometimes instead of choice there was dictate which, strangely enough, is how I became a quarterback in the first place—reluctantly.

I didn't know it at the time but the first important crossroad occurred in high school, and I had nothing to do with the route I was to follow. I was pushed against my will to change positions from end to quarterback as a sophomore.

At St. John's Catholic grade school in Deer Park, a Cincinnati suburb, I'd been a halfback and fullback. Running with the ball was my thing, natural and instinctive, and I would never completely get it out of my system. I came out of grade school as a 125-pounder, added a lot of weight over the summer and reported for the freshman high school team at about 155 pounds.

Football was a big deal at Purcell, an all-boys Catholic school with an enrollment of around 1,200 students. At least 100 guys tried out for the team. I knew I could catch and run with the ball but I'd never thrown it much so being a quarterback never entered my mind.

On the first day of tryouts I saw two lines of players at positions that interested me, running back and receiver. Even in those days I was impatient to compete so I picked the shortest line which was for the ends. That was my position as a freshman and I wound up having an excellent year.

I anticipated catching more passes as a sophomore but it didn't happen. At that point the late Jim McCarthy, Purcell's head coach, began shaping my future. The best sophomore quarterback had been called up to the varsity and Coach McCarthy wanted him replaced. The way McCarthy later told the story, he asked who was the best athlete-leader among the incoming freshmen and the coaches said it was me.

"Then make him a quarterback," he told them.

I heard that Bernie Sinchek, the freshman coach and still a good friend, and the others were against the switch. So was I, figuring I'd been a good receiver and should stick with it. But McCarthy was a lot like Tom Landry as a coach. He was somewhat distant as far as personal relationships with players. He didn't tell me about the move. He told other coaches to tell me. That's the way things were done under McCarthy. He said how it would be and there was no arguing. Like Landry he had this mystique about him and when he said something, everybody took notice.

I was not an instant success. Sophomores rarely played on the varsity anyway and I wound up as a reserve. Make that injured reserve, to borrow a term I'd become familiar with in the National Football League. I broke my left hand and played only two games.

As a junior I was second-string quarterback and starting defensive halfback. Actually my senior year was the first season I saw consistent game action at quarterback. Gradually I'd started to like the position. I liked the idea of running with the ball again. My future wasn't at halfback. I probably wasn't fast enough. But at quarterback I could drop back to pass and take off running. I made more yardage from the *threat* of passing than actually putting the ball in the air.

There was nothing wrong with the strength of my arm. I knew that from the way I could throw a baseball from the outfield. But I was a wild, inefficient passer. The potential to become a good passer was there but that wouldn't develop until I spent the first year after high school graduation under coach Bob Shaw at New Mexico Military Institute.

Funny what a great passer I've become since Purcell. We were city co-champions my senior year but not because I bombed anybody's secondary. I ran for more than 500 yards and you only have to know one thing to grasp my early tendencies: we didn't have any running plays for the quarterback.

As a passer I was more like Rex Barney, the major league pitcher who had such a great arm but couldn't throw strikes. Like Barney, I threw high and outside a lot. Yet as the years went by I got better and better at Purcell. The truth is I completed less than 50 percent of my passes.

But the first what-if had taken place. Coach McCarthy's instincts were right. Quarterback was where I belonged. As a receiver I wouldn't have become the next Lance Alworth. I doubt there ever would have been an NFL receiver called Roger (Bambi) Staubach.

The next decision concerning my future involved the question of where to attend college. I'm still a bit mystified as to why I eventually decided on the Naval Academy. There was no military background in our family. I'd never had any boyhood dreams of going to sea. You don't hear a lot of talk about oceans in Cincinnati.

I was confused about what to do, and also upset during my senior year in high school because of what was happening at home. My father was sick with diabetes. Part of his toe was amputated and this came as a tremendous shock to me. I knew he was diabetic but didn't understand the severity of the disease. There were 40 scholarship offers to consider and because of my father's situation I was thinking of staying around locally, either at the University of Cincinnati or Xavier.

Something inside kept resisting the idea. I had high aspirations. Staying in Cincinnati wasn't the problem. I liked the city. But I was thinking more on a major scale in football. The local colleges were fine schools but not really competing on a national level. I had ambitions of someday playing in a bowl game or having a chance to be on the No. 1 team in the country.

Staying in school locally just didn't meet those high aspirations. I knew it would be a dead end to some degree. But here was the irony. Cincinnati and Xavier, the colleges I had reservations about attending, were among the ones who seemed to want me the most. The school that intrigued me at that time—Notre Dame—didn't make a recruiting move.

Playing for Notre Dame seemed like a natural choice since I'm Catholic and was attracted to the school's tradition and national football reputation. Joe Kuharich was the coach then and their recruiting program was down. They didn't even come to our school which was ridiculous because we had a good program. Even after Chuck Lima, a Purcell fullback at Notre Dame, sent film of me to his coaches, they failed to follow up. All I heard was that they said their quarterback quota was full. If they'd pursued me at that moment there's a very good chance I'd have gone to Notre Dame.

Of the schools I visited on recruiting trips I best liked Purdue and the Naval Academy. I even committed to Purdue by signing a scholarship tender: what's called grant-in-aid or letter of intent in other parts of the country. Then all of a sudden I thought, *Purdue seems so big and it's just not right for me.*

Meantime, I'd taken College Board exams for the Naval Academy. I scored high in math but low in English, too low to meet entrance requirements. Things were now very complicated. I didn't want to go to Purdue. Despite the darnedest sales pitch I ever heard, from Coach Woody Hayes, Ohio State had been eliminated by the tender I signed with Purdue. Then after the Ohio High School All-Star game—I played defensive back and spent most of the night tackling the Most Valuable Player, a halfback named Paul Warfield—Notre Dame suddenly became interested. Their quarterback quota sprang a leak and I was offered a four-year scholarship. Because of the earlier snub I wasn't interested.

Where was I going, anyway?

To this day it's hard to exlain why I kept being attracted to Annapolis. I did like the people I met there. The environment and atmosphere were impressive to me. Although I was a little leary about being a military man, at this point in my life I was drawn to the aspects of receiving a good education and still being involved in athletics.

I remembered the instructor-pupil ratio. It was one professor per 20–25 students. We were assured of individual attention which is so important. I had the foresight to know that an education was going to be important. Frankly, I also realized my study habits weren't all that great. I needed discipline in this area. I felt it was necessary for someone to sit on me academically so I could get the education I wanted.

To pursue enrolling in Annapolis required another choice with two alternatives. Each involved one year of preparatory schooling so I could take another crack at the College Board. The Naval Academy people first suggested I attend a prep school. I rejected that idea as a waste of time. The other option was to enroll in junior college. This became sort of a compromise solution, and the place in mind would introduce me to military life. It wouldn't take long to determine if I wanted four more years of the same thing at the Academy.

That is how I ended up going to New Mexico Military Institute. What an amazing development when I think of it today. I believe the Lord must have sent me. I prayed hard about that decision. Yet, logically, there was no reason a homebody from Cincinnati should wind up in Roswell, New Mexico. I was homesick as a dog for a long time and still worried about my father's condition. But it was on the road to the Naval Academy and for some reason I thought I should go there.

The kicker is that the Naval Academy never should have let me in. Not because I busted the College Board. I passed that breezing. But I failed another test—an eye test. What the Naval Academy didn't discover until too late is that I'm partially color-blind. Had this been known earlier I would have been disqualified from entering.

My preentry physical for the Naval Academy was taken at Fitzsimmons Army Hospital in Denver. The seaman administering the eye test was just going through the motions, not really paying attention. He was in charge of the white, red and green dot test. That's the one where they flip white over red or green over red and you have to say what color the numbers are. I finished the test and the guy behind me said, "Hey, you missed quite a few." And I said, "Oh, I always do."

If the seaman at that moment had put down "Fail" on the eye test it would have been all over for me. The Naval Academy was very strict about waiving people in on color blindness. They just weren't doing it.

I've never been able to pass a strict color-blindness test. At a distance, light green and white look the same to me. Dark colors at a distance just look dark; I can't distinguish them as blue or red. I don't have any trouble with a technicolor movie and before anybody asks the question I'll answer it: No, it never bothered me on the football field. I didn't throw a few interceptions against Philadelphia because the Eagles wore green and white jersies.

After enrollment at the Academy the eye problem was discovered during the first physical there. "How did you get in?" they wanted to know. I remember someone expressed what I was thinking: "You are one lucky fellow."

The next thing they told me was that I wouldn't go Navy line or be a flyer. I was restricted and the Academy doesn't like to do that. They'll wind up restricting guys in later years if their eyes get worse or they get hurt. But they don't bring in people knowing they're going to be restricted. I was headed for a staff-type position from the outset.

I couldn't fly because of the carrier landings. Particularly at night the signals are transmitted through red, green and white lights, just the colors I have trouble with at a distance. It's the same with being a line officer on a ship.

Again they are distinguishing port and starboard lights, and the colors are important. It's not overly significant but a navigational error *could* hinge on something like that.

One thing that ticked me off later was that the Naval Academy took some criticism after it was discovered I was color-blind. People were saying they broke the rules to get me in which is baloney. At the time they didn't know what kind of athlete I was going to be. They knew I was good but no one could predict what was going to happen. Remember, they wouldn't let me in straight out of high school because of the English problem on the College Board. It would have been easier to enroll me then if somebody were interested in cheating. They weren't, of course. The odd fact stands that I got into the Naval Academy through a foul-up in the physical.

But what if I had not?

I probably would have thought again about Purdue or maybe Notre Dame. By then I had established myself as an All-American junior college quarterback. I'd had a tremendous season at Roswell. Even a lot of schools from the Southwest that don't normally recruit in Ohio were now interested in swaying me from the Naval Academy.

Had I been ineligible for Annapolis then it would have been a different ball game entirely. There would have been a more wide-open selection of schools from which to choose. I believe I would have honed back to Purdue or explored Notre Dame. I'd probably have heard again from Woody Hayes, who called seven straight nights before I signed the tender with Purdue. Since everything turned out all right at the Naval Academy a lot of credit should go to that lazy seaman who was goofing off during my eye test.

The color-blindness issue sort of figured in why the Cowboys drafted me in 1964 on the tenth round. Those were the days when the NFL allowed teams to select "future" choice, a practice since abandoned, and because of that junior college season I was eligible to be picked a year before I graduated from Annapolis. Gil Brandt, player personnel director for Dallas, said I was drafted on the basis of athletic ability *and*, at least the way the Cowboys heard it, a question of whether the color blindness might prevent me from serving four years of active duty.

The post-graduation summer of 1965 was one of proposals. I received two and made one. They turned out to have the happiest, most long-lasting impact of anything in my life. The proposal I made was to Marianne for a September marriage, and the best thing about that was she agreed.

The proposals made to me were NFL contract offers from the Kansas City Chiefs and Dallas, in that order. This is where Danny Petersen, an assistant basketball coach at Navy, helped turn my professional career toward Texas. It was Petersen who tipped off the Cowboys that I had received a serious bid from Lamar Hunt, owner of the Chiefs.

During that period there was an American and National Football League and, consequently, two drafts. The leagues would merge in a few years but at this time they drafted separately and bidding between them for players was fierce. Anyway, that's how I wound up being courted by different teams since Kansas City also picked me in 1964 on the fifteenth round of the AFL draft.

Lamar himself came to our home in Annapolis to outline his deal. As I remember it he said Kansas City would give me a $5,000 signing bonus and $250 to $300 per month while I was on active duty with no strings attached. If I decided to stay in the Navy after my four-year hitch was up I kept the money. I also would sign a future contract for three years at $25,000 annually plus receive another bonus of $50,000 should I choose to leave the military.

"Would you be interested?" asked Lamar. "Oh, yes, this sounds great," I told him. "But I have to get it approved by the Navy."

I took the contract to Captain Paul Borden, a legal officer at the academy. He cleared it. I knew the Cowboys were interested but to what degree I wasn't certain. One thing for sure though. Lamar Hunt was one jump ahead of them.

Word of my meeting with Hunt got around the Academy where I was serving as an assistant coach while waiting for stationing orders. Brandt said years later the Cowboys had in mind an offer similar to Hunt's but admitted that since the NFL season was underway they were busy and didn't realize I viewed my signing situation as urgent.

Petersen changed that with a phone call to Brandt in which he said, "If you're interested in Roger you better step on it." Captain Borden and Brandt then talked, with Gil stressing that Dallas definitely wanted to make a bid.

What if the Cowboys had said, "Well, we can't worry about that now"? Then that's where it would have ended. I'd have signed with Kansas City. But it happened that Dallas was playing in Philadelphia a week or so later on the same weekend as the Army-Navy game there. Captain Borden, Brandt and Dallas general manager Tex Schramm arranged to meet then. My idea was to get one offer from each team to avoid haggling with anybody.

The Dallas proposition went like this: a $10,000 signing bonus and $500 per month while I was on active duty. There were no give-back restrictions if I stayed in the Navy. When and if I reported to the Cowboys they would pay me $25,000 per season on a three-year contract in addition to another signing bonus option. I could take $55–60,000 up front or, what I decided was best, $100,000 deferred over a ten-year period. When Captain Borden outlined the deal over the telephone I told him to accept.

In turn I called Lamar and told him I'd worked out an arrangement with Dallas. "I'm sorry," he said. "I wish we'd had a chance to get back with you."

There were three reasons why I picked the Cowboys over Kansas City. The money was better with Dallas, the Cowboys drafted me higher and at the time the NFL was considered the better brand of football.

Now when I look back on that situation I see that there was a fourth reason, the most important of them all. That was Danny Petersen's phone call which alerted the Cowboys to Hunt's offer. Incidentally, Petersen came to Navy from Michigan State where he'd also been sort of a talent scout for Dallas. It was from the Midwest campus that he recommended a basketball player whom the Cowboys signed as a free agent in 1964. The way things turned out at first the Cowboys thought he'd done them a favor but I'm not sure they still feel the same today. The player was Pete Gent.

Three years passed, one of them the longest of my life spent as a supply officer in Vietnam at the height of that sad country's conflict. Even there football and the possibility of playing again lay heavy on my mind. Around Chu Lai where I was stationed I'd throw passes in spare moments. The terrain was so rough I wore out the football, wrote Brandt for another and he obliged by mailing one. Back in the States I was assigned to Pensacola Naval Air Station in time to shake some football rust by playing a so-so 1967 season with the base team. Soon it was time to determine my future either as a Navy man or a pro quarterback.

The Cowboys talked to me about spending time with the team in training camp the next summer. The idea appealed to both sides. They were curious to see what I could do after such a long layoff. I wanted to see myself.

I never told anyone the importance I placed on the training camp test of '68. If I'd been a flop I never would have left the Navy. I would have said, "I'm staying in." I had no problems with the service. Marianne and I enjoyed it. In the Supply Corps there would not have been a lot of sea duty. I would have stayed in Pensacola a bit longer and then gone off somewhere else. Unless something in the business world caught hold it was the Navy for me. At that time there was nothing in business. As far as any other avenue of interest outside the Navy, football was it. It was football or the Navy and the '68 training camp would tell me which way to go.

I believed I could play again. But I also was realistic. If I went to California and discovered that after three years a comeback would be an insurmountable battle, then I'd have to give up football. I also prepared for going out there. I worked very hard—which was almost my undoing.

In May, only two months before camp opened for me and the rookies, I developed severe pain in my right shoulder. I'd throw passes one day and the shoulder would be killing me the next day so much I could barely lift a football. I kept going to an orthopedic surgeon on the base for treatment. He prescribed anti-inflammatory medicine and therapy. None of it did any good. I was in a sweat. Camp was around the corner. In my present condition if I threw passes one day I'd have to lay off for two weeks before the pain went away.

Eventually a friend recommended I see a doctor in town. I'm embarrassed to admit I don't remember the physician's name. Of all the people who've contributed to my career none was more important than this man. We'd gone through the same routine of therapy and so forth until one day he decided to give me a shot of cortisone. He must have hit the right spot. What apparently had been a bad case of tendonitis subsided. Usually cortisone offers only temporary relief but the injection plus a change in my warm-up routine cured the only sore-shoulder problem I ever encountered.

Warming up properly is imperative for young quarterbacks. I never used to do it. I'd just hit the field and start throwing. It finally caught up with me in the form of the shoulder pain. This was such a scare that I developed a fetish I followed throughout my career in Dallas. I always put "hot stuff" like analgesic balm on my shoulder before practice and iced it down after a hard day of passing. Without the cortisone shot I couldn't have put this new lesson of a disciplined, slower warm-up to work. But together, they got me ready for California.

Early in June the shoulder returned to normal. I spent a solid month of passing in preparation. Many of the workouts were with Kaye Stephensen, who went to quarterback for a while with Buffalo. I was keyed up for the trip, too. The waiting made me so jumpy I'd rush out of the house at 10 P.M. just to run around the block. Anything to keep active. Once my shoulder came back Marianne knew I had to go out there and determine whether I could play or not. Thanks to the anonymous doctor in Pensacola I would get the chance.

I took two weeks' leave to go, which many players thought odd, to say the least. But those 14 days were without price because everything clicked in Thousand

Oaks. I played well in scrimmages against San Francisco and Los Angeles. The Rams were then coached by George Allen and I recall his saying I ran like Fran Tarkington but had a stronger arm. As for Landry, he had questions about me because I *did* run frequently. Except for Tarkington, running wasn't considered an asset for quarterbacks in those days.

I believe that's when Dallas knew I could play. To me it meant I definitely was getting out of the Navy. I went back to Pensacola sky-high emotionally. It was like I'd won a championship. I kept thinking to myself, *Boy, I really set 'em on fire.*

Something else told me the Cowboys were favorably impressed. I had their playbook to study for the next year. Coaches told me they'd wanted to send me a playbook before I came to that camp but Landry wouldn't hear of it. After those two weeks he gave me one. That was a positive sign and I recognized it.

Back in Pensacola I was thinking I could whip the world. I had a great season with the Goshawks, the base team. We won our first seven games. I was back in the groove again.

Amid the initial excitement I didn't stop to consider the reality of my competitive situation with the Cowboys. Meredith was the starting quarterback in 1968 and only 30 years old. He took the team to a 12–2 record that year, the best in franchise history, although it ended with an upset playoff loss to Cleveland, 30–21. Meredith's peak seasons, many of them, you'd think, were to come. Morton completed his third year as Meredith's understudy and looked like the guy who'd take over some day for Don. I remembered Craig from 1965 when we were together on the College All-Star team and knew he had a tremendous arm. Since the Cowboys drafted him No. 1 it was evident how they felt about him. For a No. 3 quarterback there was Jerry Rhome whose edge on me was more mental than physical—five years of pro experience. And there I was, pumped up about being a 27-year-old NFL rookie.

Only through hindsight do I realize what a close call I experienced. Had the shot not helped settle my shoulder it would have been practically useless to go to camp. I could have lasted one day, maybe two, on adrenalin and guts. Probably all I could have done was get some advice from team doctors on how to rehabilitate.

A number of things might have changed if the Cowboys had not seen me in action. Rhome might not have been traded, even though I understood he wanted out. The Cowboys may have brought in another quarterback. Because I did well I think their attitude toward me altered a great deal. Now I was in their plans. The shoulder problem *could* have been a career-finisher if it hadn't cleared up quickly because I didn't have a lot of time to decide on whether to leave the Navy or not.

I wasn't oblivious to the quarterback situation ahead of me in Dallas. I looked at it this way. First, when Rhome left I had a chance to make the team. Second, they were going to keep three quarterbacks. Third, I just wanted to establish myself, to make it somewhere. I thought there was a definite chance that would be with a team other than the Cowboys.

I'm convinced that's what would have happened if the status quo had remained with Meredith. The only way it could have been different was if Craig had asked to be traded because of Don's seniority and stability as the No. 1 man. Then I would have been Meredith's backup. As matters stood the team was coming to the point at which Meredith could get over the playoff hump that was stopping Dallas. All I knew was that at age 27 I wasn't patient enough to sit around four or five years waiting to play.

On July 5, 1969, five days before my reporting date to camp, I was in Pensacola when the phone rang. It was Curt Mosher, the club's publicity man, who said to expect some calls from the press because Meredith had just retired. I was shocked.

I'd taken leave to attend quarterback school in Dallas that spring. Rhome had been traded so Craig, Meredith and I remained. Going through quarterback school Meredith gave no indication he was going to quit. He even invited me to dinner one night at his home but never dropped a retirement hint. I didn't know Merdith very well but I liked him. He was a fun-loving guy.

As Mosher forewarned my phone rang. The press wanted to know how I felt about suddenly being the second-team quarterback. Naturally I was ecstatic. It meant I was closer to getting a chance to play. I even joked about the situation to Marianne by telling her, "Pro football isn't so tough. I've gone from No. 4 to No. 2 quarterback without doing a thing."

Incredibly it was true. Meredith retired at age 31 and his departure stunned everyone. In hindsight I can see what a fateful decision that was for me. If Meredith hadn't retired I would have been an "also-ran" in Dallas. He definitely could have had his best years before him and in that case it would have taken a long-shot break for me to get playing time.

Craig took over for Don with a lot of maturity about him initially. Then he began to have injury problems. If Craig had a failing I think it was that he didn't work as hard as he should have to recover from those injuries. Craig was a tough guy. He could take a beating. So could Don and so could I. Every quarterback has to do that.

Craig did play hurt. He played with a bad shoulder in

'69 and underwent an operation after the season ended. But he didn't take time to rehabilitate himself. That was his problem. I think if he had it to do over again he would have come back in better shape for the 1970 season. He just wasn't back all the way. He had the whole offseason to get ready and didn't do it. He came to training camp and had some trouble with his arm which led to bone chips in his elbow.

I'd spent the previous year in typical fashion for a Dallas rookie, being seen or heard from rarely. There *had* been one heady moment. Because of another injury to Craig I started and finished the first NFL game for which I'd put on a uniform. The thrill was multiplied by the fact we beat St. Louis 24–3 and I threw my first touchdown pass, a 75-yarder to Lance Rentzel.

With Craig hurt as the '70 season opened I started the first two games. That was the year Landry said everything was up for grabs, all positions open to challenge, and he established "performance levels" as guidelines. If you didn't meet those standards you didn't start. I knew they didn't apply to me because there was no way Landry felt I was ready to play full time. It just wasn't going to happen.

Craig took over for me in St. Louis, after I'd thrown a second interception that gave the Cardinals a 6–0 lead in the second quarter. When Landry sent him in, I felt humiliated. Never in my football experience had I been sat down after starting a game. It made me hot and I said so on the sidelines. It made me hotter that we went on to lose 20–6.

At midseason the Cowboy's record slipped to 5–4 with a 38–0 loss to St. Louis in the Cotton Bowl, the only time Dallas ever has been shut out in 20 years. Ironically, Meredith was in the press box as an announcer for ABC-TV and the crowd started hollering, "We want Meredith!" over and over. The plea was ironic for Don, too, because so often during his latter years he'd heard the crowd yell, "We want Morton!" Don simply waved and said, "No way you're getting me out there again."

After that game Landry decided he would call plays for Craig and we won our last five regular season games. The same defense which earlier in the year cratered in a 54–13 defeat to Minnesota turned magnificent. During a six-game span leading up to Super Bowl V opponents scored only two touchdowns and a field goal against us. Landry maintains to this day that, for brilliant defense over a sustained period, the '70 Cowboys were the best he ever fielded.

During the pre-Super Bowl countdown against Baltimore, the Cowboys were tagged as "a team without a quarterback." That was a tragic, unfair situation for Craig, and I think it had some effect on him entering the game. Baltimore won 16–13 on a last-second field goal by Jim O'Brien, which brings up the biggest what-if of my career in Dallas.

What if . . . the Cowboys had won Super Bowl V?

There's no question we should have and would have, except. . . . We were ahead 13–6 in the second quarter and had the ball second down, goal–to–go at the Baltimore one-yard line. Craig handed off to Duane Thomas who hit the middle and fumbled. An official, Jack Fette, flubbed the recovery call and gave possession to the Colts. Dave Manders, our center, actually fell on the ball and Billy Ray Smith one of Baltimore's defensive linemen, later admitted it. Billy Ray could afford the admission since it was his frenzied shouts of "Colts' ball! Colts' ball!" that helped fake out Fette. The way our defense was playing, a 20–6 lead would have been almost insurmountable but Baltimore dodged the bullet right there and went on to win.

I was going crazy on the sidelines, rooting so hard all

the way. It never dawned on me that there was no way I would have had an open shot at quarterback the next year against a guy who led his team to a Super Bowl victory. I see that today but then I didn't.

Instead, something very low-key yet dramatic happened as the Cowboys' team charter flew home from Miami. Landry was visiting in the players' section, stopping here and there for a few words. He sat down with Marianne and me and said to me, "You'll have a chance to start next season." That got my competitive juices going immediately. Next day I was at the practice field working out.

The same feeling struck Danny White when I retired. I'm sure his adrenalin was pumping a mile a minute. It was a different approach for him. He was going to *play*. The identical thing happened to Glenn Carano, who went into training camp as Danny's backup. Glenn was saying to himself, "Even though I'm probably going to be second team I am one step closer." That's the emotion I had when I stepped off the plane from Miami. It was like a new lease on life.

Had the Cowboys won that Super Bowl, Landry would not have been encouraging to me. I don't know what my attitude might have been under those circumstances. I'd have been back in that limbo status again, knowing I was a year older and going on 30. I would have asked to be traded. I'm sure of it. I would have had to.

Landry was true to his word in 1971. I did compete with Craig as an equal. Unfortunately for everyone we hadn't settled anything after six games and the team struggled with a 4–2 record. I'd start, then Craig would start and the team sort of drifted. I think Landry was indecisive about a No. 1 quarterback. He kept hoping the question would resolve itself on the field but it didn't. In all honesty I suppose any decision at that point was a coin flip, but I still think Landry let the situation drift too long.

On one side he had Craig who was an experienced veteran. Then he had me, an untested commodity, a guy with potential but an experience variable working against him. Craig and I were caught in a situation that couldn't go on and on.

Landry knew neither of us was a George Ratterman-type who could be happy as a backup throughout our careers. It'd be the same on any team with two quarter-backs close to the same age. In our case I was one year older than Craig and by a wild coincidence we shared the same February 5 birthday. This situation will be a problem with Danny and Glenn, too. That can only go so far. They're both excellent quarterbacks and Glenn is not going to stay put.

Landry didn't make our situation any better by what he proposed to do when we played Chicago. During a team meeting he almost casually mentioned that we were going to have *two* No. 1 quarterbacks against the Bears. Craig and I would shuttle on alternate plays. We almost fell off our chairs. We looked at each other and rolled our eyes. In all the years I was in Dallas that has to be the worst decision Landry ever made.

The system rolled up a lot of yardage but not enough points. I don't know if the Bears taunted our shuttle system or not. Whenever anybody was tackled I was trotting to the sideline. "You guys looked like two ships passing in the night," somebody cracked in the locker room.

Chicago won 23–19 and during the last few minutes of the game Landry left Craig in control. His explanation was that it became important at that time to have one quarterback in there for the sake of continuity. Right there

I thought it was over for me, that he'd made his choice and it was Craig. I figured since he turned the game over to Craig I had lost my chance as a starter.

Next night in Dallas there was a team party. The wives were holding their annual Las Vegas Night function. The way I saw it everything had come up snake eyes for me and the Cowboys. Ralph Neely, our starting offensive tackle, had broken his ankle in a motorbike accident. Also earlier in the day defensive end George Andrie was taken to a hospital complaining of severe chest pains. He feared a heart attack but his symptoms were soon diagnosed as acute indigestion. With a 4–3 record the whole team felt like burping.

I was no exception. My mood that evening ran the gamut from dark to discouraged (which isn't very far when you think about it). Yet an encouraging word *was* heard. Ray Renfro, an assistant coach, pulled me aside to whisper, "You're not supposed to know this but . . . you will be starting this week." Renfro added he was informing me at great personal peril that included his job and both ears. Landry would have them all if he knew.

The point of the alternating-quarterback episode was that if we rallied to beat the Bears behind Craig, I *wouldn't* start the next week. Certainly the team's performance from then on might have been as it actually occurred—a 10-game winning streak culminated by victory over Miami in Super Bowl VI. But I would not have been a part of it in that instance. As it was, the opportunity became mine and the moment pivotal to my career. Had Craig won that game against the Bears . . . who knows?

I think Landry's confidence in me wasn't 100 percent despite the promotion. Only four weeks earlier he'd benched me at halftime against the New York Giants in a game we were leading 13–6 and eventually won 20–13. I wanted to tell him to trade me then but I didn't. It was the middle of the season and I didn't want to ruffle the water. Nor had I forgotten being sat down early the year before against St. Louis. Both incidents made me furious with Landry because he didn't allow me to finish what I'd started.

Marianne reminds me that I used to talk about being traded all the time—around the house. She said one year I had the kids convinced we were moving to Green Bay. Another year I decided Atlanta needed a quarterback. Only twice did I directly suggest to Landry that he trade me. The first time was during another Who's No. 1? crisis with Morton in 1973.

I had to ask for a trade rather than sit on the bench any more. You can't believe the sensation that leaves. The game is over and you've contributed zero. It's the pits. I didn't feel I should be in there because I was so superior to Craig. I never held it against Craig personally because he was playing. I just wanted an opportunity. I wanted to *play*. How I would get that chance I didn't know. Dallas didn't seem to be the place my career would continue for much longer.

Craig had some bad luck and I mean that sincerely. Craig also wasn't settled into a lifestyle of really dedicating himself to football. He couldn't get away with doing that. He was trying to be Bobby Layne or somebody similar, and he didn't have the disposition for it. I think he was a great athlete and quarterback. Injury problems hurt him and affected his concentration, I think. I used to watch Craig throw and there wasn't anybody better.

You take all these what-ifs and how do you explain them?

I think God knows how our life is going to go. We are predestined from the standpoint of his knowing. We have a free will and determine our own fate, though. God just knows how it will turn out because he can see. He is all-knowing. I believe that.

I think prayer is very powerful. I've prayed hard about the direction I've taken during my life . . . about going to the Naval Academy, my various situations with the Cowboys, retirement. Afterwards I became at ease with the decision. Prayer isn't the cure-all, however.

The Bible says, "Knock at the door and it shall be opened; seek and ye shall find." Some people who take that literally believe all they have to do is sit back and their prayer will be answered the way they wish. I think prayers sometimes are answered, "No." I also believe that along with prayer a lot of effort must go into a decision.

My view is that if a lot of hard work and effort are put into anything, good things will happen. Sometimes you don't even realize they're good. They may look bad. But this approach is the best of other alternatives.

Let me give you some personal examples. Early in my sophomore year at the Naval Academy I wasn't playing much and thought to myself, *This is ridiculous*. But I was still working hard every day. If I had let that state of mind prevail to the point of affecting my physical effort then I was finished. Too often people let their state of mind affect physical preparation. They get down and depressed. They quit trying.

I've been down but never to the point where I haven't worked hard. After the St. Louis game when Landry took me out and after the New York Giants game when I was down in the mouth, I still hit the practice field the next day going full blast. I continued to prepare for my career. *It might not be with the Cowboys*, I thought then. Wherever it might be I wanted to be ready.

Fate is something too intangible for me to understand. I'm more receptive to the idea that we determine where we're going and how we get there by the effort we put out.

When I pray for help in making a decision I'm never sure my prayer has been answered. I simply have confidence that it has. There are no visions. The clouds don't part and no voice speaks to me. There's no lightning or thunder. Quite the opposite.

I receive a sense of peace in knowing I've done everything I can in making a decision. I don't second-guess or dwell in the past. I *do* think about the past and learn from it, but I don't let past mistakes become an obsession.

I don't look back and say, "Well, if I hadn't gone to the Naval Academy I would have been able to play pro football four years earlier." I deal with decisions as I've made them. A lot of effort went into them. They were thought out. Afterwards, off I go.

It was like that with retirement. I didn't suddenly wake up one morning and think, *I'm going to retire.* That decision was well thought out. I weighed things and prayed about it. This season I'll say, "Gee, I wonder whether I should have retired," but it won't be something I'll dwell on. It will just be a passing thought. Probably a natural thought and a healthy one.

There may be momentary regret but I won't second-guess what I've done. This fall, as I am watching the Cowboys quarterbacked by someone else, I *won't* be saying to myself, *What if . . . ?*

III

The Super Bowls

This game is a big one but I'm not sure how much bigger it is, in comparison, than the Army-Navy game when Roger was so much younger. Every midshipman, ever officer—why every admiral in the fleet—were all on Roger's shoulders. But he thrives on pressure. He seems to respond to it perfectly."—Cmdr. Paul Borden, USN (Ret.), prior to Super Bowl VI

Some people may find it trite when I describe the Super Bowl as the end-all. Certainly Duane Thomas would. It was Duane who as a rookie offered the classic analysis of why he felt the Super Bowl wasn't the ultimate game. "If it was the ultimate game," Duane said, "they wouldn't be playing it next year."

Yet from the annual perspective of the Cowboys,

Super Bowls were the ultimate. I agree with that view. Every drill we completed, every play we ran, every push-up we did in training camp, every weight we lifted . . . all of it was done for the purpose of winning the Big One.

To me Super Bowls are like the Army-Navy games. They represent the epitome of the sport, the reason we're playing. They are what motivates us to sweat, strain, hurt and keep going.

As long as I played for the Cowboys, winning the Super Bowl was our objective every year. Such are the welcome pressures on a team that consistently had world championship ambitions. We never thought the goal was unreasonable or unrealistic.

I was the starting quarterback in four Super Bowls and don't believe I performed badly in any of them. Neither do I credit myself with being the difference in the two we won. All in all I think I just did my job.

In order, I remember the capsule highs and lows of each Super Bowl like this:

VI—Dallas 24, Miami 3. There was more personal pressure in this one than any to follow because it was my first to be active. I'd started our last nine straight games but less than 20 against NFL competiton in my career. So my inexperience was a potential factor. It was crucial that I avoid mistakes, and I did [12 completions in 19 attempts, 119 yards, 2 TDs, *no* interceptions]. I didn't think I had a great game but they gave me the Most Valuable Player award. Actually our record-setting running game was the key to victory.

X—Pittsburgh 21, Dallas 17. Of a total of four interceptions I threw in four Super Bowls, three came in this game. Only one was crucial since it followed a fourth quarter blocked punt, which turned the outcome in Pittsburgh's favor. Until then we had a surprising 10–7 lead. Considering the pass rush pressure [seven traps] I thought my passing was OK [15 of 24, 204 yards, 2 TDs]. The major disappointment was the way our two-minute offense functioned when we had a chance to win in the final minute.

XII—Dallas 27, Denver 10. I think I played a positive role in not giving up an interception and hitting key plays to keep our drives going. My performance [17 of 25, 183 yards, 1 TD] was more consistent than sensational. Our defensive play was magnificent and dominated a game the media built up as almost a personal duel between me and former teammate Craig Morton. The saddest feeling I've had during a Super Bowl, other than in losing, was in watching what happened to Craig.

XIII—Pittsburgh 35, Dallas 31. Other than an interception by Mel Blount on a pass play that led to sharp words between me and Landry afterwards, I look on this game as pretty decent personally [17 of 30, 228 yards, 3 TDs]. I regret that pass more than any I ever threw. I still believe the game was greatly influenced by the worst penalty ever called in a Super Bowl, the tripping infraction on Benny Barnes in the fourth quarter. Unfortunately, it also decided the question of which team dominated the decade of the 70s.

Talk about your what-ifs. A Dallas player could drive himself nuts dwelling on the three Super Bowls we lost. Against Baltimore in Super Bowl V an offical named Jack Fette mistakenly gave the Colts a fumble recovery on their one-yard line.

We felt officials let Pittsburgh get away with too much roughhouse stuff in Super Bowl X without drawing a single penalty, especially Jack Lambert who kneed people and once turned Cliff Harris upside down and dumped him on his head. Then there was the Lynn Swann–Benny Barnes penalty in XIII.

But to keep complaining about those calls detracts too much from Pittsburgh's great play. The bottom line was that the Steelers made the big plays and deserve credit for them. When a team goes 4–0 in Super Bowls over a span of six years, as Pittsburgh did, it stands alone.

The sheer excitement of playing in Super Bowls never became old hat to me. The thrill increased because of the opportunity to enhance the history of the Cowboys. Entering the last one I played, Super Bowl XIII against Pittsburgh, we were assured of setting one record and had our eyes on another. Dallas was appearing in its fifth Super Bowl and, like the Steelers, shooting to become the first three-time champion. To that point no other team had played in more than four Super Bowls or won more than two.

One feature of the game did change for me and the team over the years, though. We were able to handle the pregame atmosphere better. The first Super Bowl for the Cowboys, the one I didn't play in against Baltimore, was an experience in distractions because we didn't know what to expect. Both teams have to go through them but if they've been through the hoopla once they're not surprised, irritated or unbalanced by the scene. Super Bowls are special in a crazy kind of way.

Players are required to attend picture-taking and interview sessions for four days. People are calling their rooms. Then there's the ticket situation. *Everybody* needs tickets so they worry with that. For a week they're working out in unfamiliar surroundings which is a difficult adjustment. So it's a definite advantage for a team that's been through the hectic countdown before. Since both teams were experienced in the pregame ritual neither the Cowboys nor Steelers had an edge here prior to kickoff.

Other than Thomas Henderson's holding court with the media there wasn't much controversy or lively topics. Normally there's a theme the press, radio and TV people harp on. Prior to Super Bowl VI it was whether the Cowboys finally would win the Big One and, if they did, whether Duane would talk about it. The buildup to Super Bowl X featured us as Cinderella in cleats, the only wild card team ever to qualify for the title game. Before we kicked off against Denver in Super Bowl XII, everything possible had been written or said about Craig and me. By comparison Super Bowl XIII was quiet.

Most of the questions I handled were the old ones about playcalling. When I answered seriously it was to say I thought playcalling was more important in the running game than in the passing phase. I slipped in the usual joke about Landry telling me when I was 42 he'd let me call plays.

The only other subject that got a lot of attention was whether I thought the American Conference was stronger than the National. I agreed there probably wasn't the overall strength in the NFC but two or three teams were just as strong as any in the AFC. I also pointed out there were many positive signs in the NFC that indicated AFC superiority would turn around soon.

For instance, the NFC has by far the greater number of top running backs. The AFC's only great breakaway threat is Earl Campbell of Houston. Franco Harris ranks with the best anywhere but his style is different from Campbell's. For exciting runners the

NFC now has Ottis Anderson, Walter Payton, Tony Dorsett, and Wilbert Montgomery. If there's a noticeable difference between the conferences, it's that quarterbacking in the National is less experienced and consequently not as strong overall as in the Americn. The point was illustrated by the fact that prior to the '79 season only four starting NFC quarterbacks had thrown as many as 1,000 NFL passes—Jim Hart of St. Louis, Archie Manning of New Orleans, Mike Phipps of Chicago and I.

So a lot of pregame focus was put on the AFC's general superiority and the fact that Dallas had been the only NFC team to win a Super Bowl since the 1967 Green Bay Packers. The media latched on to one obvious angle—Dallas vs. Pittsburgh would be the first rematch in Super Bowl history. The same teams which contested Super Bowl X were back again.

We planned a Big Play offensive attack against the Steelers with emphasis on taking advantage of their blitzes in the passing game. Our definition of Big Play was one with instant touchdown potential. Each was an out-of-the-ordinary play, the kind the writers in Dallas described as "exotics." One was a fake wide-receiver reverse in which Drew Pearson passed to tight end Billy Joe DuPree. Another featured me handing off to Tony Dorsett, taking a pitch-back from him and throwing deep for Tony Hill.

Neither worked. The first ended in disaster and subsequent controversy. The other misfired because a Pittsburgh blitz ruined the timing. Both failed because of our lack of execution rather than sharp defensive play by the Steelers. Yet our passing game and third-down conversions were excellent overall. We made nine of 16 third-down opportunities, 56 percent, which is ultrasuc-

essful against any defense and more so against a team
s good as Pittsburgh.

The Steelers are pretty predictable defensively, but
don't mean that as a criticism. Basically they broad-
ast what they're going to do. The problem is that they
lay their defenses so well the fore-knowledge doesn't
elp that much. Still, we felt we could hurt Pittsburgh
assing on third down to the inside.

In those situations, Pittsburgh's defensive backs
ike to take away those inside routes—the ones toward
he middle of the field—so our receivers worked on
pecial techniques to compensate. Instead of releasing,
hat is, starting their pass routes, with an inside move
hey would drive straight upfield a couple of steps.
Depending upon the position of the defensive back they
night even start to his outside, which would be toward
he sideline. In either case only *then* would they make a
reak for the inside.

We made these adjustments because of all the
rouble our receivers had trying to shake Pittsburgh's
econdary in Super Bowl X. In that game if the receiv-
rs had an inside route, right off the bat they'd try to get
nside and found it impossible. The bump-and-run was
ermitted all over the field in those days and they
vound up being manhandled. Golden Richards, for
nstance, left the game with broken ribs.

But with contact permitted only within the first five
yards downfield in Super Bowl XIII our guys had an
easier time getting open. Drew had some good inside
outes and twice in the first quarter our preparation for
Pittsburgh blitzes paid off to other receivers. With
inebackers coming, Butch Johnson caught a 26-yard
ass and Hill a 39-yarder for our first touchdown.

The running game was critical for us, and although

we opened strong on the ground we didn't maintain the threat, Pittsburgh played Joe Greene, their left defensive tackle, in a strange way, sort of angled toward the center-guard gap. Then they overshifted the line either way. One of their major objectives was to protect their linebackers, especially Lambert in the middle. Our counterpriority was to block him but we didn't do it well enough. Lambert became involved in a game-high 12 tackles and Jack Ham, the All-Pro outside lineacker, wasn't far behind with 10. Together, Pittsburgh's linebackers were credited with 22 primary tackles and 11 assists, an uncommonly high total.

They had to be wondering what was going on during our first series, though. Dorsett gained nine, 16 and 13 yards on successive carries. In four plays following the opening kickoff we moved from the Dallas 28 to a first down on the Pittsburgh 34. At that point, because of our philosophy of trying to hit the Big Play, Landry called for the fake reverse-pass.

I pitched out to Dorsett on an apparent end sweep, the play he'd twice gained big yardage with already. Only Tony was to hand off to Drew coming back the other way. Then Drew, a former quarterback at Tulsa, would throw long for DuPree. The play worked all week in practice but here it backfired and was heavily second-guessed when the game ended.

What happened was Tony and Drew mishandled their exchange and fumbled. Pittsburgh recoverd on our 47 and went into score their first touchdown. Afterwards, there were two ways to analyze the wisdom of using that play. One point of view was that the timing was never better since Pittsbrugh was Dorsett-conscious because of his earlier gains and thereby more vulnerable to a fake. The other was, why use a pass when the running game was going so well? In other words, keep running until they *make* us pass.

The answer was that we'd planned it that way. We weren't going to be conservative. We wanted to hit Pittsburgh early, make the Steelers play catch-up. Our idea was to run on them, beat the blitz passing and hit a few Big Plays. The reverse pass was one of them.

I didn't see it as a bad play in the context of what we had set up. I wasn't surprised when Tom sent it in. I knew his feeling about how we'd attack and this play was part of that approach. The timing was proper because it *is* a first down play. If I questioned anything, and that was only later, it was calling the play on their 34-yard line. At the time I didn't realize we were down there that close, almost in field goal territory. But all in all, I still think it was a good call.

I can't say the same for another that Landry went with late in the second quarter. It was the wrong play at the wrong time, resulted in the only interception I threw in the game and harsh words between us on the sideline. Of all the passes I ever threw that didn't turn out right this one will haunt me the longest. In a game we lost 35–31 this play resulted in a definite 7-point swing in the final score and potentially 10 to 14 points.

I'm not saying it lost the game entirely, just that we made a huge strategic error which most observers overlooked. It was a shame, too, because offensively we scored more than we thought necessary to win. Going in we felt somewhere in the area of 24 points would be enough. We surpassed that figure, scored enough points to win any Super Bowl ever played except this one, and more points than any losing team in the game's history.

To that point the game had evolved this way. Pittsburgh quarter-back Terry Bradshaw passed 28 yards to John Stallworth for a 7–0 lead after defensive end John Banaszak covered the Dorsett-Pearson fumble. Hill caught my third-down pass from 39 yards out for a 7–7 tie after one quarter. We went ahead 14–7 when linebacker Mike Hegman ran 37 yards with a Bradshaw fumble but Stallworth made it 14-all by turning a simple square-out catch into a 75-yard touchdown play.

That was the situation when we established a first down on the Pittsburgh 32-yard line. This would be the second play of the two-minute period before the first half ended. It ended in an interception by cornerback Blount, a bad personal foul penalty on DuPree when he tackled Blount and eventually Bradshaw's seven-yard TD pass to halfback Rocky Bleier with 26 seconds left on the halftime clock. Pittsburgh would lead after two quarters 21–14.

What Landry called was a lay-action pass. It was the same play we've used against them time after time, and they look for it every time. If I've ever questioned a call I did that one. It wasn't even in our two-minute drill game plan.

I know Coach Landry's thought was that the play had been successful in the Super Bowl of '75. It's the one we used to get a 29-yard touchdown with Drew to open the game. But a pass off the same formation later in the game had been intercepted by strong safety Mike Wagner. Wagner shouldn't have been near the play but he was. He recognized it and reacted. In this instance, so did Blount, because otherwise he had no business being deep enough to make an interception on the 16-yard line.

If Blount was doing his job on the defense they were playing he should have been up short. But I know they recognized the play immediately and, I'm sure, had an automatic with the linebackers. Without that check-off, Blount would have been up short to take Billy Joe. Instead linebacker Dennis Winston stuck with DuPree.

I'm the first to admit when I foul up and since this pass ended in an interception I accept part of the blame. But the wrong set of circumstances existed for what we tried to do. First of all it was a play-action pass in the two-minute period. Pittsburgh was not looking for a run at that moment. Lambert dropped straight back. He didn't go for the run-fake at all. Instead he became a problem for me trying to hit Drew coming across the middle. Meantime Blount saw the play developing and took off for the middle of the field while Winston followed Billy Joe running a crossing pattern.

This gets a bit technical but here's what should have happened the way their defense was set. Cornerbacks come up. Linebackers and safeties drop into zones. Therefore, with Winston taking his drop at the same time Blount broke to the middle, DuPree *should* be left uncovered. He wasn't. Winston was all over him as the films later showed.

Afterward I came off the field and Tom said, "Why didn't you throw late to Billy Joe?" And I snapped back, "Why did you call the play? It was ridiculous. We've got a two-minute offense. Why were we running *that?*"

I didn't like the play to begin with. Play-action is set up to hold the linebackers, make them respect the possibility of a handoff. In doing so the quarterback has to fake well, then all of a sudden look up and find his receiver. Unlike a straight drop-back or a pass from the shotgun formation, the passer doesn't have as much time to find his receiver. What also complicated things on that pass was that I got hit just as I threw.

But the idea behind the play-fake is to make the linebackers at least hesitate before they get into pass coverage. Lambert didn't, because in the two-minute period he's not looking for a run. So it was a play that didn't make sense. However, it's one we've used successfully in the past and one of those things that Tom goes back to in an uncertain situation.

Sometimes, because of the pressure, a play like that isn't analyzed as far as down and distance. We've used play-action passes before on second-and-10, 11, and 12, when there is limited respect for the threat of a run.

As for the mechanics of what I did, I would have felt a lot worse if Billy Joe had been open on the sideline. The fact is that neither he nor Drew was clear, and I got hit. If I had had a split second longer there's a chance I would have seen Blount. Without that protection the only person I saw was Lambert. I knew I had to get the ball past him so he couldn't intercept. I threw it just past Lambert . . . and that's where Blount was.

During a game errors like that don't stick with the players. Only later do they magnify. While we're playing all our attention is focused on the next play and executing it properly. It was obvious during the third quarter that we weren't moaning about Blount's interception. Pittsburgh got zero against our defense and made only one first down while we threatened to tie the game at 21-all.

Momentum was ours, and to me momentum is a state of mind. It's sensing that something good is about to happen on this play or the next. We felt that emotion while driving to Pittsburgh's 10-yard line. yet the fact we scored only three points from the threat would hurt tremendously after tight end Jackie Smith and I misfired on a wide-open touchdown pass. The difference between a field goal and touchdown—four points—would stand as the difference at game's end.

I've gone over that pass to Smith time and time again and there's nothing untold about it except. . . . Landry tried to change the play but couldn't.

Part of it was our own fault. We were facing third-and-three from the Steelers' 10 when Tom sent in the play designed for Jackie. But the call, along with necessary substitutions to run the play, got to the huddle late. Setting up the pass required a man in motion and then a run-fake to one of the backs. The problem was that I wound up strapped for time. There wasn't enough left on the 30-second clock to get the man in motion before the snap. Sometimes I didn't use the motion man if the play came in late but in this case he was the key to the whole play. So I called time out and went to the sidelines to discuss the situation with Landry.

We talked about switching to what we called a 17 route where Billy Joe goes down and turns out. The fullback goes out in the flat. It has been a good play for us, DuPree catching many touchdown passes on it around the goal line. But somebody on our sideline said he didn't think we could bring out the substitutions who just entered the game. I ran half-way out on the field to ask an official and he said, ''That's right. The subs have to stay in the game for at least one play before leaving the field.'' When I told Tom, the decision was made for us. We had to stick with the original call to Smith.

Everything worked beautifully except the pass and catch. Lambert blitzed and Scott Laidlaw, our fullback, decked him. Blount followed another receiver the corner. I came out of the play-fake, looked downfield and there was nobody near Jackie.

I don't think Jackie realized how wide open he was because he kept running and, according to the philosophy of the play, went too deep in the end zone. He kept going 18 or 20 yards downfield whereas the way we'd worked on it, normally from the two or three-yard line, he would have been eight to 10 yards deep. When I spun around I figured he could just stop on the goal line and the closest guy to him would be somebody in the end zone bleachers.

So I sort of lobbed the ball in there and didn't get enough velocity on it. He went deep in the end zone and either got tripped or slipped. Seeing the play later from an end zone camera, the ball hit Jackie right in the chest as he was going down. If the ball had been up I know he would have caught it. I'd like to have thrown a better pass because in all honesty the ball came in low, although still catchable. But it wasn't the easy catch it should have been.

We kicked a field goal to make it 21–17 but the psychology of the moment was important for the Steelers. They hadn't done anything in the second half but were off the hook. Again, it was not a play we dwelled on during the game. I felt nothing at the moment except the usual impatience for another shot to score.

Midway through the fourth quarter Pittsburgh still led 21–17 when the game blew up in our faces. The most controversial penalty in Super Bowl history started it. Even NFL commissioner Pete Rozelle later publicly admitted we were victims of a horrible call.

The penalty was called against Barnes for allegedly tripping Pittsburgh wide receiver Swann. I never could figure out how Benny could be running fullblast down-field and intentionally trip a receiver *behind* him, which is where Swann was. The whole thing took place near our bench. I was standing right there and saw it. When I saw the flag I thought it was interference on Swann for pushing or something like that.

The official right on the play was back judge Pat Knight. He made the first signal, waving his arms back and forth for an incompletion. Then here came the flag from over in the middle of the field. All our guys started yelling because they thought it was interference on Swann. Incredibly, field judge Fred Swearingen saw the play differently from everybody else in the Orange Bowl. His penalty stood, cost us 33 yards to the 23 and from there Pittsburgh scored for a 28–17 lead.

Some strange things happened on the way, though. On third down from our 17 Bradshaw was trapped for a 13-yard loss by Henderson on a blitz, but a delay of game penalty against Pittsburgh took precedence. Instead of fourth and 17 from our 30, with Roy Gerela looking at a 47-yard field goal, Pittsburgh had third and nine from the 22. Franco Harris burst up the middle to score on the next play while strong safety Charlie Waters, who had a chance of stopping him in the secondary, was inadvertently screened out of the play by an official.

That whole chain of events was ironic. Swann's play was the biggest of the drive yet wasn't the result of anything he did. It was some idiot official throwing a flag when he's out of position to see the play right. And another official standing on top of the play allowing himself to be talked into a penalty that wasn't there. We can justify those complaints. But having Randy White where we did on the following kickoff was our fault.

A defensive tackle, Randy was positioned short in the middle of the field to lead the blocking wedge on the runback. Odds on the kickoff going to Randy were almost nil, but it did. Putting White anywhere close to where he might have to handle the ball was unwise because Randy was handicapped by a cast that protected his broken thumb.

It seemed like even when Pittsburgh did something wrong it turned out right. Gerela normally would have kicked off as deep as possible but this time he slipped. The result was a low bouncer to White who had trouble tucking the ball with that cast. Randy was tackled hard, fumbled and Pittsburgh recovered on our 18-yard line. Bradshaw passed to Swann on the next play for a 35–17 lead. Within the space of 19 seconds Pittsburgh had scored 14 points and iced the game.

In the remaining 6:51 we scored twice on passes to DuPree and, with 22 seconds left, to Butch Johnson. I think Pittsburgh was a little tired at the end but that hardly matters because the Steelers won 35–31.

Super Bowl XIII was a key game for the Cowboys as far as the overall concept of the '70s is concerned. Pittsburgh, not us, became the first team to win three Super Bowls and went on to make it four last season by beating Los Angeles 32–19.

Historically, then, Pittsburgh finished the decade as the Team of the Seventies. They wrapped it up against the Rams. When it's all said and done they were in four Super Bowls and won them all. Of the four we were in when I played we won two and lost two. Both of the losses were to the Steelers by a total of only eight points but I don't think too many people remember that. They only remember who won.

That's why Super Bowl XII against Denver is more

enjoyable to replay. On the basis of personal accomplishment I've never felt better after a Super Bowl. In the first one we won against Miami the excitement was overwhelming. That game was the biggest victory in Dallas history because it lifted a load from the franchise, lifted that can't-win-the-big-one onus from the Cowboys. I was part of the '71 team mostly during the second half of the season. I felt I contributed but I still wasn't an established, consistent quarterback by any means. I was part of the momentum that overtook the Cowboys at midseason. Everything just clicked all at once.

In '77 we were coming off a season that left me depressed. I had the finger injury, felt I'd let the team down and even gave Landry carte blanche to trade me. Our offseason attitude was good and like '76 we started off strong. I was confident we wouldn't tail off at the end like we did in '76 because we'd picked up Tony Dorsett. Our running back situation hadn't been solid for a number of years because of injuries to Newhouse and Preston Pearson. Tony coming on the scene would give us a consistent threat back there, I felt, even though he was a rookie.

When we hit a midseason rut and lost to St. Louis and Pittsburgh, people begn saying it was like '76 all over again. But it wasn't. First of all, I wasn't hurt and we had Dorsett. I thought our running game, even if it had a problem here or there, would always come around. So that season was most satisfying. We controlled things.

I really think we were the best team in football that year. Pittsburgh was having an off year. Denver beat them twice, in regular season and during the playoffs. Denver also beat Oakland twice, so the Broncos had a great year, too. Dallas and Denver each finished with 12–2 records, best in the NFL, so there was little doubt that the strongest teams were meeting in the Superdome in New Orleans.

The only thing that made me a little nervous was competing against Craig, my former teammate-rival in Dallas who was quarterbacking Denver. The media was into comparing us every which way. Craig was coming off a tremendous season and because I liked him personally, I was happy for him. Since he left Dallas I had established myself. He'd gone to the Giants, on to Denver and now to the Super Bowl.

If anyone wanted to second-guess the decision that resulted in my staying with the Cowboys and Craig's leaving, at this point they were forced to admit it was good for both of us.

I felt at the start it would be an offensive game. By that I mean the offense that could sustain itself longest without making mistakes would win. We would compete against a great defense. Denver faced the same situation because our defense was at its peak. I knew their offense would have to have an unusually sharp performance to get much done.

Tom's game plan against Denver was to run the ball. The Broncos play a three down linemen—four linebacker defense, what we call a 3–2, and it's tough when they put you in must-pass situations. Therefore, running was critical. Blocking Randy Gardishar, their excellent inside linebacker, was another key objective. We wanted to make sure we went to our backs or first-down passes to avoid the second-and-10s. We had some play-action passes mixed in and a few Big Plays but overall our approach was conservative.

Then why did we open the game with a reverse

from Dorsett to Butch Johnson? The ball was fumbled, and we were fortunate to recover for a nine-yard loss on our 20.

That play was well calculated. Denver's defensive strength was its unbelievable pursuit. The Broncos flowed to the ball "like field mice to a haystack," as Cowboys special assistant Ermal Allen told us. It was very difficult to run wide on them. They would bottle us up. If we tried to cut back inside, the pursuit took care of the runner.

With that reverse we told them, "You better stay home and play your positions. We have some things up our sleeves." There wasn't any other meaning than that.

What we didn't have in hand early in the game was the ball. Tony Hill fumbled a punt on our one-yard line and made a miraculous, touchdown-saving recovery. Dorsett also fumbled into Denver's secondary but somehow center John Fitzgerald beat four Denver players to the ball. Within the first five minutes of the game we fumbled on our 20, one and 22-yard lines without suffering any damage.

. No question we were jittery. We were really slopping around on offense at first. Newhouse was yelling to me in the huddle, "You gotta keep these guys under control!" Everyone's a nervous wreck from the Super Bowl, the Superdome and the fans. An indoor atmosphere for that game is crazy and I think both teams were fighting the noise, the hoopla. The sound is overwhelming if you're not accustomed to playing indoors.

The game turned on the fact that we made mistakes that didn't hurt us. Denver made mistakes and we capitalized on a lot of them. Some we didn't but at least the turnovers meant field position and kept them in the hole. They never got untracked against our defense, yet at the half we had only 13 points.

One reason was that Efren Herrera had a poor day. He missed field goals of 43, 32 and 44 yards. DuPree also fumbled a completed pass on their 12 so we should have had the game locked up by then instead of leading only 13–0. But I think Denver was demoralized offensively, and with good reason. Our defense had made seven turnovers— interceptions by Randy Hughes, Aaron Kyle, Mark Washington and Benny Barnes; two fumble recoveries by Hughes and another by Bruce Huther.

Denver got an early third-quarter field goal that we countered a few minutes later with an improvised play on third-and-10 from the shotgun. Bernard Jackson, Denver's free safety, had been hanging in the middle. He wasn't dropping into deep zone as he should. Our receivers had mentioned it to me and I remembered that in the huddle. Butch wasn't supposed to figure in the play but I told him, "Run a good post route."

When I faded I saw Jackson hadn't dropped quickly enough. He was a step off. Steve Foley, their cornerback, did a good job on the play and was right with Butch but Jackson should have stopped the play. When I threw I thought the ball was too long. I couldn't believe it when Butch made a sensational catch in the end zone for a 45-yard touchdown.

Our lead swelled to 20–3, then slipped to 20–10 after Rick Upchurch returned the kickoff 67 yards and reserve quarterback Norris Weese took Denver in from our 26.

On the next series, as the fourth quarter began, I broke the tip of my right forefinger while being sacked by linebacker Tom Jackson. I left the field and went to the locker room with Dr. Marvin Knight. I got a shot of novocaine which numbed the fingertip but also meant I couldn't pass with any accuracy. Fortunately, Weese fumbled to Kyle and on the first play we ran the pitchout to Newhouse, who passed 29 yards to Golden Richards for a touchdown. That was it. The game was over.

Turnovers killed Denver. Our defensive line against their offensive line was a mismatch. Denver could have had Superman in there at quarterback and it wouldn't have done any good.

That's why I felt so sorry for Craig. People just weren't going to understand. He had an awful day under the pressure of our rush and threw four interceptions. If Craig and I had switched sides the Cowboys still would have won. I couldn't have done anything in that situation, either. Denver simply had no control over Ed Jones, Randy White and Harvey Martin. Randy and Harvey were co-Most Valuable Players and rightfully so.

Give Craig or any other quarterback some time and he'll hit those receivers. Craig didn't have a chance. He was on the run the whole time. We also had some blitzes that worked, particularly the ones with Hughes from safety. Our defense just controlled the game, that's all.

Winning a Super Bowl the first time is an unbelievable thrill. There is more maturity about it the second time. One thing it demonstrates is that the first time wasn't an accident. The history of many teams is to win the Super Bowl and then have problems. Kansas City, the New York Jets and Oakland come to mind. Even Miami took a tumble after winning its second Super Bowl. So did the Cowboys, but we came right back to become the only NFC team to win the Super

Bowl in the '70s. It showed we could play with anybody in football.

Overall I think the 1977 team was the best Dallas put on the field while I was active. The '71 team was very close to it and similar— strong running game, good passing game, tough defense.

But as far as having fun nothing beat the '75 team that wound up losing to Pittsburgh 21–17 in Super Bowl X. As the year began we were in a state similar to what faced the Cowboys in '80. People were thinking that Dallas was on the decline, and that possibility *was* greater in '75 than '80. What everyone forgot was that Landry always keeps a sound nucleus of players. They also forgot Tom's abilities as a coach. Not until the '75 season was well underway did it become evident to outsiders that the Cowboys had made a spectacular draft to add rookies like Bob Breunig, Randy White, Thomas Henderson, Pat Donovan, Herb Scott and Randy Hughes. Twelve rookies made it that season and called themselves the "Dirty Dozen."

We were underdogs when the season began. One Dallas paper picked us third in the division. A wire service forecast we'd finish last. But the '75 team kept making plays when it had to and qualified for the playoffs as a wild card team. Upsets over Minnesota and Los Angeles carried us into Super Bowl X as a popular favorite with everyone except oddsmakers.

Our game plan was to shoot the works. At the time Super Bowl games had a reputation of being conservative and boring. Since we were heavy underdogs we accepted the challenge of taking chances to make things happen. That was the reason we sent Henderson on a reverse with the opening kickoff. He returned it 53 yards and was kept from scoring only by Roy Gerela's last-man tackle. We got our idea across, though. We were going to gamble.

As soon as we got our first turnover at Pittsburgh's 29 Landry went right to our bread and butter, a pass over the middle to Drew for a touchdown. We led at the half 10–7 but missed chances to do a lot of damage. With first downs at Pittsburgh's 15 and 20, we came out with just a 36-yard field goal by Toni Fritsch.

What hurt us, of course, was Swann's making four great receptions for 161 yards. But we still had the Steelers fighting for their lives into the fourth quarter before the game turned on a blocked punt that rolled out of the end zone for a safety.

Pittsburgh got good field position after the subsequent kickoff from our 20 and took its first lead 12–10 on a field goal with about nine minutes left to play. Then we went for the same pass to Drew which had scored earlier but Wagner saw it coming and intercepted. His runback to our seven positioned Gerela for a short field goal that put us down 15–10. The capper came on the next Pittsburgh possession when we blitzed Bradshaw on third down but neither linebacker D. D. Lewis nor safety Cliff Harris got to him. Swann took Bradshaw's pass over his shoulder at the goal line for a 64-yard touchdown.

We trailed 21–10 with 3:02 left and still almost won. After I passed 34 yards for a TD to Percy Howard, Pittsburgh made a mistake. On fourth and nine from the Dallas 41 the Steelers ran off tackle instead of punting. With 1:22 on the clock we got possession on our 39.

The Cowboys two-minute drill wasn't as refined in those days as it is now, and that cost us. There was sideline confusion over what we wanted to do. We weren't as organized as we could have been. We had no time outs left and things went wrong. There was a bad center snap and our ball carriers didn't get out of bounds, all of which kept the clock running. Looking back, I think we rushed ourselves into thinking we had to hit a long-gainer.

I did a terrible job in that situation. Reviewing the game I found where we ran only five plays in the final 82 seconds, an average of 16 seconds per play. That was not good when you consider what they were: my scramble for 11 yards, a pass to Preston Pearson for 12, two incompletions and a game-ending interception by Glenn Edwards in the end zone.

Instead of trying to hit the big play we should have gone for something over the middle, attempted to force them down around the 20 and back into a normal defense instead of the "prevent" they were playing. Our two-minute offense just wasn't as smooth then. A year later we could have torn up the defense they were in, as we did in Super Bowl XIII three years later on our last touchdown drive.

I wasn't aware until later that the Steelers hadn't drawn a penalty throughout that game. I remembered Lambert kneed Preston Pearson flagrantly and the referee only warned him, which was a joke. They should have called a foul right away. Lambert and Swann were the instrumental players in that game; Swann with his catches and Lambert with his screaming, hollering and great performance. I think Lambert even intimidated us a little bit.

But the officials were letting him get away with murder, too. I mean, they *warned* him about kneeing Preston. That's an automatic flag. Pittsburgh was the most penalized team in the NFL that year and wound up with no penalties in the Super Bowl. The Steelers were knocking down our receivers all over the place. I still think there's a legitimate gripe there.

I harbor a complaint about Super Bowl VI as well. Not with the result, which found us beating Miami, not with my helping the Cowboys end six years of playoff frustration, but with being named the Most Valuable Player. That was questionable even though I completed 12 of 19 passes and wasn't intercepted.

The postgame squawk was that maybe Duane Thomas should have been MVP. Duane did have an excellent game with 95 yards rushing and a 5.0 per carry average. He certainly deserved consideration but I would not have voted for either of us.

Of all the Super Bowls this was the one where an offensive lineman should have been singled out. We rushed for 252 yards, a Super Bowl record that still stands, and I had beautiful pass protection all day. They could have picked anybody from the line and not gone wrong—Dave Manders, Blaine Nye, John Niland, Rayfield Wright or Tony Liscio.

There wasn't an overwhelming sense of joy in beating Miami. The team felt relieved more than anything. It had been a tense season because Duane had withdrawn to brood. It had been a grim season for a nucleus of Dallas veterans who had been sardonically labeled "Next Year's Champions." They had been beaten twice in the final seconds in NFL championship games against Green Bay, twice upset by Cleveland in playoffs and lost Super Bowl V on a last-gasp field goal to Baltimore in successive seasons.

It was Bob Lilly who epitomized the internal rage and despair of the era when Jim O'Brien kicked the field goal that beat the Cowboys 16–13 in Super Bowl V. Lilly sailed his helmet 40 yards upfield. He knew his years were numbered. A lot of guys felt if we didn't do it in '71 their last chance would be gone.

Frusatration ran deep on the '71 Cowboys and the countdown to Super Bowl VI was equally cheerless. Duane was playing the sphinx. His only pregame comment to the media came during picture day when, after sitting alone and silent on a stand of bleachers, he asked a reporter, "What time is it?" He was widely quoted, too.

On top of that a Monday locker room fight broke out between fullback Walt Garrison and wide receiver Margene Adkins for reasons I never learned. Landry clamped down by announcing that anyone who embarrassed the team in any way the rest of the week would be fined $5,000.

Once the game started everything smoothed out. We dominated on both sides of the ball and got rid of the tag of not being able to win the big one. I remember the faces of Bob Lilly, Mel Renfro, Cornell Green, Chuck Howley, Lee Roy Jordan, Dave Edwards, George Andrie . . . all the veterans who looked like the weight of the world had been lifted from their shoulders. Although they had retired before the Cowboys won again in 1977, they had accomplished their goal. They were world champions once and no one can ever take that from them. The victory took a lot of pressure off of everyone, Coach Landry included. I think it removed more from him than anybody. Those moments in that cramped, steamy locker room in Tulane Stadium were the highlight of my career because there's no feeling in the world to replace the feeling that goes with winning the first Super Bowl. Not winning the second one or whatever follows.

The Cowboys were playing in those days under a

stigma. We could feel it and certainly we heard and read about it often enough. As Lance Alworth remarked after we beat Miami, "This has been a team with a mission ever since training camp." Here's a contrast: When the '71 team won playoffs against Minnesota and San Francisco there wasn't a great uproar in the locker room afterwards. That team knew the season wouldn't be a success until we won it all. Whereas in '75, we weren't supposed to win anything and after each playoff victory there was bedlam.

A team can go through all sorts of problems but when they've won the whole thing, even if it's only once, they've done something. They can always defend themselves. Otherwise the Dallas players of the '60s would just be able to say, "Well, we were always in the playoffs," or as Minnesota says: "We were always in the Super Bowl." But the Vikings lost four of them without ever winning once. I'm in agreement that just getting there is a tremendous feat but that's not how the public looks at it. If a team can say, "We *won* a Super Bowl," then they can justify themselves completely.

Take Kansas City right now. The Chiefs haven't done anything in a long time but they can point to the Super Bowl they won. The same with Oakland. The Raiders have had some trouble since they won it all, but the pressure is off somewhat now. Before Oakland claimed a Super Bowl it was a winning franchise for a decade or more; yet people maligned the Raiders because they hadn't won the Big One.

So it was with the Cowboys in 1971. The pressure was off. Even in the difficult years that followed we could return to the satisfaction of winning the Super Bowl. There is a feeling inside that's hard to explain. I think we were a bit more sober when we won the Super

Bowl again. We reflected more on the fact that it means the first one was no fluke. Each is great, and I'm sure Pittsburgh felt great after every one of their victories. But I believe the Steelers would agree that the first one is the most special. It was for me.

IV
The Unforgettables

"Duane Thomas has become for the Cowboys what Russia was to Churchill; the proverbial enigma wrapped in a riddle, doused with tabasco sauce and stuffed in a cheese enchilada."—Cowboys's defensive end Pat Toomay

They weren't necessarily the best or the worst although Thomas Henderson, the All-Me linebacker, will argue the point. Hollywood would say—and has often enough—that he's the best-ever which, of course, is nowhere near the truth.

Henderson can claim one distinction, regardless of whether he wants it or not. He is a starter on my all-time team of Most Memorable teammates and/or opponents. Each leaps to mind for specific yet unrelated reasons, most of them sad or unpleasant. Probably that's the common denominator that makes them unforgettable.

In summary they were distinguished as the following:

A running back who wouldn't talk.

A linebacker who wouldn't stop talking.

A richly-talented but personally eccentric wide receiver.

A defensive tackle who would not shake hands with me.

Another wide receiver whose troubles led me to courtroom testimony in a narcotics trial.

A quarterback with whom I had two fights.

First and foremost, since he thinks of himself that way, I'll start with the rise and fall of Henderson. His failure with the Cowboys was a simple case of self-destruction. The way I saw it he was devoured by a feeling of self-importance and in a strange twist, eventually undone by what he considered his greatest triumph.

Henderson's fourth year in the NFL was a success. In '78 he was named to the Pro Bowl for the first time. He made some big plays along the way, the most prominent being a 68-yard interception runback for our final touchdown in the NFC Championship against Los Angeles. We beat the Rams 28–0 in a game a lot tougher than the final margin suggested.

The Los Angeles situation put Hollywood in the headlines because he had predicted in a newspaper story the Rams would "choke" against Dallas. The interception return gave him a platform from which to expound and he took advantage. No one else on our team taunted the Rams like that, but Henderson more than offset the respectful things others said about the Rams.

The beginning of the end took place in January,

1979, the week prior to our Super Bowl XIII loss to Pittsburgh 35–31. It was there and then that Henderson began to lose his grip on reality. The Super Bowl countdown triggered what was to follow in November when Coach Landry kicked him off the team.

Once we arrived at the Super Bowl site Thomas was besieged by the media. Since there was no other controversial subject about the Cowboys and Thomas was a breezy, easy interview, reporters honed in on him. He had something new for them every day. Frequently it was something outrageous. Eventually it was an insult to Pittsburgh quarterback Terry Bradshaw. "Bradshaw couldn't spell *cat* if you spotted him the *c* and the *a*," he said.

Henderson became such a Super Bowl subject that both coaches were asked what they thought about his conduct. Landry was clearly uncomfortable with it for several reasons. He has a well-defined code of behavior and, to him, Henderson was not acting like a profes-sional. I think Landry also believed Thomas was riling the Steelers, something we didn't need, and may have been distracting his teammates. He never said any of this publicly but I do remember one of his responses which was to come true in November. "When it gets to be a problem with the team then I'll do something about it," Landry said. Chuck Noll, coach of the Steelers, brushed off Henderson with an acid remark that "empty barrels make the most noise."

A comment one day in our locker room drove home the point that Thomas was headed in the wrong direction. He came up to me and said, "Hey, I really got you. I got you now. I replaced you in *Newsweek*. Bradshaw and I are on the cover of *Newsweek* maga-zine!"

That summarized Thomas's problem. He was really into the publicity thing. An indication of how deeply it affected him was his belief that it would bother me if I weren't on the cover of *Newsweek*. Frankly, for me it was better because he took some of the pressure off of everyone else since reporters worried so much about him and what he might say next.

Henderson's ability to manipulate and dominate the media, his concern for attention and publicity, just finally overwhelmed him. It hit him and it was too big for him. He didn't put it in perspective. He didn't take advantage of it the right way.

I believe the Super Bowl experience was the key to what happened later. He was the center of attention all the time. Instead of playing with it and enjoying it, he took it seriously. I get a lot of flattering letters and sometimes there's a tendency to think, *Man, you are really something special*. Then I remember there are more people out there who *aren't* sending anything. Thomas received a lot of fan mail which said, "We are all behind you," but didn't take into account he probably was hearing from one-half of one percent of the people out there. You have to keep things in perspective. He didn't.

I felt that was a big factor in the way he approached the 1979 season: how many times he worked out in the offseason and how much he put into practices. Later on that did affect his play.

Thomas had the world by the tail if he had just done it right. But he was carried away with all this hoopla. He never understood the reason behind his reputation——that he was a successful football player on a successful team. You don't create a personality without the proper surroundings. The Cowboys were his surroundings but he didn't grasp that fact. Thomas felt *he* was the personality and looked at everything else as secondary. If he'd looked at it the other way he could still have been as colorful and flamboyant as ever. Just as long as he did his job on the field.

I talked to Thomas about this during training camp. "Look at the big picture . . . you still have to abide by the rules, the curfews and practices," I told him. Some days he didn't feel like practicing, but other guys practiced when they felt the same way. That became a big problem. The situation finally came to the point where he stopped working as hard as he could. It climaxed in the Washington game, but there were a lot of things leading up to Landry's decison to let him go the next day.

Basically, Henderson didn't feel like making the effort he once did. That affected his play and it also affected his relationship with teammates.

Then Pete Gent was quoted in a Dallas newspaper as saying one of the reasons they cut Henderson was that he wouldn't conform to the Cowboys's image. And further, that the rest of the team wouldn't stand up for him. What a joke.

Gent, who last played for the Cowboys in 1968, had no conception of the Henderson situation. His reaction was typical of someone judging a case which he didn't understand. Gent did get one part right, but for the wrong reason, when he noted that teammates didn't squawk when Henderson left the team. That was a perfect indication they felt Landry had done the right thing.

We aren't a bunch of machines. If Thomas had been getting a bad shake everyone would have stood up. Nobody felt *good* about it. Nobody disliked Thomas.

He just wasn't doing his job, not in practice, not on the field. Even if you're making mistakes on the field and still working hard no one holds that against you. But if you're dogging it . . .

Thomas wouldn't recognize that. All that ability and talent and he was blind to it. He couldn't see he was affecting his teammates and affecting his play. That was the shame of the whole affair.

Then last spring, after he'd been traded to San Francisco, Henderson made everything worse for himself with an interview in a national magazine. In the past he knocked teammates like Cliff Harris and D. D. Lewis, and in this article he came down heavy on Harvey Martin and Billy Joe DuPree. He said Harvey wasn't much of a defensive end and that he'd kicked around DuPree at tight end for five years in practices.

That was camouflage for Henderson's own failings. The guy didn't want to work. He quit working on the practice field and it affected him in games. He didn't play well and at the end when the Cowboys got rid of him the players were basically saying, ''Thomas, it's your own fault, nobody else's.'' Some of these guys he picked on give 100 percent and expect others to do it. So they didn't have any parting praises or sympathy.

Thomas went after them with a vengeance because he didn't recognize his own problem. If he'd been kicked off the team only for waving a bandana on TV or yelling before the camera—which he did in Washington— players would have rebelled against Landry. That wasn't it at all. It was a combination of not working and then going to Washington where the game meant nothing to him.

He plays when he wants to play. He's not a team man. That's the bottom line. Until Henderson changes he will constantly have problems. It made me sick to see him pick on DuPree, who only gives 100 percent *all* the time. DuPree plays hurt and practices hurt. He's gone out there with a sprained ankle and worse. Henderson wouldn't practice if he had a scrape on his elbow.

None of these guys are going to pop back at Thomas. They have too much class about them. If you polled the team on who was the most valuable linebacker, Henderson or D. D. Lewis, 90 percent would be for D. D. He is consistent game in and game out. He was more valuable to our team than Thomas.

Henderson's potential is among the best in football if he applies it. So far he hasn't. There are guys with potential all over the world who never live up to it. He has in certain games but not on a consistent basis. That is what counts. *That* is how you measure a player. Maybe in San Francisco, Thomas will apply himself every day. But if he doesn't he'll jeopardize his career.

Those were some of the ideas I tried to get across to him during our training camp talks last summer. He would be understanding one day but on the next it was as though the hoopla and attention got to him and he felt bigger than the system.

In fact, one night Henderson and Tony Dorsett dropped by my room to say they were leaving camp. Both had been fined for curfew violations and were upset about it. Thomas owed $300 and I said, "I'll get your fine money back if you just don't leave camp." I wasn't going to get it from the club because I knew the Cowboys wouldn't refund. I would have figured some other way, though. Anyway, they decided to stay and the situation cooled off without my having to raise the money.

I find it totally absurd that guys can't live within

the rules for four or five weeks during camp. When they don't they just put the burden on Landry. If a guy gets away with something there, he'll try to do the same thing when the rules are critical. He won't show up for meetings on time. He'll be late for a game.

Rules are there for a reason and they are very simple. We don't have any tough ones. Training camp and the night before *road* games are the only times we have curfew. How hard is it to live by those rules? It's crazy to stay out two hours late in camp when for eleven months a year you can stay up until 6 A.M. if you choose. All that does is jeopardize the whole team because if guys start flaunting those rules then the club will start making tougher ones.

The Cowboys are a well-run team from that standpoint. We're on and off the field after a certain length of time, even if the workout is a bad one. We're not overwhelmed by rules. Players who've gone to other teams have made that discovery. They've come back later and said, "I didn't realize how good I had it here."

I remember Otto Brown, a defensive back, and some other guys traded to the New York Giants were real impressed at first. They said, "This is great. We went up there, met the coach, had a beer with him and everything was lax." But they didn't win and pretty soon figured out why. Otto said, "I didn't realize how fortunate I was to be with a winning system. You need rules to win. You just can't start to do anything otherwise."

Rules are necessary to run a team without distractions. In many cases they're mandatory for the success of your team. There are teams in the league where players walk in on the middle of a meeting. That is a distraction.

Teams make rules for about 10 percent of the players. Call a meeting at 9 A.M. and 90 percent will be there on time. It's the 10 percent you're battling all the time. Rules, including a schedule of fines, are necessary for that 10 percent. If we didn't have them then the rest of the guys, the 90 percent, would be affected.

Like we all were in 1971 with Duane Thomas.

That was one time in his career that Landry slackened his rules. He made exceptions for Duane. It became a double-standard situation. Duane got away with talking back to coaches, not answering roll call, not wearing a tie on road trips. He even skipped a practice in Dallas before the Super Bowl and there were rumors he might not even play. Duane became an introvert. He withdrew from everyone. What the players saw, however, was that he was being handled as a separate case.

Landry really tried to work with Duane. Anyone who says otherwise doesn't know the facts. Landry went out of his way to solve an unsolvable situation. Yet in doing so Landry created unrest among the team with his separate *and* unequal treatment of Duane.

I still don't know what the real problem was there. Some said it was drugs but there was no evidence. Physically, the way Duane played, there was no evidence at all so I rack that up to speculation. I do know Duane's first agent was a bad one. Duane came to mistrust the man completely. Being black, Duane had a natural distrust for society on the basis of how he and his ancestors had been treated. I suppose he wound up mistrusting everyone and simply went into a private shell which no one could penetrate.

I tried. So did others. None of us got through. I always felt there was something warm and very vulnerable behind the sullen, angry mask Duane wore. Only Duane knows the why of it all. I never read or heard an explanation of what compelled him to follow a course which amounted to professional suicide. He once told me on the practice field, "You shut up." He ignored or cursed reporters covering the team. Coming off the field after a brilliant touchdown run one afternoon, he walked right past Landry's outstretched handshake.

During Duane's most famous tirade against the Cowboys he called Landry "a plastic man, no man at all," Gil Brandt "a liar" and Tex Schramm "sick, demented and totally dishonest." Schramm made a tongue-in-cheek reply, "Well, that's not too bad. He got two out of three."

I'd put Duane at the top of the list of wasted talent I saw during my NFL career. He was a great, great athlete. What impressed everyone was his football intelligence. He was *very* smart, moved from halfback to fullback, picked up his new position quickly and made few mistakes. The Cowboys were just right for Duane in that his running style fit what we were trying to do. To see all that go down the drain was a tragedy.

Other than someone cut down early by injury, I can't think of another player who might have been one of the greatest running backs ever and didn't make it. Now he will be just a guy who had a year or two. That's the shame of it. Duane's history could have been something special on the order of Jimmy Brown, Gale Sayers or O. J. Simpson.

One day Duane holed up in his dorm room, refusing to practice. Landry had returned to single standard rules by then and his patience was exhausted. He gave the trade-him word and Duane's career with Dallas ended. The Cowboys parted with him during the summer of '72 in a trade with San Diego for wide receiver Billy Parks and running back Mike Montgomery.

Insofar as leaving the Cowboys, I wasn't far behind although my absence was less permanent than Duane's. Two weeks later during an exhibition game against the Rams, I made an all-time hardhead decision. I chose to accept rather than avoid a sideline collision with linebacker Marlin McKeever, who probably didn't feel the impact. I did. The tackle separated my right shoulder. That injury prevented me from making a worthwhile contribution to the season until a divisional playoff against San Francisco, and it would help start the only bitter feud I ever had with an opposing player.

He was Diron Talbert, defensive tackle for the Washington Redskins. Our relationship over the years deteriorated to the point where we didn't even shake hands when team captains met for the pregame coin flip. He called me the "wrong quarterback" to start the '72 NFC Championship game. I referred to him as "a mediocre defensive tackle." Those were about the kindest words we ever exchanged. To this day my feelings toward Talbert haven't changed a lot.

Here's how our squabble began. Landry sent me into the San Francisco playoff with us behind 28–13 late in the third quarter. Craig Morton came out but not so much for anything he'd done wrong. As Landry put it afterward the team was playing "lousy" and collapsed around Craig. With 1:53 left to play we trailed 28–16 but suddenly I could do no wrong. I passed 20 yards to Parks for a touchdown. Toni Fritsch trick-hit the onside kickoff—he swung his right leg *behind* his left—and Mel Renfro covered the resulting fumble. I wound up throwing a 10-yard TD to Ron Sellers for the winner. Coincidentally, our game followed the Immaculate Reception playoff between Oakland and Pittsburgh, the one where Franco Harris ran for a disputed but decisive touchdown with a deflected pass in the final seconds.

A writer named Jerry Magee from San Diego captured the essence of both games in one sentence. Someone showed me the story and I remember it went something like this: "Dallas scored 14 points with less than two minutes to play to beat San Francisco 30–28 Sunday in the most miraculous playoff finish staged in the NFL in the last three hours."

The victory qualified the Cowboys to meet Washington in the NFC Championship at RFK Stadium. It also presented Landry with a quarterback problem. Would he start Craig, who'd taken the team to a 10–4 record during regular season? Or would it be me? I'd thrown only 20 passes late in the year after returning from the shoulder injury and about as many more against the 49ers. Late in the week Landry said I would start.

Washington beat the tar out of us 26–3. They shut down Walt Garrison and Calvin Hill with about 30 yards rushing. Every time we ran a pitch-out Jack Pardee, the linebacker who's now Washington's head coach, would knock Calvin for a loss. We were second-and-15 almost the whole game. I was the leading ground gainer which is not the way it's supposed to happen. We could have had King Kong in there and it wouldn't have made any difference. I didn't throw any interceptions but that's no brag, either. It wasn't a good game for me but neither did I think we lost on account of quarterback play.

That's why the criticism hit me pretty hard. I couldn't believe it. Why pick on me after the game? Why weren't they talking about the great things they did like stopping Hill and Garrison? That was the difference, because when we played Washington earlier that season Walt and Calvin gained more than 200 yards and killed them. But no, the finger was pointed at me.

Here's where Talbert came in. After the game he said I was "rusty" and "the wrong quarterback" to be playing. And here's how I feel about that. I have a fetish about not name-calling other athletes. The things the press and other people say about you are upsetting to a degree but I can forget those. But when your peers start bad-mouthing that's something else. Better than anyone else they know what you go through to play the game. To do it when you're down . . . I have no respect for that.

I realize now that Talbert was part of the psychological program in Washington. After that playoff game it was his job to get in a psych that might be useful later. Plus I realized he and Craig were good friends. Maybe he was even right about it. If you looked at the whole season maybe Craig *should* have played that game. I wish he had. But what made me so mad was that the game had ended, they won and were going to the Super Bowl, and all of the sudden he started firing salvos.

Then in 1975 there was a national story about homosexuality in pro football. Supposedly there were three homosexual NFL quarterbacks. I'm thankful to be heterosexual but that didn't stop Talbert from using the story as another ploy against me. During our game against the Redskins he called me a "fag." He knew that would get my goat. But this time it backfired on

Washington. I had a great game after that and we beat them 31–10 which put us in the playoffs as a wild card team. The whole subject bugged me, though. I'd rather be called anything but *that,* unless it's a coward.

Talbert said other things if they made a play or were beating us. He loved it then. As for me I used some questionable language which I'm not proud of— words you say but don't really mean when you're competing. In the heat of the battle he brought out the worst in me in that respect, so I was just as bad about using some questionable language.

Talbert's next deal was refusing to shake hands. I went out before the game with the captains, stuck out my hand and he ignored it. I tried to shake hands with him before the next game and he did the same thing. So after that I never tried. It was another psychological maneuver on his part. I'm sure down deep he had a personal thing for me. He was a George Allen man and the Redskins always seemed to have some personal campaign going against Staubach.

One time I did say, "I guess the way a mediocre defensive tackle can get some publicity is by bad-mouthing the other quarterback." I'd like to set the record straight on that. Talbert definitely wasn't mediocre. He was the kind of guy you'd want on your team. He gave maximum effort. A lot of Redskins were out of that mold . . . Billy Kilmer, Ron McDole, Chris Hanburger, Kenny Houston. Those were some tough cookies. They came to play all the way and you had to respect that. I want them to know I did.

The only other opponent I had something going with on a fairly consistent basis was Jack Youngblood, defensive end for the Rams. Now there was a tough one. Youngblood would get on my case sometimes. One playoff game he kept hitting me late, I thought, but the referee wouldn't call a penalty. Jack was just mad because they were losing.

Anyway I threw a pass that was tipped up and he went to intercept. I tackled him before the ball got there, and the whole Rams team got upset with me for saving an interception. Like I'd done something illegal. I really hit him good, probably the hardest tackle I ever made. Jack and I have nothing personal going. I've talked to him at Pro Bowls and consider him a phenomenal football player. I'd have to give Youngblood the vote as the best defensive player I ever competed against.

Normally I say very little during a game. I have been accused of cursing and I have said a few words I regret. But if *I* say something everybody makes a big deal out of it, like it was the Pope talking or somebody holy. One time I called Bill Bradley a "chicken s——" because he hit me late. He started whooping and pointing his finger as though he'd never heard the word before. "I thought you were a Christian!" he screamed. Finally, I told him, "S—— is *not* a bad word, you jerk."

Honestly, I didn't say much to anybody on the field. If I did it was because I was mad at myself. I do recall an instance when I lost my temper again against the Rams. This time they were beating us in a regular season game and I got knocked out of bounds right by their bench. From all the hollering I thought they were filming a sequel to *The Exorcist* on the sidelines. Guys like Lawrence McCutcheon, Billy Waddy and some others started screaming at me. They had the game won and were cussing me out.

I turned around and said, "Well, you front-running b——s!" I did *not* call them, "choking sons-of-b——s!"

which is what everybody quoted me as saying. What I did call them was true. They were front-running; the game was almost over and they were cussing at me. On top of that after the game they couldn't wait to tell everybody Staubach used bad words. I mean, any of the other guys could say that and it would be nothing, right?

For conversations on a more lofty plane, Billy Parks provided a sounding board. He was a real character. Because of his frizzed blond hairstyle plus some of the things he did, Parks was nicknamed "Harpo" after the silent member of the Marx Brothers. In one respect Billy was misnamed because he wasn't quiet on certain subjects.

Parks was anti-Nixon and anti-Vietnam War to an almost violent degree. Before one of our games Secretary of Defense Melvin Laird held a military induction ceremony at Texas Stadium. When Parks saw that, he was so upset he almost refused to play.

Billy and I used to battle it out on social, economic and military issues. He was a smart guy, a good person, an idealist. He and I disagreed about whether we should have been there in the first place, and I still feel what we tried to accomplish in Southeast Asia was a better alternative to what's happened. Parks had deep concerns about people and the world in general but not football.

It bothered Billy that football was so important. He believed the game's value in terms of helping society was out of whack. The ideal football game to Parks was a choose-your-sides contest on a vacant lot attended by no one. He resisted the notion that football was meaningful and, to him, it wasn't. Therefore, as a player he was undependable. Parks played when the mood—or maybe the moon—was right. Sometimes he felt bad about playing in front of Lance Alworth. Once he declined to play at all, claiming a sore knee, upset that his good friend Tody Smith had been deactivated that week.

Parks was a tremendous receiver when everything clicked inside. But football wasn't his No. 1 priority. He let other things interfere with his game and you can't do that. You have opinions and philosophies but after hitting the football field you have to go at it. That includes practices and everything else. Parks couldn't or wouldn't. The Cowboys traded him after one season to Houston and he drifted out of the game after another season or so. Parks couldn't have been more than 28 years old.

Years later, another Cowboys receiver was responsible for one of the most uncomfortable episodes in my life. In his behalf I found myself sitting in a court of law, testifying under oath as a character witness. What made me ill at ease was that the case involved narcotics and I am inflexibly opposed to drugs. Yet friendship and what I knew about Bob Hayes compelled me to take the stand.

Hayes and I go back to the College All-Star game in 1965. I dislocated my shoulder in the first quarter but because the ambulance was enroute to the hospital with Paul Warfield—he'd broken a collarbone—I was still in the locker room at halftime. Bob spent most of halftime with me, one of the few who did. He showed genuine concern. I had a good rapport with Bob then and it was the same when we both came to the Cowboys. Bob also had come to our aid at the Paul Anderson Youth Home in rounding up some athletic equipment for us. He was a fun guy, a likeable person.

Why his career faded so abruptly in Dallas and ended after the 1974 season is debated to this day.

Through his prime years Hayes was more effective than any receiver who ever played pro football. He was *the* dominant force. I've looked up some of his club records and they are staggering. Bob caught passes for 246 yards in a 1966 game against Washington. One season he totaled 1,232 yards in receptions over a 14-game schedule. His first seven years in the NFL Bob caught 67 touchdown passes. He *averaged* 20 yards per catch over a career, which is similar to a quarterback hitting 65 percent of all his passes.

Bob's last three years in Dallas were unhappy ones by comparison. In '74 he caught only seven passes for one touchdown—his 71st and last. I threw it to him, a 35-yarder with a few seconds left against the New York Giants. Ironically all it did was prevent a shutout in a game we lost 14-6.

Probably a combination of factors caused Hayes to be ineffective toward the end. His knee began swelling on him. Also, the game was changing into zone-type coverages. Teams began playing looser with not as much man-to-man coverage. Again, the irony was that, more than anyone, Bob forced those changes with his speed and ability to run past people. Then he didn't adjust to the zones as well as he could. Speed was Bob's major asset. He wasn't like Lance Alworth, who could start to lose speed but develop a knack of getting open. Some critics faulted him for not being able to make the tough catch over the middle. He wasn't the best at it but I don't see that as a glaring weakness that helped push him out of the game in '75 after he'd been traded to San Francisco.

I knew some people would misunderstand when I testified at Bob's trial. Sure enough, they did. They failed to make the distinction that was foremost in my mind when I agreed to do it. Bob already had pleaded guilty to selling narcotics to an undercover agent. He admitted guilt. Therefore, my part was not concerned with determining guilt or innocence. I would *not* have gone to court under those circumstances. I tried to help Bob in the *punishment* phase of the proceedings. I did it for two reasons. He asked me. And I think Bob is basically a good person.

The prosecution had tape recordings of conversations between Bob and the undercover agent. They were pretty incriminating. Knowing that information there was no way I could have testified in Bob's defense if the question of guilt or innocence hadn't already been established. I wasn't trying to get him off, either. What he'd done and pleaded guilty to were the very things I've preached about to youth. I felt Bob deserved to be punished.

But knowing Hayes and how he goes about his life I also felt he'd been used by the people he was working for. I felt he could withstand the punishment and come out a better person. So I told the judge that the qualities I knew in Bob were good ones, that he did have good in him and definitely had the potential to rehabilitate himself.

Obviously, Bob didn't make smart choices. He might have thought he was really helping those guys. I don't know. There is no justification for what he did—yet he's not a bad human being. I think Hayes can do a lot of good, and that was all I really said to the judge. Still it was tough for me to do because I knew somebody would get the picture of an athlete making a mistake and getting off because everyone rides to his rescue. Since the guilty plea had been made, that wasn't the situation. It didn't stop the negative letter-writers from asking, "What are *you* doing down there?" They weren't even listening to what I said. Even the prosecutor, Dick Zadina, said he appreciated what I said because I wasn't up there trying to get Bob off the hook.

Finally, I come to the most unpleasant personal chapter of my NFL career. During the final week of the 1976 training camp I was involved in two fights with backup quarterback Clint Longley. At least they were described as fights. Actually the first was more of a brief wrestling match and the other just a blindside punch by Longley.

I have no feelings toward him anymore. I will admit bitterness over the way everything took place. I also feel partly responsible for the circumstances leading up to it. But the *way* it happened remains a bitter thing with me. That will never go away.

From the beginning then. Longley and I got along very well the two seasons he played for Dallas in 1974–75. He used to sit with me on the plane all the time and say things like, "I used to watch you when I was in college at Abilene [Abilene Christian College]." Our relationship was friendly. I was the older, established quarterback, he was the young guy coming up and we were at ease with each other.

The Washington game of '74 gave Longley credibility as far as his future with the Cowboys. Good ol' Talbert said before the game if I scrambled and the Redskins knocked me out, the game would be virtually over. Diron was half right. I got hit in the third quarter and never came out of the fog in time to play again. We were behind 16–3 but Longley, then a rookie, passed us to a miraculous 24–23 victory with a 50-yard TD to Drew Pearson with only seconds left.

Longley could see a future with Dallas but he still

didn't want to settle down as quarterback. He wasn't serious about learning the game, studying it. He felt I was the quarterback and he could just do what he wanted to since he was on the team now. I think he was satisfied with the understudy role. At least he never complained about the role, and he never did much about changing it by studying and preparing for a game.

Longley was a gifted athlete who had an excellent college career at ACC. He especially liked to throw long and developed a nice touch on deep passes. Because of this tendency, and the time he bounced a pass off the tower where Tom watched practices at training camp, he earned the nickname of The Mad Bomber.

Even though Clint had physical ability he didn't take the game seriously. That's the way he was—a free spirit. And that is what really came back to haunt him. Jim Zorn, then a free agent with the Cowboys who's now a star with Seattle, almost beat out Longley in '75. If not for the Washington game the year before, Zorn would have been on the team. But Landry had this mystic feeling about Longley from the Washington game. I believe to this day that's the reason he kept Longley. I'll bet if you talk to Dallas coaches today they'll say the decision to keep only two quarterbacks, and to keep Longley over Zorn, was not unanimous.

Longley went through his second season and played one game start to finish. I cracked some ribs the previous week against Washington so with a playoff spot assured, Landry went with Clint who did a fine job in beating the New York Jets 31–21. We upset our way into Super Bowl X in a tremendous finish for a team coming off an 8–6 season. Everyone was happy but not for long.

In the spring of '76 Danny White came to quarterback school. He joined the club after two years as a starter in the World Football League, which had gone broke. Within that two-week period something became very evident to everyone—Danny White knew our offense almost as well as Longley. They really grill you in those two weeks, and I'm sure Clint felt threatened.

All of a sudden the Danny White influence was being felt. The press began writing about Danny and a lot of positive things were happening to him. Just as suddenly Clint said, in effect, "I don't want to have anything to do with it anymore," and would not communicate with me or Danny. This was a tremendous change from the previous two years, and I was baffled.

It got so bad Clint wouldn't even throw passes with us at the practice field. If Danny or I were out there throwing, he'd leave and come back later. His whole personality changed.

I think it was the threat of White, the threat of losing the backup job. I believe he made up his mind he was going to lose it. He had enough ability to battle for it. He was in the driver's seat. He'd been with us two years. But since he hadn't applied himself enough during those two years he wasn't ahead mentally. Danny bridged that gap real quickly.

One day in the locker room I asked him, "Clint, what's wrong?" He just said, "I'm going to do my own thing. I don't want to throw with you guys. I don't want to have anything to do with you guys." It was such a complete change all I thought was, "I hope he gets over this."

Clint never did. He never changed. There was no communication at all. The day we got on the plane to go to Thousand Oaks, he wouldn't even talk to Marianne or the kids. We were all standing there and he never said a word. In training camp it was the same thing.

I went to him again out there and said, "Clint, what *is* the problem?" He wouldn't talk and I could sense his growing dislike for me. I didn't know why but I recognized the way he'd begun to feel toward me.

Not long afterwards we exchanged sharp words. We had laps to run and he was skipping his. "Why don't you run your laps like everybody else?" I asked him. "You aren't my coach," he snapped back. Later he blamed our problems on the fact I nagged him like a coach all the time, which was absurd. I'm not a coach-person and never have been with Danny, Glenn Carano or the receivers. I didn't tell those guys how to do things, but there was a normal interchange if something was obviously not right. If I was not setting up properly one of the other quarterbacks would mention it. Sometimes a quarterback would tell a receiver, "You weren't quite deep enough on that pass." But that's everyday stuff, not out of the ordinary at all.

There was one other incident before things got physical. One night we came out of a meeting and Clint was walking with Golden Richards. I yelled to Golden and Clint said to him, "Don't wait on that a—hole." Golden told me what he said so I went to Longley's room and said, "Clint, there is something wrong. Whatever kind of person you want to be and however you want to do things is fine. Just don't talk behind my back again."

Once more, he said, "I don't want anything to do with you. You go your way and I'll go mine." I said, "Fine, we'll leave it at that." Nothing had changed from what he'd told me two months earlier in the locker room in Dallas.

Clint had this chip on his shoulder, and it got to

me. Maybe that was what he was trying to do. Seeing him act childishly became a constant irritation. The lid began to blow on a Tuesday when we were throwing to receivers after practice. Everyone was tired, sore and sick of training camp.

Longley threw a pass to Drew Pearson who dropped it. Clint cursed at Drew. He was half serious, half joking, so right there I could have let the thing pass. But I didn't because he'd already been talking behind my back. I said, "Clint, I'm getting tired of you talking behind people's backs. Somebody is gonna knock those Bugs Bunny teeth of yours in." He said, "Are you going to be the one?" and I said, "Yeah, I'd love to do it."

Up to that point I don't know what I could have done that was different to prevent it. Maybe nothing. But right *there* I could have. Maybe I shouldn't have confronted him with what he'd said about Drew. Except I was mad again over his talking about people like that, saying things he wouldn't dare say to their faces.

We walked over to a baseball diamond adjacent to the practice field. He said something about, "Let's take off our shoulder pads," and I said, "No." We threw our helmets on the ground. What I wanted to do was get in a good wrestling match with him and get it over with because I was thinking, *Man, if we start swinging I could break my hand or something.* So I made up my mind I would wrestle him.

Then he hauled off and took a swing at me. That set me off. I was walking over there thinking to myself, *I wish there was some way to get out of this.* Not that I was worried about fighting this guy. That was the last worry I had. It was just that here I was 34 years old and headed for what amounted to a schoolyard scuffle. I recognized all the problems it was going to create before it started. But once he took that swing I didn't care anymore. All I knew was a guy tried to hit me.

He tried to sucker-punch me. I ducked and his punch grazed the left side of my head. In fact, my head was sore for three or four days every time I tried to put on my helmet. He hit me hard enough so that I just went crazy. I lunged at Clint and immediately wrestled him to the ground. It wasn't long before Danny Reeves, an assistant coach, pulled me off.

When I got off I said, "Clint, the next time I'm not gonna let you up." I was still plenty mad because of that first swing he took. Reeves walked back to the locker room with me and along the way he said, "Roger, I'll tell you one thing. Don't turn your back on him again. If I were you I'd be careful. I wouldn't turn my back on him."

Tell you what. That was what you call a real prophecy.

When Landry heard of the incident his reaction was terse. "It better not happen again," he told us. That's all he said. At the time I believe we both thought it was over but later I found the reasons the worse was yet to come.

The previous Saturday night had been a bad one for Longley. We played Los Angeles in a televised exhibition game. Clint didn't play the second half. His pride was going downhill quickly because of the developing quarterback situation. Danny now looked like he was moving up as No. 2 although it still wasn't clearly defined. But I think Clint began to gear himself mentally to be third-team quarterback, and he wasn't going to take it. Danny played the second half against the Rams, looked good, and that increased the pressure Longley felt.

Mel Renfro told me he heard Clint talking to a friend in Denver, saying, "I'm going to be leaving the Cowboys. I'm not gonna be here any longer." Renfro said Longley went on to talk about not playing in the Rams game.

Longley did take pride in playing and had showed moments of greatness. The Washington game wasn't an accident because the potential was there. But I'd have more forgiving thoughts if he hadn't hit me the way he did. I was lucky he didn't break my jaw.

Longley also was proud to be No. 2 but most of all showed a lingering fascination with his great performance against Washington. He had a tape of that game he used to play frequently during training camp. People were praising him all the time, probably telling him he was better than I that year. Maybe he was. He sure was on that Thanksgiving Day against the Redskins.

In other words he wasn't just another quarterback. He had done something. He had an identity. Now out of the blue came this guy Danny White who's an NFL rookie from the World Football League and he's outshowing Clint. It got to him. There's no question in my mind that is what changed his character.

Danny stayed away from Longley. He never said anything to him. I saw how Clint had changed but Danny didn't know Longley any other way. I did, and it bothered me. If I had ignored Clint I don't know what he might have done. Probably he would not have taken out his frustrations on me. I suppose I helped that process because I was irritated by what he was doing and how he went about it. To some extent I was instrumental in what happened.

For three days after our first encounter Longley and I did not speak to each other. I had no idea how our differences might be resolved. I never dreamed the end would include my sitting in a hospital emergency room, in full pads yet, having nine stitches taken over my left eye.

Only afterwards did the pieces fall into place.

Landry scheduled a private meeting in his room with Longley before Friday afternoon practice. I never learned the purpose of their talk. Clint didn't show. By then he'd made up his mind what he was going to do. Renfro told me he'd overheard Longley say to one of his friends in Denver, "The way I can really leave this team is if I hit Staubach."

Meantime I'm happy as a lark. It was the last day of practice at Thousand Oaks, always the most beautiful day in the year for me. I'm the world's happiest human being on the last day of training camp. I can't wait to get home. So I came into the locker room joking and laughing. What Harvey Martin said later was that Longley had been sitting in a chair in the locker room for the last hour. He didn't go to the meeting with Landry. His bags were packed. His check had been cashed.

On the basis of that evidence I'd say what he did was more than a little premeditated. I wasn't aware of these things at the time or I wouldn't have forgotten Reeves's warning earlier in the week. I wouldn't have turned my back on Longley.

He was sitting on that chair about six feet from me and at an extreme angle to my left. My initial memory was that I was just putting my shoulder pads on when I got hit. But Lee Roy Jordan told me I actually had them on and was starting to buckle them. That's probably the way it was because I remember trying to throw the pads off. I wanted to get enough freedom of movement to fight.

I made a vulnerable target. I was standing, loose as jello and ecstatic over the prospect of being home the next day. Both hands were on the shoulder pad straps tightening the buckle. Doing so meant my head was down in almost a chin-on-chest position. It also meant my vision was riveted on a piece of equipment about eight inches in front of my nose.

That is when Longley struck.

He'd been sitting there waiting for the right moment. There weren't many players around. Some had dressed and left. Others hadn't arrived. No one was looking, especially me. He picked the perfect instant for a blindside punch.

I knew two things right away. I knew what had happened, and who did it. But I *was* dazed. I remember one time as a kid I ran into a tree. This was the same feeling . . . boom!

I remember reeling down and Clint jumping on my back. I couldn't quite get with it. There were about ten seconds in which I was having problems clearing my head. I'd been knocked into a set of floor scales. Whether I was cut from his fist or the scales I never determined.

Then all of a sudden I had complete control of myself. All I wanted to do was get the guy. I remember being very coherent when I turned around and stood up. Players had us separated. They grabbed me and wouldn't let me go.

"The damage has been done!" I shouted. "I've

got to get this thing over with.'' Longley was screaming like a maniac. I was trying to get loose to get at him. But the players wouldn't let me go because my eye was bleeding.

Don Cochran, our head trainer, took me to the hospital for stitches. On the way back to the locker room Cochran slowed the car near the dorms and I jumped out. I headed for the dorm where Longley stayed. I didn't think he'd leave. I thought I'd see him that night but I wanted another meeting as quickly as possible.

Frankly, I went around the outside of the dorm first because I knew he had a couple of guns in his rooms. One of Clint's hobbies was hunting and he brought firearms to camp to target shoot, sometimes in an open area behind the dorm. I realized he had a rifle and pistol and I wondered if at this stage he was dangerous. But he was gone. He was long gone.

I met some sportswriters who said a reporter from one of the Dallas radio stations had given Longley a ride to the Los Angeles terminal. Before Clint left he claimed I had provoked his punch by pushing a chair at him. If that were true someone would have seen it and he wouldn't have run.

I learned something about myself in the next few days that I didn't like. I had tremendous hate festering in my heart for three or four days to the extent that I wouldn't have been able to turn the other cheek. I would have taken physical action if I'd seen Longley and that is wrong. Hate and revenge are not part of the Christian faith.

When it was over I had other thoughts about Clint. Here was a guy who had a chance for a bright career, who could have been salvaged in Dallas except for circumstances that were out of control. He did have opportunities in other places. I've forgiven and tried to forget the incident. I was wrong having revenge and hate in my heart.

But what keeps me from forgetting entirely is the way it happened. I could easily have lost an eye or had my jaw broken and might never have played football again. The way he did it was a bad act. I haven't seen Clint Longley since that day. I'd prefer to keep it that way, too.

V
When We Were Young

"It's easy to tell my children the ideal way to do things but I always remember there's a chemistry—an electricity—between parent and child that can come back to haunt you. If I don't try to live that way and do those things, they won't either."—Roger Staubach

Dominating the landscape around the village of Lauterbrunnen in Switzerland is a waterfall which drops an impressive distance over the face of a mountain. It is from these cascading waters that the village was named: the German-English translation breaks down into *Lauter* (pure, clear) and *Brunnen* (spring or well).

Another name apparently derived from the waterfall. As the water descends from the great height it breaks into a spray that from afar resembles diffused dust (in German, *Staub*) which eventually disappears below into a brook *(Bach)*. Logically enough, the place was called Staubbach (Dust Brook) Falls and, for that matter, still is. Situated nearby is the three-story Staubbach Hotel, which I not only don't own but was unaware of until Sheila Wells of Amarillo, Texas, sent me a picture of it.

From *Staubbach* to *Staubach* was a natural transition which genealogists theorize my forefathers made centuries ago from their proximity to the waterfall. No one can prove it by written records, but tradition has it that as a family designation the name was in use in that area in the time of Charlemagne (747–814). The earliest established proof I've seen of the Staubach name is from an inscription on a church memorial stone in Herbstein, a village in Germany. A former town elder and master of the tanner's guild, Zacharies Staubach (1608–82) is buried there.

There is no question that I'm descended from the Swiss Family Staubachs. On my father's side the heritage is Swiss-German. On my mother's it's Irish (her maiden name was Smyth). Staubach relatives who have traced the family name found ancestors who were everyday people in everyday occupations. Staubachs have been merchants, policemen, farmers, teamsters and the like. As far as I know none was famous but more importantly, neither was anyone notorious. The Staubachs have been solid, hard-working, God-fearing people, and if I received no other legacy I would be proud of that.

With one exception there was no athletic strain on either branch of the family tree. I understand that Uncle Harry, my mother's brother, had fantastic athletic ability but wasted it by not applying himself. The family talk was that grandmother spoiled him and sometimes he wouldn't even show up for some of his games. When I began to develop as an athlete relatives would say that all came down through my mother's side from Uncle Harry.

My dad had three brothers and none was involved in athletics. Neither was my father, beyond some semi-pro baseball and football. Yet in a physical sense I was fortunate to be born of Robert and Elizabeth Staubach. Both were strong, tall and sturdy. Dad stood a fraction over six feet tall and weighed about 195 pounds. Mother was around 5–7, maybe 140 pounds. It was because of them that I grew to 6–3 and carried 200 pounds as a professional athlete.

Being blessed from birth with physical equipment is no advantage unless you're competitive. Where I got my streak of competitiveness I'm not sure. The instinct to excel just seemed to be there naturally. I never thought about why or where it came from. Perhaps it was from my mother. She was more ambitious than my father. Whatever she did, singing or playing the piano, she wanted to be the best. Dad wasn't overly competitive. He was easy-going, the kind of guy you wanted as a friend because nothing seemed to bother him.

I was attracted to athletics by the neighborhood environment. My parents didn't push me in that direction. All I had to do was walk out either door of our house and there was a game in progress. Across the street a man named Tom Brannen had a basketball goal behind his house. Down the street lived the nine Bien children whose yard was large enough for football. Our backyard was tiny when I think of it today, but at our age and size then it satisfied the dimensions of a softball diamond. We were running, throwing or dribbling almost every day. By present-day standards our neighborhood would be classified as lower middle class, but to us kids it was a paradise of fun and games.

My first experience with organized athletics was at age eight when I joined a Pee Wee League baseball team. I was lucky to be coached by a man of infinite patience, John Fink. He let us throw, hit and even call balls and strikes. Kids that age can't get the ball over the plate, so an inning might last an hour. But Mr. Fink never gave any indication it bothered him. He was a teacher. He stressed fundamentals and having a good time—just the right approach for children starting in athletics.

Best of all Mr. Fink didn't discourage anyone. We played in a low-key atmosphere in which winning wasn't the only objective. Later in life I came to appreciate how important that was because it helped me develop a healthy attitude toward sports in general. Some kids are lucky enough today to join leagues like this which have their priorities in order: children, not coaches or parents, are the first consideration.

Winning is fun and it's the American way. I believe in it. But for kids at a young age, athletics should be stressed for the pleasure of participating. If a child is provided with the proper environment he will begin to learn the lessons of athletics which are useful in everyday life—working as a team, self-discipline and personal sacrifice. But if he's thrown against must-win pressures and chewed out if he doesn't, athletics becomes a negative experience and he soon will drop out. A kid isn't mature enough to handle the psychology of someone being mad at him.

I'll give you a personal example. When I was in the sixth grade I was the catcher and my good friend Vince Eysoldt was pitcher on a baseball team which won 39 straight games and the state championship. When I was in the seventh grade our football team didn't win a single

Roger limbering up his arm at six months.

With Heisman Trophy won at Navy in 1963.

Roger running sprints...

Staubach scrambling *(Cowboys Newsletter)*.

Examining bad center snap from shotgun formation *(Cowboys Newslett*

Breaking away.

Roger dodging Minnesota defensive end Jim Marshall... a ballet of elder statesmen in 1978 (photo by Russ Russell, *Cowboys Newsletter*).

Roger Staubach prepares to release a 39-yd. touchdown pass to Tony Hill in the Super Bowl XIII *(Cowboys Newsletter)*.

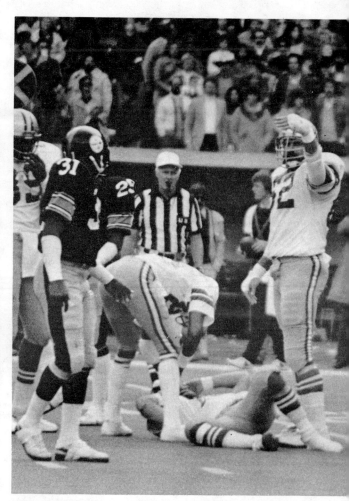

Staubach down with a concussion in the 1979 Pittsburgh game. Center John Fitzgerald is waving for team doctors; Drew Pearson is leaning over stricken quarterback *(Cowboys Newsletter)*.

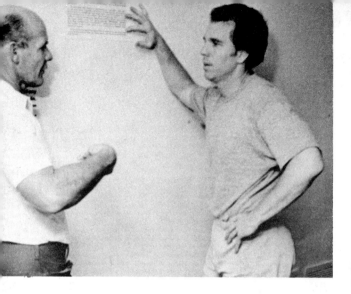

Coach Tom Landry in conference with Staubach *(Cowboys Newsletter)*.

Roger leaping into Ron Springs's arms after throwing game-winning touchdown pass against Washington—see Chapter XI (photo by David Woo, *Dallas Morning News*).

Roger and Marianne, 1973.

Signing autographs on a
street corner in Dallas
(Cowboys Newsletter).

Marianne and Roger, 1980.

The Staubach girls at their home. Left to right: Stephanie (11), Amy (3), Michelle (12), and Jennifer (14). (These and all following photos copyright 1980 by Jerry Cabluck.)

Jeff Staubach (5½)
in fine passing form.

Roger and Amy shooting baskets.

Marianne

The Staubach clan at poolside.

Family portrait

game. Sure, I enjoyed the winning season more but I learned from both years. Fortunately, we had a coach, Paul Risenberg, who wasn't high-pressure during the all-losing season so I didn't become soured on athletics. Then in the eighth grade, under the same coach, we won all our football games.

Winning is nice at any age, even as early as seven or eight years. Given a choice it's natural to pick winning over losing, but losing shouldn't be a big deal at that early age. If a kid loses, he shouldn't worry about it, but learn from the experience. He should be able to have fun and enjoy the sport, whatever it is. In fact, at these early ages I don't think they should even keep score.

As he gets into high school then winning and losing become more important. He is now part of a team concept and the emphasis on winning is greater. At any age I think an athlete should compete to win with the best of his abilities. But what's critical is how he handles the losing at this stage of his life—how he accepts it and what he does about it. The attitude of coaches, what they say and do, also becomes vital in providing a healthy athletic atmosphere. If he loses I think the best approach is to say, "We did our best. Let's go out and have a milk shake and forget about it." Losing shouldn't become a stigma or leave psychological scars in high school.

In college the emphasis on winning increases. But by now the athlete is more mature. He can go after the winning more because he can handle the losing better. He can still function as a person if he loses. Criticism shouldn't bother him as much because of his maturity.

At the professional level there is no substitute for winning. That's what Vince Lombardi meant when he said, "Winning isn't everything; it's the *only* thing." An athlete's career is based on winning in the pros because it's his profession, the way he makes a living and supports his family. It's the same as selling life insurance or real estate. To be successful he has to win.

At the college level he can still win or lose and grow as a man. He can learn what sports are all about and apply those lessons to life. What athletics teaches is the self-discipline of hard work and sacrifice necessary to achieve a goal. Nowadays, too many people are looking for a short cut. They want a free ride, a handout. For guys who've been in athletics this shouldn't be true because they know what it takes. There are no short cuts to success. Just the blood, sweat and tears which produce results. Life is the same as athletics. You have to work to accomplish anything.

To be a success in any endeavor also requires a knowledge of fundamentals. Regardless of whether one's an athlete or not, a sound academic base is mandatory. Kids should begin forming the educational foundation of their lives in grade school. They should learn the fundamentals of how to study which will carry them into college for the culmination of the educational process.

The mistake many youngsters make is emphasizing athletics to the exclusion of their education. They become big stars in high school but then discover they're not good enough to play in college. Then what do they have? If they are without an academic background they will have problems, perhaps lifelong difficulties.

To any young person interested in athletics, I'd have to say at no stage of your life should you totally gear toward becoming a professional athlete. The odds are simply astronomical against you. The first thing in your temporal life should be an education. Competition in the business world can be tougher than the athletic world. The mental aspects are much, much tougher in business.

Look at it this way. If you're 5–6 and want to be a wide receiver in professional football, you have no chance. But the guy who is 6–4 and did play wide receiver someday will be out of uniform and into the business world. Then you'll be competing against him in an arena where size and physical skill don't make any difference. The man who wins that battle will be the one who's best educated.

Ideally, as you prepare for your life work, you should also be preparing for your eternal life, which means developing a relationship with Christ.

Sports and religion have been twin focal points for me almost as long as I can recall. As a preteen I was aware of my athletic ability, that for some reason I had instincts which put me at the head of the class in sports. In baseball I had good hand-eye coordination and wound up having one of the best batting averages in the Pee Wee League. When we played sandlot football or even tackle on the playground—those games were on *asphalt,* which I find hard to believe today—I was always the hardest guy to bring down. I was more aggressive than anyone although, again, I never stopped long enough to wonder why. On my first basketball team in the fifth grade I was the leading scorer, but that I could understand. I shot more than anyone else. In modern-day terminology I was a gunner.

But that's the way I was as a kid. I wanted the ball hit to me. I wanted to shoot it. I wanted to run with it. Wherever the action was I enjoyed being in the middle of it. Sure, I liked being good because there was a certain status that came with the attention. But as good as I may have been there was something inside which always made me press to be better. Therefore, whatever skills I had I applied and constantly tried to improve.

Baseball was the center of my early attention and the Cincinnati Reds were *it*. Everyone idolized Ted Kluszewski, the home-run-hitting first baseman. He lived about four miles from us and one of the thrills of my youth was just riding a bicycle past his house. I remember all the Reds players of my childhood . . . Roy McMillan at shortstop, Johnny Temple at second, Ray Jablonski at third, Kluszewski at first. Wally Post, Jim Greengrass and Gus Bell were the outfield. Andy Seminick and Ed Bailey caught. Going to a Knothole Gang Day at old Crosley Field in Cincinnati was the biggest day in my life.

I didn't become attached to a football team until after I started playing the game in the seventh grade. Then I idolized the Cleveland Browns: quarterback Otto Graham and other stars like Ray Renfro, Marion Motley, Lou Groza and Dante Lavelli. One reason Cleveland became my team is that the Browns were the only ones we ever saw on television. TV was new in those days. We were among the last families to get a television set, so before our 10-inch black and white set arrived I'd go to other people's houses to watch the Browns.

At the Naval Academy I began following Baltimore and Johnny Unitas. He was in his prime when I was at Annapolis. I'll never forget a game he played against the Chicago Bears one Sunday. I saw this one from New Mexico Military Institute, and it left a lasting impression about a quarterback who would never give up.

The Bears had a defensive end named Doug Adkins, who at 6–8 was a virtual giant in those days. Adkins just beat Unitas apart. I think Unitas even wound up with a punctured lung or something equally as bad. He was bleeding and they took him out. But Unitas came back in and threw the game-winning touchdown pass to Lenny Moore down the right sideline. I have always remembered Unitas for that display of physical courage and perseverance.

During the late 1960s I began following Dallas because of Don Meredith and the fact I'd been signed by the Cowboys. That's when I also became intrigued with Bart Starr of Green Bay. I was impressed by his sense of command on the field. So my early football heroes were first Graham then Unitas then Starr.

None of them influenced my habit of play as a quarterback, though. I developed my own style and it came from baseball. I was a baseball quarterback, no question about it. As a youngster I played outfield, pitched and caught. Each is a position that requires some sort of wind-up throwing motion.

To this day when I wind up to throw a football there is a little hitch in my passing motion. It happens fast but it's there. When people talk about having a quick release they mean taking the ball back and flicking it with the wrist like, say, Joe Namath does. I never really had that.

But I was a strong thrower. I threw the ball hard. Throwing hard wasn't best in every situation but it's a nice asset when it's needed. My arm strength meant that I could get away with that little hitch because I made up for it in velocity. Terry Bradshaw of Pittsburgh and Bert Jones of Baltimore are two of the strongest-armed quarterbacks in the NFL, but I'm up there with them in velocity.

That developed from baseball. Playing baseball was how I learned to throw the ball. That's how I first learned to throw anything. Remember I wasn't a quarterback until my senior year in high school. All they knew about me then was, "Hey, this kid has a great arm."

I had no control over my arm back then, but I'd played halfback in grade school and could run with a football. As a young quarterback I relied on what I did best—run—because my arm wasn't disciplined. I became a scrambler because there was more security running than passing and I was successful at it.

Coming out of high school I wasn't established as a passer. College recruiters looked me over and said, "He has a strong arm, excellent running instincts and fairly good size. We can develop his arm."

At this stage of my life I probably was a better baseball player. Bernie Sinchek, my baseball head coach, felt this was the sport in which I had a professional future. I'd started out to be a heckuva basketball player in high school and had colleges interested in me as a junior. But as a senior I leveled off and didn't have a great year. The problem with continuing to play baseball was that there weren't many scholarships in that sport.

I had a chance to get a football scholarship, and that was the name of the game. My parents would have had a very difficult time sending me to college on their own. They would have done it. They would have figured out a way to do it by scrimping and saving and sacrificing. My father was a manufacturer's representative in the shoe, leather and thread business. I'd estimate he probably made only $50–55 a week although the job did provide a car. But it was obvious the family's finances were tight because when I was nine Mother went back to work as a secretary at General Motors.

Football gave me the opportunity to attend college so it became the emphasis in my life. I spent the summer between high school graduation and entering junior college in New Mexico throwing a football. The work paid off because I had improved by the time I came under the influence of Coach Bob Shaw at NMMI.

Shaw was a former pro receiver for St. Louis whose name is still listed in the NFL record book. During a 1950 game against Baltimore he caught five touchdown passes, a feat never duplicated. Shaw ran a pro-type offense which was ahead of its time at the college level. The emphasis was on passing, so it was at NMMI that my arm began to smooth out. I became a quarterback with passing promise. The transition took place during a period of less than a year, between the end of my high school days and the conclusion of the football season at NMMI. A strong football arm developed from a strong baseball arm during that period.

During my formative years when I was so heavily involved in athletics my parents never cautioned me about taking sports so seriously. They were very even-handed about athletics. Mother once tried to make me into a piano player but those plans blew away during my first recital when I forgot all the notes to the *William Tell* Overture. When I received athletics awards they didn't brag about it. They were humble about things like that.

I never felt parental pressure to become the best baseball player or the best football player in the world. They just loved me and wanted me to be happy in what I did. Their ambition for me was to get an education and be a good person. That's what they were—good people.

They would never step on anybody to gain something for themselves. My dad wouldn't do it. He'd give you the shirt off his back and be happy about doing it. Mother was like that, too. They gave a lot more than they took. As a child I couldn't have been luckier to have parents like that. They didn't have money yet I always had what I needed in school because they pinched and saved.

Because I was an only child most of their life was directed toward me. Of all the gifts they gave me none was more important than their living the life they told me about, the kind they wanted me to live. They were tremendous examples.

People have asked me who my biggest hero was, and I tell them it was my dad because he had the greatest influence on my life. If he had turned out to be bad, I would have been in trouble because I adored him. When he left to go on business trips, I remember how upset his absence would make me. I remember how much I just liked being around him.

As naturally as I slipped into athletics, religion became an important and serious side of my life at an early age when I attended a Catholic grade school. It wasn't hammered into me by anyone despite the scare stories you hear about nuns being so harsh. Yes, the nuns *were* tough but they were true, loving servants of the Lord. They not only aroused my curiosity to learn more about religion but gave me a great foundation for my faith.

Somehow, from somewhere inside of me, an instinct said, "This Lord is forgiving." That thought really became important to me. I remember going to my parents and saying, "Mom, Dad, I did this wrong thing yesterday. Do you think if I start over today the Lord will forgive me?"

I learned the personal anguish of asking for forgiveness when I was about seven years old. The incident remains one of the most traumatic experiences of my life. I stole from a religious store, of all places. I took a little statue of the Blessed Virgin and a medal. I also took money off a neighbor's table—50–60 cents worth of change— and put it in a drawer in my room. I didn't spend the money. It just lay there where I'd see it every day and get more and more upset about being a thief.

One night I was lying on the couch and burst out crying. My mother thought I was sick until I told her what had happened. I knew what I'd done was wrong and I'd let my parents down. My remorse was overwhelming. To this day when I go back to Cincinnati and drive through that area I can picture where that religious store was located. It's not there anymore but in my mind I see it the way it was, right down the street from the doughnut shop.

The family from whom I took the money was named Cross. Mother told Mrs. Cross what I'd done, returned the money and made me apologize to them. It was the most embarrassing time of my life and I dreaded ever seeing the Crosses again. Today, I wouldn't take a paper clip if it didn't belong to me.

I was coming to know and understand more about the Catholic faith almost daily. No one had to brainwash me. I was fascinated by this forgiving Jesus. He not only died for our sins but forgave our sins. The concept intrigued me.

As a result I wanted to know more about Him. On weekdays, even when it wasn't necessary, I'd get up early and go to Mass. During Lent I went all the time because I wanted to be a part of this faith that made so much sense to me. My parents and others were instrumental in helping me to know Jesus Christ, but it was through a personal commitment above and beyond them that I came to Him. The lure definitely was the God-man. I had a feeling about Him.

While learning more about faith I became mesmerized by the Apostles. They were just like all of us. Even at the final hour Peter denied Christ. Then Thomas, who still didn't believe He had risen from the dead, had to stick his hand in Christ's wounds. Then I found out these same men, who were so fickle and inconsistent, martyred themselves for Him. The Apostles actually *saw* what we were learning about in the Bible—the death and resurrection. They were human and their frailties were universal, but they had the opportunity to see Him and be with Him.

That was when I began to realize the importance of faith. I didn't have the answers to all the questions. I didn't have the answer to my mother dying painfully or my dad being so sick. I didn't have the answer to someone else, a child or friend, dying too young. Faith is the *only* answer to things we can't understand about God's eternal plan.

The essense of my faith is that as a Christian I believe Jesus Christ died for our sins on that Friday, that He came back from the dead on Sunday, and His resurrection gives us a chance for everlasting life. That is the faith which to this day I practice through the Catholic church.

A firm religious foundation combined with wholesome parental example helped me as a youngster to withstand peer pressure. Because of these influences I could overcome the temptation of joining a crowd doing something I knew was wrong.

I remember another incident from my youth as an example of facing down temptation. It was on an elementary scale but this is where self-discipline begins. Resist on such a simple level, and it's easier to do so later when the issues are larger and the consequences more severe.

We lived on a circle drive adjacent to Ohio Avenue, a main drag with a heavy traffic flow. My mother told me never to cross that street on my bicycle. One day there was a fair in Silverton, and all my friends got together and said, "Let's ride over there." I got right up to the end of North Berkeley Circle but wouldn't cross Ohio Avenue.

A neighbor who lived in the corner house overhead the kids saying, "C'mon, Rog, let's go. We'll ride over there and get back and no one will know." But I resisted and wouldn't cross Ohio Avenue. The neighbor told my mother about this scene. Ironically, it was Mrs. Cross from whose home I'd stolen the money. I wouldn't cross the street because of my parents—not that I feared them or feared I'd be punished but because I loved them and didn't want to disappoint them.

This is the sort of relationship we're trying to develop in our family. Kids growing up today are confronted with issues that are much tougher than those in my time. I believe there is a spiritual solution to problems we encounter like peer pressure. If there are ten kids at a party and nine are smoking marijuana, what's the tenth one going to do? If he has a solid relationship with his parents that will help. If he has a relationship with Jesus Christ he can walk away from that temptation.

The love I felt from my parents, the examples they set for me, and my Christian faith were instrumental in molding the kind of person I am today. It was by example that my philosophy on race relations was formed and my mother was largely responsible. A black family was moving in close to our neighborhood, and people were upset about it. I recall my mother chastizing the neighbors about their prejudice. I was in another room but I could hear everything going on in the house.

"How can you call yourself Christians?" mother said. "How can you hold something over the blacks because of the color of their skin, whether they want to move in next door or whatever they want to do? It goes against everything we believe as Christians."

Mother not only talked a good game but practiced it and tried to get others to practice it. That always stood out in my mind. In forming opinions about other people you must have understanding. You have to put yourself in their shoes. I was taught to judge a person on who he is and what he stands for instead of his color.

Like my mother, I am upset by religious hypocrisy more than anything. Jesus Christ would jump out of His skin at such a two-faced attitude. The second greatest of the Ten Commandments is to love your neighbor as your-self. Yet there have been Christians through the years who've prevented people from joining their church because of skin color. This is a disgrace. There is no worse hypocrisy in all of life than a Christian prejudiced toward another human being.

Everything we do on earth is temporary. We have our temporary joys and sorrows, for which there are temporary solutions. The permanent solution is that relationship with Christ. That is the bond which extends beyond this earth.

First as a child and now as a man I have been fascinated by this thought. For a long time I've had an awareness of who I am, where I am and where I'm going. I've always had an instinct about that. I never dwelled too much on the past. The present is important to me in relation to the future. What is the future, not only on this earth, but when you die?

Learning the Christian faith formed the answers for me. It's not like having a crutch, because the concept is sound. It's a proven plan, not something made up. God put it together in his infinite wisdom by sending His Son here. I believe that Jesus christ was the Son of God who died for our sins and came back from the dead on Sunday to give us our salvation. That's what it's all about.

VI
The Family

"I think we are coming into a hard period for Roger because, not having any sisters, he has no idea of how girls react. Half the time he doesn't even know how I am going to react, much less a teenage girl."
— *Marianne Staubach*

The bottom line in a family is love. Everything revolves around and depends upon that emotion sooner or later. Love makes the good times better and sustains a family through periods of stress, anger and heartbreak. Love makes being a family an enriching experience for parents and children.

I learned that growing up as an only child and now am trying to apply the knowledge as a father of five. Marianne was exposed to the same warm, close household except she had one advantage which proved valuable as a mother. Her parents, George and Anne Hoobler, had five children, so with four brothers and sisters Marianne was accustomed to a boisterous atmosphere around the house. I've had to make an adjustment to the clatter and chaos five active, healthy children create.

I don't think we're overly strict parents. There is organization in our family structure, responsibilities for everyone within the unit. Marianne has seen to that. She keeps a chart in the kitchen to remind the kids of their duties—the everyday things you find in many homes, like setting the table and clearing it, doing the dishes and taking care of their part of the house where each of them has his or her own bedroom.

Since we were able to afford it financially, I felt it was important that each child have the privacy of a separate bedroom. At the same time we've let them know that it's something special, that living in this home has been a very, very big step for us. Marianne and I saved for ten years, cutting back in many areas, to build a large but not extravagant or ostentatious house.

Part of the children's responsibility is to help maintain it neatly. We have other guidelines for them concerning when they can go out, whom they go out with and what movies they can see. For instance, we don't let them see many movies, even those with Parental Guidance ratings, unless one of us has seen it. We're not different from many other parents when it comes to television. There are rules about what they can and can't watch.

Neither of us is a fanatic about demanding perfection in our children's behavior, or inflexible over an occasional exception to the rules. It's normal for every kid to test his parents at some point just to see how far he can go, what he or she can get away with. Yet I believe the child feels better and more secure in knowing there *are* boundaries which he's not allowed to go beyond. In this way he learns what his parents consider acceptable in areas ranging from speech, dress, behavior toward others, manners and so forth. If it's handled with an eye toward being constructive, discipline ingrains into the child his parents' value system.

[Marianne:] *Jennifer is the easygoing, friendly type. She's the Good Samaritan, always willing to help people. She'd rather be doing something for someone else than studying. Jennifer would rather give Amy a bath in the evening than do her homework. We have to save her from herself sometimes.*

She will volunteer to do anything at school. If they want someone to put up a bulletin board she says, "I'll do it." If the cafeteria needs cleaning she'll do it. Jennifer's not this way just to get out of class or avoid studying. She simply volunteers because she is always willing to help.

Our oldest daughter is not real big on neatness, and this may drive Roger to drink if that's possible. One night he came in from a speaking engagement and went up to tell the other girls goodnight. Jennifer's room looked like a cyclone had hit it. Roger went through the roof. He told the other girls he was going to bed but to tell Jennifer her room had to be clean before he left for 6:30 Mass in the morning. She got in about 10 o'clock and was up until about 3:00 A.M. cleaning her room. There was a swim party the next day, and Roger had said if her room wasn't spotless when he left for Mass, she wasn't going.

So that's Jennifer. She just rolls with things.

Eventually all children require discipline because it's natural for them to push beyond the allowable limit sometimes. Our kids aren't any different. Nor is our range of punishment out of the ordinary. Depending on the severity of what the kids have done, we reprimand in several ways: a verbal correction, withdrawal of a privilege, being sent to his room or a spanking. We have used a paddle but only on the bottom and mostly for the young ones. I can't remember the last time either of us spanked the older girls. The little ones, Jeff and Amy, still catch it but not very often and only for something significant.

Regardless of how our children have been disciplined, we try to impress several ideas upon them: First, that we're not doing it because we feel hostility toward them. Second, they are punished because we love them. Third, we fully explain the reason for the reprimand and emphasize that what they have done is bad. We avoid telling the children they are bad. The burden goes on what they've done, not on themselves as persons. Psychologically, there's an important difference to a child's self-image between *doing* a bad thing and *being* bad.

Frequently after one of our kids has been punished I start feeling worse about it than they do. So I go to them, we have a talk, and I hug them and say, "We love you, but this was why it had to be done." In most cases they understand. Amy and Jeff don't so much, but it's always explained to them why they were paddled and sent to their rooms or whatever. The older girls are better about seeing our point of view. Actually this cool-down period can be a time of intimacy with the child which leads to important heart-to-heart talks.

I want my children to be children for as long as it's healthy. I don't want to stifle their growth but neither do I want them growing up too fast. What we've tried to establish is a delicate middle ground. *Delicate* is a word for it, too.

We have a rule for Jennifer, for instance, about when a boy can actually call on her and take her out on a date. She won't be able to do that until she's sixteen. Here's the way I feel about that and other similar instances. Give children permission to do things now—things that maybe they *could* have or do that aren't even harmful—and then they will want more. If she's already done this, then next she'll want to do that. The situation escalates and the child winds up trying to grow up too fast.

We've had a big family to-do about the girls' getting their ears pierced. There is nothing wrong with it except it is a step, a growing step. They don't need them pierced at age ten, eleven, or twelve. So we set a time frame on it. The reason was once they got their ears pierced they would want something else. They might want to wear make-up all the time. We let them wear a little on occasion, especially Jennifer who's old enough now. But even that is part of the growing process. They need to grow gradually.

Like every parent we hear our children say, "But so-and-so gets to do it, why can't we?" Peer pressure is enormous, and I think it's worse for girls than boys because so many feminine elements like clothes, make-up, boy friends, dating and so on confront them daily. We've tried to let our children know although it may be that way with others, because of the love we have for each other, our family wishes to handle it differently. If there is enough love and respect at home, kids can overcome peer pressure whether it's in the area of drugs, morality or what have you.

[Marianne:] *Michelle is very meticulous. Her room is spotless all the time. She is very organized and has a fantastic memory. Recently Roger and I were looking for a tennis club membership number but couldn't find the card. Michelle said, "I think it's 983, mom." Sure enough it was, and I'll bet she hadn't been there in almost a year. She remembers phone numbers, everything.*

The children all have jobs in the summertime. I keep a chart in the utility room with their duties. I never have to tell Michelle, "Today you have to clean the play room or sweep the patio." She has hers done by 10 or 11 o'clock in the morning. Consequently she ends up doing more than the others because they fink out on theirs.

I don't know how we got one like that, but she is very disciplined. If she has homework, she comes in and gets it done. The minute she gets home she'll say, "Mother. I need a poster board, construction paper, etc." instead of waiting until 10 o'clock that night.

I don't think we raise them any differently. They're just born like that. Michelle is very regimented. If things don't go according to schedule, it throws her off. She doesn't bend very easily.

Faith is the heart of our family relationships. The children know that Christianity is the core of our life, that it works in our life, and we want them to see it doing so. They know we want Christ to be part of their lives, too. We read Scripture together at home, although not often enough. Now that I'm retired from football and will be home more, I can be more involved with my children and spend quality time with them, which, to be truthful, I have not been able to do as much before.

I have tried. On most occasions I've been there when they needed me. But I've not had quality time with each of them on an individual basis. With five kids, that's tough to do. I could use my whole day just meeting their needs. I hope to attain a happy medium now.

During every training camp my mind was always at home with the family. But sometimes at home I found myself taking the children and their needs for granted. I liked to hug and hold them, do things with them, yet I know there were times when I was isolated from them by football. They were going about their business while my thoughts were on the pressures and preparation for the next game. I wasn't able to get inside their heads as much as I should—something I plan to correct.

One way to do that is to take each of our children on a trip. That's an opportunity to be with them on a one-to-one basis. It's good for them because their individual personalities emerge. They like being *the* only one for a change. It's great for me, too, as a chance to better understand how distinct each of them is when removed from a group atmosphere.

When football kept me busy from July into January, there were instances when I missed the children's school-related functions. Therefore, I tried to keep my spring schedule as open as possible to avoid similar conflicts. This was difficult to do, and people with speaking requests often didn't understand it. If I had had a speaking engagement on the day Jennifer graduated from grade school, that would have been a disaster. So I have to say no a lot because of the children's activities. There are soccer games, father-and-son nights, graduations, confirmations, communions, birthdays . . . many activities I want to be a part of. It's fun for me, and the kids take pride in their parents' being there.

I don't know how my kids perceive what I used to do. Sometimes they didn't even seem aware of it unless they went to a game. After I retired a bunch of honors came along and Marianne suggested we take the older girls to one of the functions, but I was reluctant. We've tried to keep them out of the limelight.

We've been told that our children have been good about not trying to capitalize on anything I did. Teachers have said the girls don't like to be referred to as "Roger Staubach's daughter." They love me and I'm sure they've been proud of what I did, but they shy away from a direct identification. They don't brag on it like, "Hey, my dad threw four touchdown passes." They're just the opposite—very quiet about whatever happened during a game.

They'll even joke about who they are, like I do. Someone will ask, "Aren't you Roger Staubach's daughter?" and they'll say, "No sir, my father runs a grocery store."

I do the same thing when someone rushes up and says, "Aren't you Roger Staubach?" I mean, what am I supposed to say? "Yes, it's me, in living, breathing color"? So I say, "No, I'm Harold Swartz." Once I was getting off a plane in Minneapolis and the stewardess said to me, "I know I've seen you somewhere. I know you from somewhere." This was one of my best lines because she had to be about eight to ten years younger than me. I told her, "Well, you ought to. We went to high school together." The funny thing was as I walked away, I heard her say, "Oh, what high school did you go to?"

As I said, though, my kids aren't braggarts and that's good. It's extra good because I didn't always have a great game. Since my children didn't boast about me when I did something good, the other kids weren't there to jump them when I had a bad game. Staying humble is the best way to go as an athlete, too, because there's always a next game.

If you tout your skills or game or season over somebody, it'll come back to haunt you.

We've tried to condition our children to that and they caught on. I'm sure they've been puzzled by other people who ask for autographs or make a fuss over their father. To them, I'm mostly just dad. On occasion I've even been referred to as "mean ol' dad." And when I've really had to crack down, I become the impersonal "him." Such as when one of the kids explains why he or she can't go outside to play: *"He grounded me!"*

The children also know we don't take advantage of our name other than through some advertising endorsements I do. We don't go places as a family and expect to be put in front of the line. We prefer to be like everyone else, to sit in the back of the room if necessary, just as normal as possible. Anywhere we go as a family we try to be unpretentious.

[Marianne:] *Stephanie is very competitive. She's the one most like Roger in that respect. Her humor is like his, too, very dry and understated.*

She's probably the best student of all. Stephanie has a fit if she doesn't have an "A" on her report card. She's naturally bright but still works at it. She's not content to finish down the line. A real achiever. Anything Stephanie does she wants to win or finish first.

As an example, I remember a July 4th picnic and racquetball tournament we had in 1979. One of our friends, Pete Boylan, is an excellent racquetball player, and no one wanted to play against him because he could beat everybody. What we did was put an adult and a child against an adult and a child, neither from the same family. No one played with or against anyone

in his family. When I made up the tournament draw,
Stephanie ended up paired against Pete. She moped
around the house for two days until I said, "Stephanie,
it's just for fun and we've all got to play."

So she played against Pete and lost and then it
was, "Oh, mom," and "Oh, dad," until I told her
again, "After all, Stephanie, it was just for fun." And
she said, "Well, it's not any fun if you lose."

Yes, I know who that sounds like.

Marianne and I were forced to call upon our faith to
sustain us in 1971 when a tragedy struck our family.

We lost a baby girl who was stillborn. We were going
to name her Amy. The first three girls had been born
without the slightest complication and there was no
forewarning that this birth was any different until we got to
the hospital. In the labor room doctors could not find a
heartbeat and told us the chances against the child being
alive were one thousand to one.

The delivery was normal. The little girl was perfect in
every respect, a good eight pounds, three ounces. Except
she was dead. The doctors weren't certain what had
happened. They theorized that the umbilical cord was
short and she had strangled.

One day we were happy and excited over having a
baby. The next day I was standing in a cemetery watching
a small box being lowered into a grave. We put the words
Baby Girl Staubach on the grave marker. She was gone
before we knew her.

Christians view death as going to the Lord. It opens
the door to eternal happiness. Christians who have died no
longer have to endure the trials and tribulations, the good
and bad times of life. Even though we know this to be true,
it's difficult to feel comforted when a loved one dies.

After that Marianne suffered a miscarriage, and then Jeffrey popped onto the scene. He's all boy and very active. I'll be honest: I'd rather he didn't play football. If he wants to play I'll let him, but I'm going to try to steer him away from it because he should have a chance to establish his own athletic identity and not be compared to me.

I do want him involved in athletics. I think that will be good for him. Now if I ever see him on a team with a coach who thinks he's a pro coach and isn't handling the children with the idea of letting them have a good time, I'll get Jeff off that team. He's just a fun-loving kid, but definitely has coordination and good instincts.

I've seen sons handicapped by having famous fathers, and I don't want it to happen to Jeff. I'm apprehensive that with everything he does people will say, "Well, you *should* be able to do it because your father did." Maybe if he played football as a halfback it would be better. If he were adamant about being a quarterback, he'd always feel second-best to his father unless he fell in love with the game and had the ability to accomplish quite a bit. Otherwise it would be a negative experience for him.

To follow in father's footsteps in business or other areas is great if it's the son's will. But for a father to force him in that direction would create a major problem. So I don't really care if Jeff ever plays football. However, I'd be very disappointed if he weren't involved in some type of sports program.

It's not that I have anything against football. But the fact is that if Jeff plays, it's going to be as Roger Staubach's son. To me that's too much of a handicap unless he understands the situation and insists on trying. What I want him to be is Jeff Staubach, with no mention of who his father is. I hope that's what he becomes.

[Marianne:] *I would say Jeff will end up like Michelle because he's like she was at his age—it's hard to change his mind. If he wants something he keeps at us over and over and over. Michelle was like that. He's not as organized as she is, but I think he eventually will be.*

Jeff's the one with the most energy, staying in constant motion from morning until night. He's a happy child. He comes down from his room smiling and cheery in the mornings.

Right now he's turned into a tease with Amy. He's the older brother we never had before. It can drive us crazy. He's always teasing and she's squealing. Amy also has learned that if she squeals before Jeff teases that gets mom's attention just as effectively.

Athletically Jeff is very coordinated for his age. He did very well when tested at his nursery school, which I would have expected. He was our only child who climbed out of a crib. He mastered it quickly. I'd put him to bed and wouldn't even be out of the door before he'd be right behind me. None of the girls ever did that. Believe me, it was a real shock when Jeff came along.

In some ways having me as a father handicapped all our children because I wasn't able to enjoy with them certain pleasures that other families take for granted. It was impossible to really relax and have a good time at places like Six Flags Over Texas, the State Fair of Texas, Texas Rangers baseball games, restaurants, concerts, rodeos, or any place there was a crowd. I understood that was part of the price I had to pay for being in the public eye. I never liked it, and when we were trying to do something as a family I resented the attention. The children suffered from it more than anyone, since it meant that instead of having their father to themselves, he was signing autographs or making conversation with strangers.

People are good about not interrupting our family when we go to an open house at one of the kids' schools. I've let them know that this is a special time with our children and we'd prefer to be just like all the rest of the parents.

Eating out was an unpleasant experience at times because of the autograph business. I don't want to turn down those who ask for them, and at the same time, I don't want to be signing my name when we're out as a family. What happened was that I became reluctant to go many places which, in effect, simply penalized my children.

I got sort of paranoid about autographs after so many years. Even if no one was approaching our table at a restaurant I came to *expect* it. If I signed one, I anticipated others, whether or not they ever asked. It put me on edge and diverted my attention. It was simply not a fun situation for me to be that way while trying to mesh myself into the activities of the family.

Marianne and I have found certain restaurants in Dallas which respect our privacy when we're out together. People may hit me up for an autograph when we're leaving, which is fine. I don't mind that at all. I'll sign as many as I can and get it done all at once.

Whatever I do or say, I want it to be a good example for my children, especially in the area of Christian faith and lifestyle. As long as your kids see you trying to live the life you talk about, they will respect your word and deed. In many, many ways children develop through parental example. They soak up everything—your language, behavior, moral standards and so on. It seems to me a solid rule of thumb to follow through life is to ask, "Would I want my child to be doing this?"

[Marianne:] *Amy is a lot like Stephanie was when she was little. In fact I inadvertently call her Stephanie sometimes. It's not because they look anything alike. Stephanie has always had dark hair and Amy is blonde. Their actions are similar and both talked a lot when they were very young.*

Because she's around older sisters and a brother Amy is more mature than the average three-year-old. It's hard to describe Amy because she's changing so fast. Sometimes she talks like an adult and will say profound things for a child her age. Amy's already showing an independent streak. She always wants to go to a friend's house, or anyone else's. She's not the least bit inhibited about going away from home or mom. And she idolizes Rog. When he comes in the door she's the one who runs to give him a hug. Or if he's leaving she has to give him a kiss. The older girls used to be like that when they were little, but then they got bigger and stopped doing it. Rog really treasures the fact that Amy still does.

We're not pushing Amy to hurry and grow up by any means. It's nice to still have a baby in the family.

I vaguely remember from the sixth grade this girl whose name was Marianne Hoobler. Some of the other guys said she was cute and liked her, but I wasn't paying attention to girls at that age unless it was to show off in front of them. Not until I reached the eighth grade did I begin to notice her. Everything else before that was all sports.

Marianne and I dated off and on through high school and while I was at the Naval Academy. We didn't lock on to each other at an early age and never date anyone else. At the Naval Academy I dated another girl for a year. Back in Cincinnati where Marianne was working as a registered nurse, she went out with other guys. Yet I always carried a special feeling for her, and we kept returning to each other until it was evident we were serious. We married after I graduated from Annapolis. We weren't too young and each of us had dated other people. To marry without having dated around can handicap a marriage sometimes. You start wondering what other people are like.

Alicia Landry once said that Tom was her best friend. Many who read that remark misunderstood it completely. By saying her best friend was her husband, Alicia was paying him the highest possible compliment. Marianne has that status with me. There is no other person to whom I confide my innermost feelings, and I probably don't do that enough with her.

I'm pretty independent and keep a lot of thoughts pent up. They eventually come out but always when I want them to. Every once in a while Marianne will get upset because she knows when something is bothering me and I'm keeping it inside. That has nothing to do with her. I think it stems from my environment, growing up as an only child without a brother or sister to use as a sounding board.

We do communicate openly and freely. She knows me through and through to the point where she realizes when something's wrong even if I'm not talking. I can sense the same thing about her. I can tell in two seconds if she's in a bad mood or if a problem has arisen.

We're no different from the average husband and wife. We have arguments, but not often and not in a loud voice. Some people say it's healthy to let off a lot of steam every once in a while but we don't. If we're about to get into a sharp exchange, it usually starts quietly with one of us asking, "Then what's bothering you?"

I have a special feeling toward women. I don't believe in screaming at them. I think a woman should be treated with love, kindness and consideration at all times. It's disgusting to me to know that some men physically abuse women. I've probably raised my voice at the children more than I should, but with Marianne I can count the times I've done that on one hand.

[Marianne:] *It's really not a fault of Roger's, but this working out and staying in shape all the time gets on my nerves occasionally. We will be ready to go out with other people and need to leave in about fifteen minutes when he comes in the front door. Instead of getting ready he'll go work out with all that equipment he has in the garage. Or he'll come in and we'll have an hour to get ready. I'll think, "Gosh, it would be just great if he would sit with the kids while they eat dinner and let me dress." But he has to work out.*

It took me a long time to realize Roger has to compete. He has to play basketball, he has to do sit-ups against somebody, he has to compete all the time. I'm not like that.

He has to be doing something most of the time. That is just him. That part of him has been hard to live with because it takes a lot of his time. But when I complain about it, he'll start working out at 7:00 in the morning which isn't like him at all, because he's not a morning person. And if he works out in the morning, then he's tired by 8:00 at night. So he might as well work out at 5:00 in the afternoon or whatever.

If Roger had his way he'd work out at 5:30 P.M. and have dinner at 7:00 or 7:30. That's just not feasible with young kids. They're ready to eat by 5:30. I don't like to sound as though we've given in to him all the time because we haven't. He's bent his schedule to fit the family. And, of course, I realize all this made him the type of football player he was.

Marianne is very smart and mixes a lot of common sense with that intelligence. Whatever she's doing, she does it right. In nursing school she was elected president of her class. In less than two years after graduation she was in charge of the intensive care unit at the hospital. When we were designing our home she immersed herself into the blueprints and could read them just as well as the architect Tom Dance or the builder Arlo Buller.

I wouldn't change a thing about my life with Marianne. I've been so fortunate to have someone who loves and understands me. In all candor I think I'm pretty easy to live with, but if I were married to someone who wanted to fight the system I'd have a problem. There *is* a system. My job was to be a football player, and if I had a wife who wanted to be an attorney, what would I do? I couldn't compromise that much. If my wife weren't willing to mesh herself into my life I would have had a catastrophe on my hands. There'd be a major confrontation. So it's been Marianne who has adapted and compromised to our lifestyle more than me.

Many women resist that role. They want to be just as independent as the man. But how can you do it? Marianne understands I am the leader of the family, and she wants me to be. Sometimes I even get angry with her for having me make every decision. When I went to training camp she just took the bull by the horns and handled everything in a fantastic way. So I know—and she knows—she's capable of doing the same thing when I'm around. Yet she defers to me, and I enjoy being the leader. Someone has to be the leader and in a family you can't have two.

We share in the decision-making process. I don't dominate to the point where there's no room for discussion. It's give-and-take, but in the end someone has to decide a course to follow. In our family that's me.

This independence we see today between husband and wife is a very difficult situation. What do you do if your wife comes in one day and announces, ''You do the laundry tomorrow because I'm going to work''? I'd be in trouble if that happened. Nor would we have a family unit the way Marianne and I perceive it.

Marianne means everything to me. She has been the love of my life. And she always will be.

[Marianne:] *I read where Bob Breunig, his room-mate on the road, kiddingly said Roger snored. I caught Roger snoring just one time and, like Breunig, I wanted to jump up and get a tape recorder to prove it to him because he's such a light sleeper. If I make the slightest noise he raises out of bed and says, ''Mari-anne!''*

He wasn't such a light sleeper until we began to have kids. That turned out to be an advantage for me because I didn't get up in the night with the children unless they were newborns and nursing. Roger would always get up because he'd hear them long before I did. That was hard on him with a lot of little ones. One night it was this one who'd be up, the next night someone different. Or they'd all be up on the same night.

In the morning Roger would say, ''Marianne, I

190

was up four times and you never even moved." And I'd say, "Well, I never heard anything." He's such a light sleeper, if I have a bad cold I'll just go sleep in the guest room. If I'm sniffling or coughing it just drives him crazy. I think Roger can hear a sparrow blink in his sleep.

VII
The Other Sides of Roger

"There is no question that Roger is this country's greatest sports hero today, maybe of our time. He is unique in that his following spans all age generations."
—Tex Schramm, Cowboys president–general manager

Dear Mr. Staubach: We were so grateful to receive the autographed picture for our son that we felt we had to write and express our appreciation. Unfortunately, he is unable to use his hands so we are writing for him . . .

For years I've wrestled with the question of where my public life should stop and my private life begin. It's been a fine line to walk and even more of a delicate subject to discuss for fear of being misunderstood.

If I said I enjoyed public attention I'd come off like an egomaniac. If I said I did not like it—which is the truth—there is a danger of sounding ungrateful. I suppose when you break it down there is something like a formula for someone in the public eye: as popularity increases, privacy decreases. You can't have both and I understand that.

What happens is almost a paradox. Someone becomes popular because of what he's accomplished and the way fans relate to his image. That's the positive side. The negative, for me, was being unable to take my children to a baseball game or Six Flags Over Texas, or to enjoy dinner with Marianne without being interrupted by someone wanting an autograph.

The only obvious line I drew was at home. That, definitely, was off limits and *very* private to me. Yet I've had people ring the doorbell of my house to ask for an autograph. Where we used to live was located on a fairly busy street and the traffic at our door reached the nuisance stage several times. One day I answered the door and there was a guy who said he was from Ohio and wanted to try out with the Cowboys. He'd found out where I lived through a friend and just wanted me to counsel him how he should prepare for the try-out.

To Roger Staubach: More than any thing else I would like for you to come to my birthday party on Sept. 18 at 4:00. My friends are all Cowboy fans too! They like you too. I am glad you are a nice man.

Dear Wade: I enjoyed reading your letter. I am very sorry I won't be able to attend your birthday party on Sept. 18, but I have football practice on that day and the coach won't let us off. Have a good day and a happy birthday.

I guess we lived in the same house so long all the kids knew our address. The doorbell rang a lot and it got to the point where I was reluctant to answer it. If one of my kids or Marianne answered the ring they were instructed to say I wasn't home. Then I'd feel bad about hiding and end up giving an autograph at the door. I'd say, "Please, don't tell you friends where you got this." Of course, the first thing they'd do is run tell their pals, "Hey, you can go right up to Roger's door and he'll sign!"

Autographing is a major problem. I can't go anywhere and be myself. Even if I go to a banquet to speak I don't feel like a person, because when I walk in I'm besieged by autograph hunters. With my head down all I'm doing is writing my name. There's no chance to know the people and to me, it's superficial. It's as if I'm a piece of machinery signing slips of paper. There's no chance to relate to anybody.

I was on an airplane once, sound asleep, when a grown man nudged me awake for an autograph. That time I did get mad. "Why wake me up for an autograph?" I asked him. "I can't go anywhere. The only place I can go is to the next stop with you. Why didn't you wait?" He said, "Well, I wanted to make sure I got it."

I don't turn down autograph seekers even in restaurants. People come up and say, "I hate to bother you . . ." and it is just one autograph for them. What they don't realize is there is just one of me and 10 million of them. Most are at least nice about it but there's always a few who don't realize there is a time and place for everything.

It's never time to ask anyone for an autograph when he has a forkful of food halfway to his mouth. That has happened to me before. Most recently it was when Marianne and I were dining out after last season's Houston game. I'd already signed autographs and we'd begun to eat when a man walked up to our table.

"I know this is really a problem," he said, "and you hate to sign these while you eat." With this he gave me four matchbooks to sign. I didn't complain but I did say, "I *do* enjoy my privacy," and wrote my name. When he went back to his table I could hear him complaining, "He didn't want to sign these," as if I were in the restaurant to sign autographs. When the guy got up to leave he looked back at us and said real sarcastically, "Go Houston." I felt like getting up and clobbering him.

> *Dear Roger: I hope you don't get tired of me writing to you but since I have to stay in bed all the time I get so depressed . . . I am enclosing a book report that my granddaughter had to make for school. She had to make it about someone she admired. She asked me if she could borrow the book you sent me. I am very proud of it so if it's not too much trouble would you please mail it back to me. I hope you don't mind me writing to you. But I get so lonesome and depressed that I feel so much better when I can write you as I don't want my children to know how bad I feel. I feel that you are like one of my sons. . . .*

If I'm out somewhere and a kid asks me for an autograph I never turn him down. There were times when I expected to be asked, such as on Saturday mornings when our practices are open and after games. That comes with the territory as they say. Even if I'm out shopping or in the grocery store I'll sign. I won't like it but I will sign autographs at restaurants—preferably before the appetizer arrives and after dessert.

Look at it from my point of view in this last instance.

For years I've been unable to treat my children to things like a baseball game. I resent that part of my notoriety. It has happened before that once I'm seated all I do is sign autographs one after another. If I went to a baseball game and got it all over within 30 minutes that would be OK. But the whole time I'm there it goes on. To each individual it's just two seconds. Like I said before, no one stops to think there is only one of me and many of those who want me to sign something.

I've learned that whenever you start signing you can't ever finish. If you don't sign at all, people think you're a jerk. And if you complain about it they think you're a fool.

I'm not totally turned off by the process. By their requests people are showing their appreciation. I do feel a responsibility to return the attention and support they've shown me over the years. Mrs. Roz Cole, my secretary since 1972, helps me try to do it. Roz goes through all the mail, handles my public appearance schedule, answers every imaginable phone call question and somehow keeps smiling. Some players deal through agents who have a secretary, but I don't think that's very personal. It *is* personal when Roz is dealing with the fans.

I'm not naïve enough to believe that I'm such a great guy because I get a lot of mail. A certain number of people will respond to whoever is in the spotlight, anybody who's popular. There are guys in jail for some pretty awful crimes who get a bunch of mail. But the people who have related to me are good, and they've done so for a reason. Then there are the kids who correspond in crayon and block letters, half their words misspelled—there's no way I can resist doing almost anything they ask. They are legitimate and so we handle that.

[Roz Cole:] *For at least three years now we've sent out about 10,000 pictures just to people who've written and requested them. During the season, roughly October through February, Roger was getting 500 to 700 pieces of mail per week. It used to sort of dribble in afterwards, but this year the demand for pictures has been heavier than ever. Since he announced his retirement people feel like this will be the last time they can get Roger's picture.*

Roger wants every piece of mail answered personally. Most of it is what we call "kid mail" and all they want is a picture. But there are some for birthdays, anniversaries, graduations and children who are sick—with those he includes a personal message. There are around 3,000 of those a year.

My philosophy on personal appearances evolved from an embarrassing beginning. When I first came to the Cowboys, I was told to ask for money everywhere I agreed to go and that would keep the volume of requests down. So I started out that way and even went to a few churches where they paid me, I'm sure, out of the youth fund. They scraped together $150 and I stuck it in my pocket just like I'd been told.

I remember walking away with a $150 check after I'd given my Christian testimony. What a joke. After my first or second season with the Cowboys the hypocrisy of what I was doing suddenly hit me. I was horrified and tried to remember some of the churches where I'd spoken so I could return the money. It wasn't *after* I had money that I started thinking differently. I simply realized that money can't be the bottom line of what I do. Money is an excellent servant but a lousy master.

That has been true with me ever since. I never negotiate with the ultimate objective being the dollar bill. We have plenty of money. I've earned it, worked hard for it. I do things with money for people outside our family. The key thing is what the Bible says about it being easier for a camel to pass through the eye of a needle than a rich man to get into heaven.

That's where I drew the line. I would negotiate in my own way, on my own terms. I'd be paid well but not end up in a hassle where the dollar was ultimate. That became true with speaking engagements, too. I decided on a nice, solid fee for business deals but would accept nothing for charities such as the Fellowship of Christian Athletes, youth and church groups, the Salvation Army or senior citizen functions.

We never negotiate money with anyone. If a business group calls Roz and wants to know my fee she gives it to them. If a youth group calls and says it will pay me a fee, she tells them there is no charge and then whether I can do it or not. There's also a thing called the honorarium which normally is associated with charity events.

I've been offered honorariums to go on telethons. The leukemia telethon would have paid me $3,000. Can you see me going on TV with all those sick kids there, asking people to give money and then walking away with a $3,000 check? That doesn't make sense at all. It blows my mind to know people can accept money for something like that.

[Roz:] *Everyone thinks since Roger retired he has nothing to do. Now all the people we've turned down over the years because of football are calling back. With just the United Way kickoff, we got at least*

20 calls wanting him to be somewhere in the Southwest. Some organizations aren't understanding when I tell them he can't come. The charitable and church functions are more persistent in wanting him because it's harder to get people to attend and they have to be that way. We realize that each one of these things is most important to the people involved and try to treat them that way.

Someone in Virginia called and wanted Roger for a Sunday function in October. I explained he had an association with CBS-TV and wouldn't be able to attend. "We were hoping he'd take a Sunday off," the caller told me. I said, well, Roger wasn't in charge of his TV schedule and since this was his first year in the business and he wasn't yet the boss, he needed to go along with their program. They still couldn't understand and wound up saying. "Talk to him and see if he can't take one Sunday off and do this."

When I've turned down others they've said, "If he can't come on Sunday what day can he come?" I try to explain that Roger doesn't do much speaking anymore, especially out of town; that speaking isn't his vocation, so because of family and business activities his ability to travel for personal appearances is limited. But if he can work it in, he will. And after I have patiently gone over all of this, they will say, "If he can't do it on this date, doesn't he have any days that are free?" There is no way for anyone to know without following Roger around just how jammed each of his days is. People don't understand that, so I have to talk to them realizing they don't. Sometimes that is difficult.

When I first started working for Roger he was

going to try to do one charity appearance for each paid appearance. Now it's more like three to five charities for every one that's paid. I keep trying to explain to him that it's not the fees which are the problem, it's the time. He's only one person. If Roger wished, he could do 15 appearances per month at $3–4,000 each. His average is two at most if they're out of town.

I enjoy talking to high school groups now and wish I had more time for it. I'd like to speak at graduations but I can't do it. As it is I mess up my schedule enough by agreeing to too many things in advance which conflict with my children's activities. Some people forget that I have five children and they need my attention and love. Jennifer had her graduation from grade school recently. Jeff had a father-and-son function at his school. Michelle and Stephanie have things at their school which are important for me to attend. It would be self-defeating for me to be appearing all over the state and country for any reason at the expense of my own kids.

I've spoken to groups who didn't care if I was an atheist or a Muslim. All they were interested in was hearing from Roger Staubach, the football player. But what I do at the end of my speech is give them a subtle message, let them know how I stand as a Christian. I think the impact is greater that way than had I been introduced like, "We have Roger Staubach, one of the finest Christian gentlemen we've ever met, one of the greatest guys ever," and so on. That gets sick.

My guess is that there are a lot of people in Dallas who don't like me because of this goody-goody person I'm supposed to be. There are probably others who are tired of hearing about Roger Staubach for any reason. I haven't gotten much negative mail to back up that feeling. It's just a hunch of mine.

[Roz:] *I met someone from out of town one night who was bad-mouthing the Cowboys and Roger. Someone in the group mentioned that I was Roger's secretary and he'd better watch out. The man spent the rest of the night trying to explain his feelings. All it boiled down to was, ''I don't know why I don't like him, I've never met him, he has never done anything to hurt me, but I just don't like him.''*

But I could tell it was because of the image Roger has and the fact that he lives up to that image. I believe some people are envious of it, resent it because they are reminded of their own weaknesses. In that context Roger makes them uncomfortable.

I always thought it was important to respond to news media—up to a point which I'll define later. After an athlete has created accomplishments on the field, the media begin molding his image to the public. This can be done any way they wish, although with only a few exceptions, the newsmen I dealt with were honest and fair with me even when being critical. I didn't always enjoy everything written about me, but I've been less upset over stories of how I played than some of the distortions I've read about myself as a person.

The way I saw it, the media and I had mutual responsibilities. It was their job to ask questions and report about the team. It was mine, within limits, to cooperate. So I did return phone calls. Well, maybe sometimes I was lax about returning one, but that was for a purpose. I wanted reporters to know that I wasn't really enjoying it. I never went out of my way to develop a public relations image with anybody because that would have been like brown-nosing. I didn't want any of them to think, "Hey, Roger really likes the attention we give him. He's into the PR bit."

I tried to find a middle road in those relationships. I wanted to be responsible in talking to them because they had a job to do. But at the same time I let reporters know, "You're not going to get any inside dope out of me. I'm not going to tell any tales. I'm going to answer the best way I can but I don't particularly enjoy it."

All the things that were written and said when I retired made me very uneasy. I got the impression that somebody important had died, not simply that an NFL quarterback decided to retire. Someday I'll appreciate the nice words, but at the time all they did was bother me. Sure, I'd have been upset if I retired and nobody noticed. But to me the reaction seemed to be the opposite extreme.

I got the same feeling during the last season when there were headlines like, "Staubach Pulls Another One Out," or something similar. That made me uncomfortable. I liked to read the story of a game, especially where I thought I had a fabulous performance and very little was written about it. A lot of what I did was taken for granted and that's the biggest compliment I could get. So there were times I felt I had made key plays but our defense had played great and we'd won. I'd be mentioned at some point in the story in the context of, "Staubach led this drive . . ." That was the type reporting I liked, where I was just in there as part of the action but not as the headline.

> *Dear Mr. Staubach: No doubt this will be the most unusual letter you have ever received. It is really a request, if you have the time, to write my little*

*eight-year-old grandson and tell him that you drank
milk when you were a little boy—or even now. Of
course, if you didn't I wouldn't expect you to do it.*

The worst misrepresentation I ever suffered was in a
Sport Magazine article written by a fellow named Robert
Ward. First of all he never took a note. Or if he did, it was
after I'd spent about two hours with him one day. I remember getting whirlpool treatment at the practice field
and him asking my views on things from Vietnam to
communism. I didn't know that was part of the article
because he wasn't writing down anything. I do know that
what I said wasn't written accurately.

He did ask me if, as a Christian, I believed in the
concept of our country fighting in Vietnam, mining Haiphong
Harbor and so on. What I told him was in retrospect we
shouldn't have gone to Vietnam but our objectives were
good. The objective of stopping the spread of communism
in Southeast Asia made sense and I believed in it.

Further, I told him that the guys who went over there
should be the biggest of heroes because they fought a war
that their own people didn't support. I said our escalation
policy was out of whack, that we should have mined
Haiphong Harbor in 1965 and it would have saved American and Vietnamese lives. It would have brought the war
to a head with the least amount of bloodshed.

But the thrust of the article was that Roger Staubach,
as a Christian, felt we should have mined Haiphong Harbor and annihilated the Vietnamese which made me look
like some kind of bloodthirsty warlord. There was another
incident while I was in the whirlpool. Jeff, who was two
years old then, was in the training room crying up a storm.
Just kidding, I said, "He's the toughest kid in the block.
Normally he doesn't cry." Darned if this guy didn't write

that I expected my son *never* to cry and that he should be the toughest kid on the block. It came out as a serious statement completely out of context.

Anyway, if I ever read another article by that guy I won't believe a word of it. He was a pacifist and expounded his philosophies through me in that story. Journalistically, it was a joke—he was not taking notes, not using a tape recorder. He had the article written before he even talked to me.

> *Dear Roger: I am having a great deal of trouble with my son, who is seventeen. He loves football, but he isn't too happy with school or here at home. He is kind of sour on life. I told him that I bet I could get Roger Staubach to write him a note. He said stars like that don't care, they're too busy with other things, and that kids like himself don't count for much. I told him he's all wrong!*
>
> *If it was only three sentences, twenty words or what have you, it would be enough. He just needs to know that someone cares and that someone is a person he cares about tremendously. It might change the entire course of his life.*

I never minded being portrayed as who I am. Being referred to as "Lt. Fair And Square" didn't bother me. But the connotation did. The inference seemed to be if I were fair and square, I also had to be dull and one-dimensional. I don't know how many people have said to me after I've given a talk, "You really *do* have a sense of humor." It was as if they expected this stick-in-the-mud to show up—somebody saluting with one hand and a Bible in the other. That's not what the Lord intended for us to be.

There *are* boundaries within which I live as far as my

faith. But that doesn't mean I walk around with a halo over my head. The way I'm stereotyped sometimes bothers me. Maybe it's unintentional but having Roger Staubach drummed into people as mom, apple pie, ice cream and the American flag often results in an entirely different image. I come out as dull.

It's as if the things I believe in reduce the enjoyment of life when compared to the playboy, wine-women-song, "whatever makes you feel good, do it" philosophy. To me that's incredible. Having peace of mind and having relationships that are meaningful are the substance of life. Those whose lifestyle is a constant parade of jumping from this to that, who always think the grass is greener somewhere else, only find insecurity. Insecurity leads them to using chemical means to take care of their lives.

Peace of mind and good relationships with those at home and with our Creator form the foundation of a happy existence. From there we can enjoy life within certain boundaries. Sure, it's probably a temporary euphoria to have one-night stands with any woman you run into. You can get a temporary kick out of drugs, although they ultimately will destroy you. But none of those experiences have permanent value or merit. They are the here today–gone tomorrow sensation, whereas God is today, tomorrow and forever.

But some people seem to think that my life is boring and tedious. Nothing could be further from the truth. I'm a happy man. I'm happy with who I am and what I am. I'm happy with my wife, my family and my God. I don't feel I'm missing any of life's pleasures or joys.

Dear Mr. Staubach: I'm so sure that the Cowboys will repeat this year I have bet 25¢ on it. Please do it!!

I have also bet that you would send me your auto-graph. Please bail me out of both situations.

Considering what we do, which is excel at a physical game, I'm often distressed by the influence athletes exert on public opinion. After all, running and jumping and throwing isn't deep background for comment on other areas of life. Yet I feel that entertainers are the worst offenders when it comes to talking about things they know nothing about. You see them on TV talk shows expounding on issues ranging from inflation to civil rights to Afghanistan. Being who they are, what they say has a big impact.

My strongest objection to what I hear from entertain-ers has been in the area of morality where they talk openly about, "I'm living with so-and-so." In doing so they are expounding a philosophy of life. They are appearing on these shows because of who they are: actors, actresses, musicians or whatever. Does that background give them the right to say, "This is the way to live?" I don't think so. Their business is acting, and they should confine their remarks to what they know.

Then we have the case of Jane Fonda, the actress who visited North Vietnamese troops during the war in Vietnam. It was her right to speak out against the conflict and be in the forefront of the peace movement if those were her beliefs. But to consort with the enemy was something else. In my opinion it was treason and the fact that she got away with it was incredible.

I've never understood why, just because a person is an entertainer or athlete, his or her opinions on every conceivable subject are so highly valued. Yet it's true and you have to deal with it. How you deal with it is the question.

In these situations I was always careful to channel my views around a common sense approach. In particular I shied away from political comment while I was playing. Now that I'm retired there are some strong political opinions I will be willing to express. To have done so as a player, I felt, would have been taking advantage of the podium given me because I was an athlete. As a citizen I have the right and the responsibility to speak out as I see necessary. As an athlete I thought I should confine myself to talking about football because that's what I knew best.

The exception was in sharing my views on faith and family life, and a very definite anti-drug stand. If an athlete believes in these things and is truly practicing them, then he has a responsibility of letting others know about it because he does have influence with youngsters. I haven't changed myself to meet these criteria. I would be who I am regardless of whether or not I compete in professional football.

When I speak to groups of youngsters I tell them, ''Don't come to the Lord because of me, just because I threw some touchdown passes.'' My point is that I'm only a vehicle to communicate thoughts and ideas, to make them think. There are people who use Christ as a cover for selfish purposes. When others see that, they say, ''This Christianity is phoney. Look at that guy.'' But that should have nothing to do with a true relationship with Christ.

For instance, if an evangelist turned out to be an imposter, many people would stop being Christians. But that shouldn't happen because an evangelist, priest, or minister is only a catalyst for people to begin having a relationship with Christ. After that is established, the human element isn't as important. To be turned away from Christianity because of the action of another human being is wrong.

After all, there are Christians fighting and killing each other in the world today, all in the name of Christ. And Christ in heaven must be shuddering. There are supposed Christians of prominence and respectability in every city who will talk about a ''nigger'' moving in down the street. Because alleged Christians have abused blacks for generations radical blacks have called members of their race who have a relationship with Jesus Christ ''Uncle Toms.'' Even the Ku Klux Klan has tried to pass itself off as a God-fearing organization. What a travesty, for that has to be the phoniest bunch of hypocrites that ever existed. Those are the kind of people who have used the Christian cover to expound feelings and philosophies which are completely against what Jesus Christ stood for.

I do have strong opinions on controversial subjects. I'm anti-abortion, as an example, and have spoken out about it. But I never used my podium as an athlete to talk about other sensitive topics. If I did, I felt people would begin to relate to me based on my stand on a controversial issue instead of as a football player. Had that happened they'd been booing if I threw three touchdown passes because I didn't like Ronald Reagan or Jimmy Carter. My objective, aside from talking about my faith and family concepts, was to maintain my identity as an athlete.

Dear Roger: Like you, I face a challenge each week. Each Monday and Wednesday a 13-year-old boy comes to my house to receive help in reading. He is presently in a special education class due to a severe reading problem. Partly, he is there because of an attitude of "I can do fine in this world without learning to read." As you can see he fails to see the importance of school.

I am writing to you to ask your help. He recently

made the 7th grade "A" football team. His dream is to be a pro player somewhere. Naturally, his favorite team is the Cowboys. My thoughts are a personal letter from you telling him "what it takes" to become a pro player with statements explaining the importance of school and learning to read would make an important impression upon him. He told me that all a player had to do was play good football . . . the teachers would pass him in school.

I have two rules of thumb about endorsing products. First, I must be convinced that the product is good and that I'd use it. Second, and this sounds almost like a paradox, I try to pick those where I won't be overexposed. Very seldom have I done local commercials. I stuck with a car dealer in Fort Worth, David Ryan, and Culwell & Sons men's store in Dallas because they were good to me when I was a rookie. In fact, they were the only ones who made an offer.

On a national level I'm involved with Fuqua Industries as spokesman for their sporting goods division, Russell Sportswear, Haggar Slacks, Armstrong Tires, Anderson-Little Men's Clothing, Mattel, Universal Gym, Avon catalogue and Xerox. I also have a pretty deep involvement with Church's Fried Chicken as major owner of the Cincinnati franchise. We have five stores in Cincinnati with plans to expand to fifteen.

All of these companies are sound and noncontroversial, and I believe in what they manufacture. Without using brand names I'll mention two products I recently declined to endorse.

One was for a breakfast cereal. I felt the cereal contained too much sugar and I didn't want my children eating it in the morning. The other was for men's underwear. The commercial probably would have been too silly so I rejected it pretty quick. Each would have paid well over $50,000.

As much as I tried to avoid controversial products, I had some problems with National Liberty Life on a veterans' group life insurance plan. People just didn't understand the product. The company has been good; I researched it. But insurance can be an inflammable subject. Show your insurance policies to two insurance salesmen and the odds are one will say what you have is great and the other will tell you it's terrible. There are 100 different faces in magazines, newspapers and on TV selling insurance and every one of them claims to have the best plan on your life. After awhile people become confused and maybe just mad. I got a letter telling me I should be ashamed to advertise for veterans' insurance as I never served on active duty. That's the kind of mail I don't like to see.

[Roz Cole:] *Roger gets many requests to visit sick children, a lot of them terminally ill. The public relations departments of Children's Medical Center and Wadley Institute screen these requests so that he gets the important ones, the ones where he can do the most good. He will do something with all of them, either call or write or visit. Once in a while he'll get a request from a five-year-old child who may not even know who Roger is. In those cases it's the parents or relatives who really want and need the visit.*

He has a good feel for some of the letters that come in. A father wrote before last Christmas asking him to send footballs to his kids. He was unemployed and one of his children was going blind. Roger sent the kids pictures and a check to buy Christmas toys. The father wrote a letter in return saying how much he appreciated it and how that had given them such a happy Christmas.

Sometimes I don't know when letters are on the level or whether we can do any good, but Roger has a sense for it. He doesn't do things like send a check with every letter that comes in with this type of request. I'm not sure what it is that clicks but he will say, "This one we need to take care of."

In the spring of 1979 someone called the Cowboys' office and told of how his son was such a fan of Roger's. The son was about 21 years old but had a serious medical problem, and so much wanted to meet Roger. Well, Roger wound up flying three people to training camp at his expense and also paid for tickets to a Cowboys game during the season. The son was absolutely thrilled. Like I said, he won't do that for everyone, but something seemed to click that this was important.

I know of many other instances of his kindness and generosity which he wishes to keep private. For one thing he can't handle each case the way he did in flying that family to camp. And the last *reason he does things like this is to call attention to himself.*

Visiting children who are seriously ill or in a terminal condition never made me feel uneasy, although I've encountered some tough situations. Some kids would rather have seen Ronald McDonald or anyone but me. Those were times when it seemed the family wanted me there more than the child and as far as the kid was concerned, I couldn't do any good.

I've been to see five-year-olds who don't know who I am. But if I can do the parents some good that's the important part. Sometimes they are in worse shape than he kids. As a parent I can understand the emotion. I'm willing to call anyone who asks. That only takes a few minutes of my time and maybe it helps.

This is where athletes are great. I don't know of any athlete who isn't sympathetic to a kid in need. There are players on the Cowboys doing things every day in some way without wanting it mentioned. I don't want the publicity, either. It says in the Bible if you start talking about your good deeds in the public square then they aren't any good.

Some places I go, such as the American Cancer Society kickoff, publicity is unavoidable. But those visits to the kids are very private. I've asked the PR departments at the hospitals not to mention them.

What's satisfying, though, is to receive a letter from the family saying that my visit produced results. There have been cases where it's made a difference in a kid's will to live. I saw a youngster once who was extremely depressed over his heart operation. He needed a positive influence, something to get him in an upbeat, optimistic mood again. The doctors said after I came to see him he took a tremendous turn for the better. His incentive returned. That made me feel great.

The only dissatisfaction I feel is that there are kids in hospitals whom I'm not going to be able to see or don't even know about. I feel guilty at times that I haven't done enough for someone else. I'll get in a rut where everything is oriented toward my business, making money or pursuing a selfish goal. I feel a responsibility to give my time, a responsibility to humanity. I would feel it even if I weren't an athlete. Everyone should. There are people in the world who need help every day.

[Roz:] *People ask me all the time, "What's he really like?" It's nice to say he is exactly the same as*

213

*his image. I've never known Roger to be hypocritica
about anything. The things most people miss are hi.
sense of humor and the fact he's a well-rounded per
son with different interests. People often are in awe o
him because they think he's just so perfect. That's only
because he says what he believes and sticks to it.*

*I can't imagine many people being pushed, pulle
and called upon for something every day as much a.
Roger. You wonder sometimes if he has a breaking
point. People can feel hectic or harassed but they are
usually going in one direction or just have one big
project to worry about. He has about ten going at the
same time in different areas while people are wonder
ing, "Why can't you do this because it's really impor
tant?" I keep wondering if there's a breaking poin
where he just throws up his hands and walks off inte
the sunset. I think because he has such definite value
and goals and knows exactly where he is going, he ca.
put it in perspective and handle everything.*

Some of these children I've visited have inspired me
Bob Breunig and I once talked with a little boy, a cance
patient, who'd been taken off chemotherapy. They wer
just giving him pain shots. He was a smart, bright kid an
knew his time was short. But his faith was unbelievable
What a great kid. No complaints, and only eleven year
old.

It's so hard to walk away from those cases. I don
understand God's way sometimes, I think of what it woul
be like if that were one of my children. Why God woul
allow children to suffer a painful, terminal illness is some
thing none of us understands. Some day I believe ou
minds will be open to know His way.

If you examine the crux of life and death, you'

ealize our life on this earth is very, very short . . . fifty, ixty, seventy or eighty years. Relative to time it is noth- ng. When you equate those years to all of time, we are ere and gone in a blink of the eye. For the Christian, the me that counts—eternity—follows this life.

> *Dear Mr. Staubach: When I received your letter and photo, it was indeed the thrill of my life. I appreciate very much the time and efforts you spent on contacting me. I showed the letter and picture to all my friends and they were thrilled also.*
>
> *You have always been my favorite football player and I am a Cowboy fan. When I grow up I hope to play football, so I have decided to drink my milk.*

VIII
The Navy Way

"Americans love a winner. Americans will not tolerate a loser. Americans despise cowards. Americans play to win all the time and every time. I wouldn't give a hoot in hell for a man who lost and laughed. That's why Americans never lost nor will ever lose a war, for the very thought of losing is hateful to an American." —Gen. George C. Patton, to troops preparing for the 1944 D-Day invasion of Normandy

Want to know the *real* reason I decided to attend the Naval Academy? Well, it was a recruiting offer I received from Rick Forzano, then the defensive backfield assistant on Coach Wayne Hardin's staff. Forzano came to Purcell High School mainly to look at Jerry Momper, our center and team co-captain with me. Apparently something I did attracted his attention while he was watching film on Momper.

Forzano, a dynamic guy with a dry sense of humor, later became head coach of the Detroit Lions. Then and now he's a persuasive fellow with words. One day at school he called me aside for a long talk about the advantages of attending the Naval Academy. At the end of the recruiting pitch he applied the clincher.

"We can't promise you anything other than when you graduate you can have your own battleship," Rick joked. We laughed and his mission was fulfilled. I was interested in knowing more about Annapolis and through Dick Kleinfeldt, a part-time scout in the area, made my first visit to the academy.

Forzano influenced my athletic life in more ways than just turning me toward Navy. After I came up short on the college board exams and was prevented from enrolling at the academy, it was Rick who suggested I try one year of junior college at New Mexico Military Institute. He then sold NMMI Head Coach Bob Shaw on taking me even though all his scholarships had been pledged. Somehow they found one for me and off I went to Roswell. There I found just the right football atmosphere for a quarterback at my stage of development.

Shaw ran a pro-type offense, the first system I was involved in that relied on the pass. At Purcell we used a very basic T-formation with all three running backs lined up parallel in the backfield. Today that looks positively prehistoric.

In a technical sense Shaw didn't change much about my passing. He saw I had the basic tool—a strong arm. With repetition and refinement he felt I could develop. I had improved considerably the summer after graduating from high school by throwing footballs to anyone who'd catch them. I realized this was my scholarship meal ticket and to be successful it was mandatory I improve.

With his background as an NFL receiver in St. Louis, Shaw was especially familiar with the passing game. He talked to me about the nuances—pass routes, timing with receivers, importance of the quarterback's set-up. It wasn't just a matter of taking the center snap, dropping back and letting the ball fly. I began to learn the reasons things are done a certain way. It was my first inkling that there was some science to the game.

Fundamentally, in the classroom and on the football field, I profited from the NMMI experience. Our team was excellent that year, finishing with a 9–1 record and flirting at one point with an invitation to the Little Rose Bowl. My study habits improved, but in another area I was having difficulty. I wasn't adjusting to what I considered the nit-picking aspects of military life.

As a plebe or freshman at the academy, I played for Dick Duden, a low-keyed, determined coach who made football fun. His personality was a flip-flop to the head man, Wayne Hardin, whom I encountered for the first time during spring football practice.

Wayne was, and still is as head coach at Temple, a tremendous competitor. He's a fiery redhead, very emotional at times and very demanding all the time. He expected everything from a player. There were always players at Navy who didn't like Wayne, but it was mostly sour grapes from B-teammers who weren't giving the game their best shot.

I liked Hardin and most other players did, too. He would get testy at times, but I think a lot of that was the result of a keen, impatient football mind. Wayne was an innovator and motivator, and offense was his specialty.

Before every Army-Navy game he always had a new

psychological ploy. Paul Dietzel, who was coaching Army at the time, referred to Hardin as the "Gimmick Coach." Of course, Dietzel ended up one year dressing his team in white shoes, which was the same thing. For some reason, as I remember it, white shoes were supposed to give Army players the feeling they were faster.

When it came to one-upmanship Wayne was a hard man to top. My freshman season he suited out the varsity receivers with florescent paint on their helmets. During my sophomore year he put a skull and crossbones on the helmets and "Beat Army" on the back of our jerseys. I got the Jolly Roger nickname as a natural extension of the skull and crossbones idea. Some people thought it was done especially for me, but it wasn't.

Hardin worked the uniforms over pretty regularly. In my junior season we still had "Beat Army" on our jerseys, only this time stitched on the sleeves. As a senior my jersey read "Drive for Five," which meant we were trying to beat Army for the fifth year in a row. Slogans didn't help us, however, and we lost 11–8.

Wayne was full of surprises on and off the field. One year we used a Sleeper Play against Pittsburgh in the Oyster Bowl and it worked like a charm. Pitt claimed that play had a lot to do with our beating them 32–9, but I didn't think so. Game officials had been told in advance how everything worked and obviously they felt it was legal. Whether it was ethical or not was the question.

Here's how it came off. After Pitt kicked off to us, one of our lineman faked a block and rolled off the field. That left us with ten men. While we huddled Jimmy Stewart, a receiver, went limping toward our bench and Dick Ernst ran on the field. It had the appearance of one player replacing another. Ernst lined up at tackle while Stewart stopped on the edge of the field—still within legal distance of the huddle and a very lonesome eleventh man. No one was near him when I threw him a 66-yard touchdown pass.

We took a lot of abuse for that play and I remember that Wayne didn't help the situation by trying to deny afterwards it was a Sleeper Play. At about the same time all of us were in the locker room explaining how it worked. So that was bad public relations. Wayne could take the heat, though, and had his crusty moments with reporters. He could be, and was, controversial.

When I was a sophomore we went out to play Southern Cal, which was enroute to the national championship, and we almost pulled the upset of the year. The Trojans beat us 13–6 in a game that began with angry overtones. Hardin noticed something on film about the way USC shifted, thought it was illegal and started pounding them in the newspapers. They were furious with us by the time the game started, but Wayne's psychology worked. We were mad, too. That was one of the best games I ever played [219 yards total offense, 18-yard TD run] and accounted for one of the strangest honors I ever received. I was named Pacific Coast Back of the Week, but by the time I heard about it, I was back on the East Coast.

Hardin stood up before a pep rally prior to the Army game my sophomore year and said, "We're gonna run up the score on Army." I don't know if he remembered that Army was a solid favorite. We arrived in Philadelphia for the game the next day, and all the papers headlined his forecast. Wayne didn't mind, especially after we did just what he predicted by winning 32–14.

Army-Navy games were special and then some. The first thing we did as plebes was start yelling, "Beat Army!" We were indoctrinated from day one. The rivalry is healthy and meaningful, rich in tradition and performances by great athletes from both sides. Intense pressure descends on the athletes because everyone is so involved.

There are 4,100 members of the brigade who are with the athletes all the time. In the mess hall there's a constant chant, "Beat Army!" The guys pick up chairs of all the players—with the players in them—and carry them around the dining area. Excitement and tension build for two weeks because each team always schedules an open date prior to Army-Navy. There are constant pep rallies, bonfires and then the crowd itself—more than 100,000 strong with the President of the United States frequently a spectator.

I never played in a bigger game emotionally than Army-Navy of my sophomore year. I remember sitting in the stands my freshman year and dreaming about playing in the game the next year. I knew I'd have a chance, but here I was starting as a sophomore. I have never since felt as much pressure, even in the Super Bowls that were to follow. Sure, there was more national interest in Super Bowls, but in the confined atmosphere of the academy there's never anything bigger than the Army game, and I felt those vibrations.

Of all the games I played before and since, this was the only one I couldn't sleep the night before kickoff. There's no way to overemphasize what Army-Navy meant. Admirals from the fleet sent telegrams to the players. The pregame nervousness and intensity of play brought to the field compare to a Super Bowl. But Army and Navy simply believe it's more important.

By that time I had overcome an early and serious problem at the academy which was self-made. I was something of a rebel about things I didn't think were important, like memorizing Reef Points and having my shoes spit-shined. Reef Points were contained in a book every plebe was supposed to memorize and some of them, to my way of thinking, were silly. Like every time an upperclassman asked us, "How's the cow?" during a meal, we were supposed to answer, "She walks, she talks, she's full of chalk, directly proportional to the number . . ." With that we told the number of gallons of milk on the table. There were others, such as, "How long have you been a seaman?" The answer was, "All my blooming life, sir. My mother was a mermaid, my father was born on the crest of a wave . . ." All that sort of stuff.

I'd never had discipline difficulties. In fact, I was president of my senior class and student council in high school. But by Christmas leave of my plebe year I had 150 demerits, mostly for not knowing Reef Points, not shining shoes, and other minor infractions. A total of 300 meant dismissal from the academy. Although the reason behind Reef Points is to teach basic self-discipline, I resisted on the basis of thinking they were insignificant. There were bigger things on my mind at the time—like beating the Maryland freshman team.

My demerit problem began to ease during the spring semester. I adjusted better to the military viewpoint and there was a let-up of what I thought was unnecessary harassment from upperclassmen. The rest of the semester I received only about 20 demerits, and no more than 15–20 over the last three years.

The best of those years was 1963. That season Navy fielded a great football team. We had a 9–1 record and were undefeated in 49 states, losing only in Texas— ironically enough, twice in Dallas. We were upset by SMU 32–28 at midseason and beaten by Texas 28–6 in the Cotton Bowl which decided the national championship.

I'm still extremely close to three teammates from the 1963 club— flanker Skip Orr, fullback Pat Donnelly and center-middle linebacker Tom Lynch. Orr was my closest friend. We also played baseball together four years and wound up being the best man in each other's wedding. Skip's now a pilot for Eastern Airlines. Pat was in our class and the three of us were inseparable. He played in the College All-Star game and impressed everyone. At about 210 pounds, he was quick and an excellent blocker. There were backs like Gale Sayers in the game that year, and Pat could hold his own. He's still in the Navy, a civil engineer. Then it was from Lynch I learned a lot about leadership. Tommy, too, is in the Navy and I feel someday he could be Chief of Naval Operations. He's dynamic, dedicated to the service, and exudes leadership and charisma.

There were so many people associated with the academy— classmates, friends, fellow athletes, officers and instructors—that I hesitate mentioning one for fear of offending another. Yet there is one man I must acknowledge. Almost 20 years have passed but time has done nothing but enrich my feelings toward Chief Donald Pelletier.

To us he was The Chief. He didn't coach or play. The Chief was assigned to the medical corps while I attended the academy, and we became acquainted after meeting at daily Mass. He was more of a father to the '63 Navy team. He adopted us and we have been like his family ever since. Through the years The Chief has maintained contact with many players and become sort of a clearing house for information on our whereabouts. We stay together in a way through him, sort of like a fraternity.

It is not far off target to say that there were fraternal aspects to having attended the Naval Academy. Everywhere I went in the NFL I was reminded of those ties. Sometimes it was someone shouting, "Hey, Roger, I was in the Navy, too." Or, "I saw you in Vietnam." I felt a kinship with all those people. And every time I was introduced before a game: "At quarterback . . . from Navy . . ." I felt proud.

For me, 1963 became a year of great personal achievement. For the nation, it was a year of tragedy. Four days after President John Kennedy was assassinated in Dallas, I was announced as the Heisman Trophy winner.

I had stretched out on my bed a few minutes before the last class of the day when I heard a commotion in the hall. There'd been trouble in Dallas. I was walking down the hall and heard somebody yell, "The President has been shot!" I couldn't believe it. No one could. No one knew how seriously he had been injured. But when we assembled in the classroom our instructor told us it was very serious, and there was a good chance he wouldn't live.

The football team showed up for practice as usual but all we did was kneel and say a prayer. The workout was canceled.

Like so many other people around the country my preconceptions of Dallas at this point were all negative. The SMU game we'd lost earlier that year was sprinkled with late hits, eye-gouging and unsportsmanlike play. Now came the President's death and with it a negative blast from the media that further distorted the city's image.

We read stories that schoolchildren cheered on the day the President was killed. To a degree that *was* true. They cheered because they'd been let out of school. They weren't old enough to be aware of what had happened. I remember that politically, it was not supposed to be advantageous for Kennedy to visit the city. He was forewarned the atmosphere wouldn't be good, but it turned out he received a tremendous reception from the people. The bottom line was that Dallas took the rap for a deranged human being, or a conspiracy, or whatever it was.

With the nation in mourning for its slain President, results of the Heisman Trophy ballot were announced. I'd won, becoming the second Navy player to be honored within four years. Halfback Joe Bellino was the 1960 winner and, like me, felt the pressure of living up to the award in the Army-Navy game. This was one of the best games of the series with Donnelly starring by scoring three touchdowns. We appeared well in control early in the fourth quarter, leading 21–7, but then Army quarterback Rollie Stichweh sparked a late rally. Army scored with about six minutes to play, gambled on going for two points after the touchdown and made it.

Our lead shrunk to 21–15; Stichweh was still hot and had Army on our seven-yard line with 1:27 left to play. At 0:29 they were on our two-yard line but had no more time outs. First, Army asked the referee to stop the clock because of crowd noise and returned to its huddle. The clock was stopped briefly, then restarted. Army lined up for the last play of the game, needing a touchdown to tie and an extra point to win, and needing a win to receive an invitation to the Cotton Bowl . . . but the final gun sounded before the ball was snapped.

So it became Navy, not Army, which challenged Texas in the Cotton Bowl. It was No. 1 vs. No. 2, with the Longhorns defending their top rank. They did it with defense, too. Even though I completed a Naval Academy and Cotton Bowl record 21 passes, we never seriously challenged. Texas had the best college defense I faced—guys like Tommy Nobis, Scott Appleton, Jim Hudson and a tackle named George Brucks who was tremendous that day.

Stories cropped up years later that Texas had our defensive signals which accounted for their offensive success. Supposedly, Army was responsible. Army scouts all Navy games and vice versa. It was said that the signals were deciphered from game film, but there's no way that could have been done. Someone in the stands could have done it, though. If he wrote down the signal, then matched the signal with the play while looking at film it could be done. Army was supposed to have figured out our signals and given them to Texas. I'd say there was a chance that happened.

About a month later I was reminded of the Cotton Bowl defeat in a very unpleasant way. The incident took place during a dinner party at the home of Undersecretary of the Navy Paul Fay. He had invited a number of people from the Naval Academy—Coach Hardin and his wife, Tommy Lynch and myself as representatives of the team. The honoree was General David Shoup, retiring commandant of the United States Marine Corps who, like Undersecretary Fay, was close with the Kennedy family. Many of the Kennedys were there—not, of course, Jacqueline—but Ted and Bobby and their wives. I was seated at a table with Ethel Kennedy who naturally was hostile toward Dallas. Yet I thought she carried it to an extreme by berating me because Navy lost to Texas. "You went down there to play in the Cotton Bowl, and you were representing the Navy and the country," she said, making it sound like Texas was an alien land.

I had no way of knowing that my best days as a college quarterback were behind me. Off and on as a senior I had trouble with strained ankle ligaments and a sore Achilles tendon suffered in the season opener against Penn State. Once I wound up hospitalized with my foot in a cast and out of action for the Georgia Tech game. The season was a downer all the way. Navy finished with a losing record, we lost to Army 11–8 and Hardin was fired at season's end.

Yet in total the Naval Academy experience was great. Enrolling there was the right move for me even though it meant four years of military duty after graduation. I'd do it again. It was a time of learning which prepared me for the rest of my life, far beyond athletic considerations. And that was my purpose for going there. I wanted to be prepared for the rest of my life.

I learned leadership and responsibility there. I learned organization. Many people today are hostile toward regimentation in any form, yet the values of that way of life are useful to me. To be untidy in dress or living quarters meant demerits at the academy, which was a lesson in neatness. To be late anywhere meant trouble, which taught the importance of promptness. Professional athletes are the world's worst about saying they'll be somewhere and then canceling out. I never do that. If I schedule it I'm there.

These habits became ingrained in me and were useful in pro football. An NFL team operates in a paramilitary manner as each day is consumed by a schedule of meetings, practices, film study and so on. Because of my service academy background and the years on active duty, I was able to adapt very comfortably to a system of rules. They were easy for me. I never thought much about them because I knew they were necessary.

I fought the NFL Players Association one year over the issue of rules. The union was trying to formulate terms of a collective bargaining agreement and one suggestion was to abolish all fines. That was crazy. Guys were contradicting themselves coming and going. On one hand there were complaints about players who either didn't come to team meetings or were late all the time. On the other hand they wanted to lift the fine system which punished them for being late. It didn't make sense. A system of rules is there to protect the 90 percent who never give any trouble and to prompt the other 10 percent to do what they're supposed to be doing anyway.

It would be nice to say, "We'll meet at 9:00 tomorrow morning but if you're not there on time there won't be a fine." Except it wouldn't work. Players would abuse that privilege. It's the same with curfew. To run an organization like a football team properly you need to have everyone doing the same thing at the same time. To get it done, rules and regulations are required. I found that quite natural.

At the academy, on active duty, and with the Cowboys in Tom Landry, I saw examples of what I consider great leadership. The key is consistency. The captain of the ship, the commander in the field, the head football coach must be consistent in handling people. If he is, you can even understand him when he's wrong. Maybe that old line from a former Green Bay Packer about Coach Vince Lombardi best emphasizes my point in a humorous way. "Lombardi treated all of us the same," the player said . . . "like dogs."

There was a sad aspect to being a graduate of Annapolis in the mid-60s. Many of us were duty-bound for Vietnam, either assigned there outright or volunteering as I did. Some of my teammates and classmates came home in coffins. If the academy is similar to a fraternity in welding lifelong friendships, there was this distinction: some of those lives were too short.

Doug McCarty, a junior college pal and teammate at the Naval Academy, was training for Vietnam duty out of Oceana, Virginia. He lifted off one day on a training flight and never came back; both he and his plane disappeared.

They found Mike Grammer and his sergeant in a Vietnamese church, their hands tied behind their backs and bullet holes in the backs of their heads. Mike and I had been classmates beginning as plebes.

Tommy Holden, a tough guard/linebacker, had gone into the marines and was a platoon leader. One day, during a firefight with the Vietcong, Tommy led a charge over a hill. As he reached the top, a bullet tore through his chest.

Compared to so many others, I had it easy during the year I spent in Vietnam. As a supply officer behind the lines, I experienced very little of the shot and shell of actual warfare. An occasional mortar round was the extent of it, and none ever fell closer to my bunker than about 100 yards.

At one point during my tour of duty I was stationed outside Da Nang in charge of a POL (petroleum, oil and lubricant) facility. The guy I replaced, Andy Havola, was one of the few supply officers ever wounded. His right arm had been shot off by one of his own men during the confusion of a nighttime sniper attack.

I never told Marianne about what had happened to Andy. The story came out later when we met in Hawaii on my R&R (Rest and Relaxation) and Andy, who was there recuperating from the wound, came to see us. Eventually he told Marianne how he came to have an artificial arm. At that point she looked at me and said, ''I thought you told me your job wasn't dangerous.''

Actually, it wasn't. Probably my most treacherous moments were on the drive from Da Nang to the POL site. The distance was about six miles through some villages, and I could have been ambushed anywhere along the way. On that drive I had a Thompson machine gun under the seat and a .45 pistol on my hip, and knew how to use them. But the thought has since struck me that if the Vietcong had been interested in stopping my truck, it's doubtful I'd have gotten off a round.

War is never pretty, and nowhere was its ghastly face more evident than in Vietnam. Death, poverty, and suffering were everywhere. As a father, I was especially affected by the plight of the children. Some moved around with bodies bloated by malnutrition; others were homeless or sick. Human misery abounded. But even though I regret the suffering caused by the war, I still believe we were doing the right thing in trying to stop the spread of communism in Southeast Asia. The concept was good and the purpose a commendable goal. We wanted to give those people an opportunity to choose how they wished to be governed. And no matter how bad some of the dictators were over there—and the Diem regime *was* corrupt—communism wasn't the answer.

Our country's motives were correct, but we went about it wrong. We tried to Americanize the Vietnamese and they just weren't ready for it. They were poor, living in squalor, yet for many of them this was an acceptable way of life. All they wanted was to be treated as human beings and go about their business peacefully. They didn't require the material things we think are mandatory. What they needed was peace of mind. But communism wouldn't allow it, as a lot of Vietnamese who resisted the communists realized.

There were those in our country who opposed the war, and that was their prerogative. They had a right to speak out against it. But those who actually supported the North Vietnamese with the misguided notion that we were persecuting this land were stupid and naïve. Did they believe the North Vietnamese weren't communists? Did they forget or ever know that communism's out-front ambition is world domination?

Without a doubt Vietnam will be considered a major event in American history. Only history determines the ultimate impact of an event, whether it's a war, surrendering control of the Panama Canal, or the Iranian hostage situation. Yet in many ways I'm convinced our country still suffers from Vietnam.

To examine those repercussions, it may be necessary to focus on the Korean War. There, for the first time in our country's history, we decided not to win. We played for a tie. To decide not to win is a major decision, and our policy makers in Washington followed that precedent in Vietnam.

America has taken a strong anticommunist stand in foreign policy, which I believe is good. In the meantime we've supported some terrible heads of state around the world. Some have been nothing more than cutthroat killers. In many of those countries it would actually be better to have a dictator—but a benevolent one who cared about the people. Impoverished and backward by our standards, the population of these countries may not be ready for the demands of democracy. In Vietnam they never had a choice under the Diem government, which we kept propped up. Diem and his followers were oppressive and unfeeling, driving around in Mercedes and throwing dust into the faces of starving kids.

Our intentions were honorable. We didn't go in there as imperialists like the French, who went in and took over. (Da Nang is all French-built, an old resort city). Yet it was depressing to see the way our military operations were handled. In my opinion the Defense Department under Secretary Robert McNamara was incompetent. Our escalation policy was nothing more than a no-win philosophy. Our attempt to modernize the Vietnamese army was woolly headed. That would have taken fifty years.

The way we handled the Vietnam war was a tragedy in other ways, too. The men who fought that war should be heroes. Instead, in many ways, this country turned its back on them. They were over there giving their lives in the most thankless circumstance—for a country that asked them to and then didn't back them up.

And where are the Vietnamese forces today? They've moved into Cambodia and Thailand. They have begun to spread into every area, and eventually all of Southeast Asia will be communist-dominated. Those opposed have lost control and, I would think, a great deal of hope.

That war hurt us beyond the lost lives and sense of failure. It created a credibility gap between the United States government and its people. Opposition to the war virtually drove Lyndon Johnson out of office. And it had a tremendous effect on foreign policy. During the Vietnam conflict we were afraid to make a move toward getting back the *Pueblo,* an intelligence-gathering ship captured on open sea by the North Vietnamese. This American ship remained in enemy hands for eleven months.

This country has been hesitant to act in almost every crisis since, including Iran. We've developed an image of being soft and indecisive, just the kind of image which gives rise to anti-American campaigns at home and abroad.

Vietnam contributed to the drug culture that plagues our nation. I think it affected our country's system of values and morality—not just morality in the area of sexual permissiveness, but in terms of integrity. Worst of all, we saw these failings in our leaders.

We learned that Spiro Agnew, Vice President of the United States, was still taking bribes from his former job as governor of Maryland. Why was this man in the White House? We learned that Richard Nixon, President of the United States, was untruthful. Nixon had many good qualities, but they were superseded by his ego and lack of moral fiber.

Is it any wonder that young people today have a credibility problem with our government? Can it be a surprise that our definition of good and evil has actually reversed itself in some instances?

Living with someone without being married is now accepted as an everyday arrangement, and a good one. What used to be an embarrassment is now a brag. In times past a guy could say he was having a lot of fun, but he never went so far as to say he was right. To me that's an example of society changing its definition of good and evil.

Examine the manner in which this country was originally structured. Our founding fathers were geniuses to figure it out. I don't think we could do the same today. We have a Congress which can't even determine an energy program or much of anything else. Yet 200 years ago there were men who could sit down, reason together, and create a structure of government that worked.

I think there was a reason they were able to get the job done. Our forefathers saw government as being responsible to the people. They didn't want the power, the money, or the slush funds. These fellows today run for office as a profession. They see it more as a source of power than as a responsibility.

That selfish attitude has been filtering down to the American citizen for too long. One result has been that most people are less patriotic. During the summer of 1980 it sounded as though we might have a revolution in this country simply because people were required to *register* for the draft. They weren't being drafted. Their lives weren't being disrupted. Yet there was resistance to even registering—an outcry against the responsibility that everyone should feel to serve his country.

I've seen enough of these guys who run around handing out flowers as if everyone were great and we all loved each other. That's not the shape of the world, like it or not. These guys want their freedom. They want all the benefits of this country. They don't want anybody telling them what to do. But did it ever dawn on them that the liberty they enjoy had to be fought for and then defended? We didn't become the land of the free and home of the brave by handing out petunias or by ducking out when someone threatened our way of life.

The no-draft, pacifist element is quite blind to facts and history. The military will be the backbone of this country as long as there is a Soviet Union in the world. Shamefully, our military capability has waned a bit since Vietnam. When we dialogue with the Soviets, when we attempt detente, it should be from a position of superior might. Since the Bolshevik Revolution in 1917, the Soviets have gone after what they wanted through cold war or outright invasions of other countries. What they want—and there has never been a secret about it—is world domination.

Once they see us as a second-rate power we will be subject to their blackmail in Europe and vulnerable to direct attack. We're fooling ourselves if we believe any other way. When we start believing we can hold viable peace talks with the Soviets while we're in an inferior position, then we've had it.

No one *wants* war. Sure, it would be a peaceful existence without any preparation for defense such as the draft. If there were no Soviet Union, maybe this world would settle down and live in harmony. Pacifism would be

OK then. But under present conditions we're like a team claiming to be the best in the NFL—if it weren't for Pittsburgh.

There *is* a Soviet Union and its goals are spelled out for all to see. We must match them with power because they won't respect anything else. The way I see it, if we don't bring our military into a superior posture against them, we will gradually destroy ourselves. If we look at historical precedent, there is no question about it.

Look again at what those men did 200 years ago. They put their lives on the line. They put their minds to work and established a system that's pretty darn good. No, it wasn't always practiced the way it was set up, particularly in the area of minority rights, but the foundation is bedrock solid. Centuries later we are still trying to adhere to the ideals of that same Constitution and Bill of Rights. We just make it more difficult than necessary.

The best explanation I heard of why this is so was from Fred Smith, a close friend of mine in Dallas. Fred is a retired business executive, a man of deep religious commitment. He said he had read an illustration of how the Constitution was all sail and no anchor. Two hundred years ago, religion was our anchor. The Constitution was set up in an environment where religion was very basic to the American public. Even people who were not Christians respected Christianity. Even though they hadn't had the Christian experience, they were aware of Christian tradition and ethic. It was part of our structure, almost like common law. So there was the Constitution on one side and religious principles on the other. Religion was the anchor; the Constitution was the sail. I agree with Fred in that it seems we've gotten loose from the anchor and are on sail.

I'm speaking about these things as a grassroots person. More people should do so, because the biggest battle we are fighting today in this country is apathy. It's important to air your personal views, and not just because the Constitution guarantees free speech. If enough grassroots people speak their minds, we will reach a majority opinion on important issues. Otherwise, it remains possible for an organized minority to govern, pass laws, and make decisions that affect all of us.

IX
Vignettes

"Roger Staubach can play until he's 40 because he doesn't know what a hangover feels like." —Sonny Jurgensen, former Washington quarterback

Salaries . . .

Maybe at times I was naïve in negotiating contracts with Tex Schramm, president and general manager of the Cowboys. Strictly on the basis of dollar signs it would look that way because my annual earnings, counting base salary and signing bonus, were $230,000 the last two years I played.

Compared to other successful, veteran quarterbacks, my figure was pretty low. According to the NFL Salary Survey, Bob Griese of Miami was the highest paid quarterback with a salary of $400,025 in 1979. Others who earned considerably more than I were Archie Manning of New Orleans ($379,000), Dan Pastroini of Oakland ($358,333), Ken Stabler of Houston ($282,000) and Bert Jones of Baltimore ($275,000).

I always negotiated for what I felt was right and fair. Money was important and I thought I should be well-paid, but there are many things I do in life in which dollars aren't the major objective. I never wanted money to become the end-all for what I do in anything. I guess part of that philosophy carried over into my negotiations with Schramm.

I didn't use an agent so we settled it man-to-man and never had any difficulty. I went to him to get what I felt I deserved, and got it. When the Salary Survey began coming out I found myself well below guys like Manning, Griese and Pastorini. My salary wasn't where it probably should have been. If I'd known what they were getting and if I'd had *all* the facts maybe I would have asked for more. But we never hassled or argued over a contract. Tex always gave me what I asked. Then again, he never told me I was underpaid, either.

For years the Cowboys have been criticized as being tight with the player payroll. Tex always denied the allegation and said Dallas was in the upper 10 percent of all NFL teams. His contention was that the club paid well overall according to a salary structure based on factors like performance, leadership, longevity and so on. Salaries are scaled top to bottom this way with no dramatic highs or lows, according to Tex.

I suppose critics now can argue that since I was the highest-paid player—and my salary was low—then the Cowboys can underpay everyone else proportionately and insist they're staying within a salary structure. Maybe if I'd gotten more money, which would have put a higher ceiling on the salary structure, it would have helped other players. Maybe not. Who knows? All you can do is look at the facts.

I went in and asked for what I felt was right. Every year I got a raise. If I was underpaid it was my own fault, nobody else's. If I should have gotten $250–260,000 then I was to blame. When I asked for $230,000, which is a good salary, Schramm wasn't going to tell me, "You deserve $250,000." He's a businessman and I realized that. I could have haggled with him or held out or raised a stink, I guess. But that's just not me.

Tarkenton . . .

Outsiders liked to joke about Landry calling plays for me. Fran Tarkenton, the retired Minnesota quarterback, was foremost among them. Tarkenton played 17 pro seasons and accumulated almost every major NFL passing record while calling plays for himself. However, the Achilles heel of his career was that he finished 0–3 in Super Bowls.

That never stopped Tarkenton from needling me. Prior to Super Bowl XIII he'd just finished his last active season and was in Miami as a TV analyst. We did a pregame interview and he was riding me about not calling plays, really getting snide on the subject. Finally, I said, "Just think, Fran, if Bud Grant were calling your plays, *you* might be here."

I must give Fran credit for getting even at a Tarkenton roast later in the year. Everyone had done a pretty good number on him and finally it was his turn to have the last word. Once again he worked me over about not calling plays. To defend myself I passed my Super Bowl ring to the dais where he stood. The inference, of course, was that he didn't have one.

Tarkenton accepted my ring. He held it up before him and slowly rotated it for the audience to admire. "Ah," he said, "so this is the ring Tom Landry calls plays for."

George Allen...

Last spring at a CBS-TV Affiliates meeting in Los Angeles I wound up talking to George Allen, the former Washington coach who was between NFL jobs. Allen was his usual enthusiastic self.

"Boy," he said, "if I can get another coaching job I want you and Cliff Harris. You are the first two guys I'd like to have."

I said, "Well, it's too late for me, George." But knowing the way George feels about older players I'm not sure he believed me.

Admiral Murchison...

Clint Murchison, who owns the Cowboys, is a very low-key person. He was so low key during my first season in Dallas I never met him. Our relationship through the years remained superficial but I don't say that regretfully. Clint had the right idea about how an owner should conduct himself.

His was a laid-back approach. Clint enjoyed coming to the games and to the locker room afterwards. He always came, win or lose, and never ranted or raved at anybody. Clint's style was the wry understatement. Again, win or lose, it was nothing serious. I thought he was perceptive about what had happened on the field. But we were too busy going in opposite directions—me on the playing field, him involved with other businesses—to have a personal relationship.

It's obvious Clint is very shrewd in business. He delegates authority and doesn't interfere with people in

242

command as long as they produce. As players we would *never* go to him with a problem. The system was run that way and must be that way. I'm sure if anyone ever approached Clint on a serious club matter he would say, ''Go see Tex.'' No player ever went to see Clint as far as I knew.

He had the right chain of command. It was like being in the service. You have a Captain, your commanding officer, and you don't bypass him to go to the Admiral. The Admiral would say, ''Go see your CO'' (commanding officer). The Cowboys operated that way, and it was a good thing.

If we had guys going to the owner and bypassing Schramm, then Schramm would lose his authority. That wouldn't work. The way authority was distributed among Cowboys management, we knew where everybody stood. That was one good thing about the team. We knew where Clint stood—which was in the background.

The breaks of the game . . .

Clint, Tex and Tom came to typify one of the ongoing criticisms of the Cowboys. The franchise is supposed to be impersonal and those three men are the established figures who made it that way.

Frankly, the Cowboys sometimes *are* cold in the way they operate. But I think every other team in the NFL operates the same way. The nature of the business demands it. Because the Cowboys are popular and have become sort of a model franchise in the eyes of many, they have been publicized more than any other club.

When I entered the NFL, I knew there was no free ride. I would be paid for what I could do. Pro football is a voluntary organization. If you choose to play you know the rules. I knew if I didn't do my job I was out on the doorstep. That doesn't mean the people who would put me there were cold-blooded. It's simply the nature of a highly competitive business. If I couldn't do it, then it was their responsibility to find someone who could.

I would have preferred to have drawn my football salary, done some off-season appearances here and there and not felt the necessity of developing my own business. I'd rather have just worked out all the time. But I got involved in business from the first year because I didn't know how long I'd last in football. I had to be prepared to do something else when I left the game. Insofar as concentrating on football, yes, the outside business sometimes interfered. But I knew the day would come when I'd need it.

A lot of players fail to recognize the need for an off-season occupation. They have money now from football and everything is hunky-dory. Then all of a sudden it's finished and they start blaming the system for dropping them. If a player leaves the game because he's disabled, that's a different thing. The NFL Players Association is trying to create benefits for that eventuality and I'm all for it.

But in general a player must prepare to do something else for the rest of his life. He can't expect football to carry him. We're in a physical game and our lifespan is shorter. The fact is, and always will be, that if you don't produce you're gone.

Incentives . . .

The second of five contracts I signed with the Cowboys was the last to include personal incentive clauses. That was by choice. The ones I had during those early years were for winning the NFL passing title or making All-Pro. What that meant was if I reached those objectives I'd receive a cash bonus at the end of the year. Persona incentives are common, especially for passers, runners and receivers who'll have clauses for number of yards gained or passes caught during a season.

From around the mid-1970's until I retired, I declined to have personal incentives. A team incentive clause, like for winning the division title, was OK because I felt that should be foremost in my mind anyway.

But I thought personal incentives for a quarterbck were bad because they created pressure on him to start thinking only of individual goals. A quarterback can't do that. For instance, assume he had a clause that would pay $2,000 if he threw 25 touchdown passes. Say he had 24 and his team was about to score from the eight-yard line. The play is a pass and the quarterback suddenly is confronted with an option: selfishly try to throw for a touchdown despite evident risk of incompletion or even interception, or safely lay off the ball to a receiver who'll gain yards but not score. I didn't want that type of choice to ever influence what I did.

Personal incentives are problem enough for a quarterback because of his receivers. Receivers who have a clause of catching so many passes will let him know where they stand. Sometimes he might feel guilty if he didn't hit them.

Howard Cosell . . .

During public appearances when there is a question–answer session, I'm frequently asked what I think of Howard Cosell, the ABC-TV sportscaster. First of all I think he's a professional. Regardless of which sport he's announcing or whether he's actually knowledgeabe on the subject, Howard *sounds* like an expert.

I don't know that Howard's ever been a great fan of mine. He's been OK to me. Like every American who's ever watched Howard, I disagree with him at times. But that's his style. He gets your dander up, gets you thinking, makes you mad or happy. During the World Series I was disappointed when he wasn't on the air. On Monday Night Football I'm disappointed if he has to miss the game. That's the uniqueness of Howard. You love him. You hate him. But you miss him when he's not there.

America's Team . . .

Every spring the team gets a private screening of the previous season's highlight film at the practice field. When we saw the one from 1978 everybody started laughing. We were labeled as America's Team and the narrator also said something about the Cowboys being "the Notre Dame of professional football." I thought it was a joke and they'd bring in the *real* highlight film next.

The players hoped that the America's Team thing would remain an inside joke. But what we feared came true: it didn't. Pretty soon that tag was everywhere. In just about every city we'd go to play a game the lead article in the sports section was, "America's Team Is Coming to Town!" I was uncomfortable with that kind of publicity and so was everyone else. I'm sure it bothered other teams because they couldn't wait to rub it in after they beat us.

Bum Phillips, the folksy Houston coach, got off a good line after the Oilers took us 30–24. "They may be America's Team," he said, "But I'd rather be Texas' Team." Then after the Rams beat us in the playoffs linebacker Jack Reynolds came up with, "Well, if they're America's Team we ought to send them to Iran."

We took it in the ear from every direction. Lewisville High School from a town north of Dallas went to the state finals and claimed *it* actually was America's Team. Local writers referred to Plano, a Dallas suburb with a long winning history in football, as America's High School. Every time we lost somebody on the other team *always* mentioned it. Of course, when we won nobody said anything.

If I'd been on another team I would have given it to us, too. Somebody trying to say they're America's Team would have been a slap in my face. As I understand, the way the label came about was through a suggestion from NFL Films, Inc. Whoever decides those things in our management liked the title and agreed to it. I didn't think much of the decision because there's always enough pressure on the team anyway. This didn't help us and I was aghast when the thing stuck.

Captain America . . .

In conjunction with the Cowboys being called America's Team, I've been referred to as Captain America. I was never comfortable with that whole scenario: the good guys . . . the white hats . . . the Cowboys are best . . . Roger is a Christian . . . Tom is a Christian. That's OK if it's subtle, but I don't like to ram it down people's throats. I do like to get my views across, but if this theme becomes overdone and repetitious, if so much is written about my being this big Christian person, then people get tired of it. And me.

The NFLPA and Ed Garvey . . .

Ed Garvey is the executive force behind the NFL Players Association. He's well educated, probably in his mid-30s, and has a quick mind. The problem with Garvey, however, is that he can be an abrasive, antagonistic guy. When someone trying to negotiate a collective bargaining agreement with NFL owners comes on strong with that sort of personality, it puts the other side in an angry, defensive posture. No one is prone to compromise when he's mad. That was basically what happened in 1974 when NFL players struck over a stalemate in contract talks.

The NFLPA's approach in '74 may have been the greatest example of poor planning in the history of labor negotiations. I went to a players' meeting in Chicago and was appalled at the tone. We were going to get our freedom. We were going to stick it to the owners who'd been giving it to us for so many years. That's where the NFLPA adopted a clenched fist logo and a no-freedom, no-football policy which was stupid.

What we were going after made sense. But the way we went about it simply played into the owners' hands. They loved it because the public was turned off. We took a beating in the media. It was difficult to appear the abused party when players showed up to walk picket lines in Cadillacs.

As a negotiator I would have gone in there and said "Pro football has been great to all of us. We love it. Thanks for the opportunity. We're grateful, but . . . let's talk about the revenue you generate and what we deserve and what you deserve." But my impression was that Garvey tried to bluff or badger the owners, and they wouldn't sit still for it.

Garvey is not the main problem with the NFLPA. The problem is apathy within the union itself. I didn't step forward enough. I paid dues and got involved with their licensee program more than any other supposed superstar athlete. They didn't have to go through an agent to use my name. I feel it's important for the membership to cooperate with the union in its fund-raising programs and express their views to the organization. Not enough of that is being done by the total membership.

But Garvey has never been able to muster cooperation from the full membership. A lot of players are involved, but the majority seem to be also somewhat abrasive. Those who were moderate, like former officers Billy Curry and Dick Anderson, have been bad-mouthed. Gene Upshaw of the Oakland Raiders recently took over as president of the union, but his newsletters read as if Garvey had written them. They're slanted and negative.

I believe in the union although I'm not certain of the ramifications of being affiliated with the AFL-CIO. But the union is necessary because otherwise management would abuse the system. This sort of behavior has been the origin of unions throughout history. Workers have been abused and, for their collective protection, have formed unions. Such was the case in the NFL.

Players do have legitimate complaints. Foremost is the disproportionate amount of money the owners keep compared to what the players receive. They tell us we're well taken care of but won't show us their accounting ledgers. We're supposed to take them at their word.

I'll admit there's been a frost on my relationship with Garvey since that strike. I didn't believe in all the freedom demands, even though as a quarterback I stood to profit more than anyone. The strike slowly began to deteriorate as veterans reported to training camps. Since the picket line was already broken I went in. That's when Garvey said, "I wouldn't have wanted to be at Pearl Harbor with Staubach." That was a perfect example of Garvey's behavior. Sometimes he puts his foot in his mouth—not a good habit for a leader.

Tex Schramm . . .

As far as I can see, Schramm and I have had a good relationship. He's a very likeable person as is his gracious wife, Marty, who accompanied us on all our road games.

But as with Tom and Clint, Schramm and I had no social ties. Other than settling my contract, I only dealt with Tex as team captain on a variety of issues that involved the players. He was always receptive and willing to listen. Maybe we needed money for a team party, for instance. Or if there was something worthwhile he felt might be done through the team, he came to me about it.

Tex has made many contributions to the Cowboys. He established the club's image and has been the marketing genius behind its rise to immense popularity. He's meticulous. Not many people know he helped design our uniforms. He's perceptive. Tex was the first to capitalize on cheerleaders at NFL games. He has vision. It was Schramm who insisted that when Dallas entered the league it be aligned with New York, Philadelphia, and Washington so the Cowboys might benefit from some of the largest media centers in the country. His ideas have influenced the success of the franchise in other ways too numerous to mention, including being the first to examine the use of computers in scouting. I like him, although I always heard stories of how tough he was. It bothered me to hear other players say they didn't think highly of him, but I didn't know enough about those circumstances to make a judgment. All I know is we got along fine.

And to think, one afternoon I came close to doing him in with a heart attack.

The Cowboys' offices are located on the eleventh story of a building about five miles north of downtown Dallas. I'd gone to see Tex, but he was busy on the telephone. (I found out later he was talking to Paul Brown of Cincinnati and other influential owners on a conference call regarding an important NFL matter.) I cooled my heels for twenty minutes, then thirty, and finally thought of a way to get Tex's attention. When I peeked into his office he had his back to the door, the chair swiveled around so he could rest his feet on a credenza behind the desk. From this position all Tex could see was blue sky because the north side of the office is an unobstructed plate glass window.

I found a maintenance man and got him to open a door to the outside on the south side of the building. I stepped out on a ledge about three feet wide. Although I was eleven stories high there was no danger. A trellis was attached to the outside of the ledge—except on the northern exposure.

I crept to the northeast corner of the building and saw Schramm still hadn't moved. There he sat talking, feet propped up. My moment came. I jumped in front of the window, spread my arms and legs in sort of a side straddle hop imitation and acted as though I were yelling at him.

Tex's eyes rolled back in his head. I mean it really scared him. He thought I was falling. He stared at me and shook his head. The guys on the conference call thought something had happened to him. When Tex gathered himself he said, "You won't believe what just happened to me. I thought my quarterback was falling from the eleventh floor."

People thought I was going a little whacky in those days. I'd ridden a camel at the practice field to help promote a movie, and I'd also been involved in a demolition derby. I've always been the adventurous sort but I guess the ledge walk topped the list. A reporter witnessed the thing from start to finish and wrote a story about it in the next day's paper. The headline read, "Roger is a Pane in the Glass."

Scrambling as a rookie . . .

When I first came to the Cowboys, I know that deep down Landry had mixed emotions about me because I ran so much. I'm sure he thought, "Well, Roger is a fine athlete and has worked hard and is just coming out of the service." He did see some characteristics that qualified me to be the second-team quarterback. That *was* a big deal. He could have easily not gone along with it.

In fact, I didn't have nearly as impressive a training camp in 1969 as I did on leave from the Navy the previous year. Whatever they saw in '68 played an important role in my future with Dallas. They made up their minds I could be backup as a rookie, but Tom had to wonder whether he'd made the right decision.

We played a rookie game in Oakland one night and got murdered. I completed something like one pass in 13, ran all over the place for about 100 yards, and thought to myself, "I am really in trouble." On top of that, I hurt my back and suffered a bruised kidney.

Next day all the veterans were out for practice. I tried to work out and could hardly move. I practiced two days before they discovered the injuries. I was out for two weeks.

At that moment Tom had to be thinking, "I have a real questionable guy on my hands, a running quarterback. I don't need that."

Still scrambling . . .

Defensive players sometimes dared me to scramble. San Francisco had a linebacker named Frank Nunley who said, "We want Staubach to run. We hope he does." That kind of talk made me run more because I knew the other team didn't want me to. The defense hates a quarterback who runs. There's nothing worse to a lineman than to see the quarterback break for a 15-yard gain after he thinks he had him trapped.

It's not good for a quarterback to think run first—but sometimes I would. I'd do it against the Redskins because I knew they hated it. They'd always say, "We hope he runs so we can hurt him," which would just help me run more. It was a challenge, and I never ducked one of those.

Getting benched . . .

My second year in Dallas Craig Morton had arm problems as the season got underway, so I started the opener in Philadelphia and we won. Next week against the Giants I started again and couldn't do anything right during the first half. I was terrible. I thought for sure Tom would bench me at halftime, and I pleaded with him to let me continue. He did, and thanks to two interceptions by Cliff Harris, we won again.

By the third week I knew the time was close when Tom would put Craig back in. From Tom's viewpoint, I didn't have the necessary experience to be the starter. I got the message one day during a quarterback school meeting when Landry said it takes four years to become an accomplished starter.

That upset me so much I confronted him before everybody. I said, "I really can't believe that. Everybody's different. How can you make a statement like that? Maybe it takes less time for somebody else."

After the meeting Tom got me off to the side and said, "It just takes time. You have to have experience. You can't just jump in there cold." Then he added, "In your case it probably will take less time because you're older." I wasn't pacified and told him, "I can't wait that many years. If I follow your timetable, I'll be thirty-one years old before I even have a *chance* to start." So we cleared the air, but I'll bet in Tom's mind he was thinking, "Well, I satisfied him for a while."

Remembering that episode and Tom's philosophy on starting quarterbacks, I felt he was mentally geared to yank me against St. Louis at the slightest provocation. I gave it to him in the form of two interceptions. Lance Rentzel also dropped a touchdown pass which meant I was throwing the ball pretty well, even if it was to both sides.

Sure enough, after the Cardinals went ahead 6–0 off my second interception, I went to the bench. I didn't say anything. I just sulked for a long time—through the second half, the postgame shower, bus ride to the airport, return flight to Dallas, and in the car with Marianne and the children. Whereupon one of the kids said, "Gee, Daddy's got his mad face on."

Benched again...

Tom took me out of another game at the half in 1971 and that time I didn't go peacefully. This was a crucial time for me and Craig Morton because we were jockeying back and forth to determine who'd be No. 1.

I was supposed to start the season opener against Buffalo but tore a vein in my leg. Craig took over and had a fantastic game (the team scored 49 points). The next week I got knocked out; Craig relieved and had another great performance (42 points). But after we lost to Washington 20–16, I started the next week against the Giants. We had gone ahead 13–6 on my TD pass to Billy Truax. But it had not been a good first half overall and Landry put Craig in. I was furious and after the game told him so. I told him he'd never understand me, that what he did to me was an injustice. Tom didn't say anything in return. He sort of shrugged. One thing about Tom: when you say something to him you don't know if it has any impact. I think it does, though. He just puts it in a mental slot. In situations like that he's not the kind to argue or even answer. It wouldn't serve any purpose for him to start yelling at me in the locker room. He just goes about his business. I'm sure what I said had some impact. Probably if I hadn't felt bad about being sat down, he would have wondered about me. I don't know for sure. He never commented on that scene.

The concussions . . .

Getting knocked out while playing football is a weird sensation— in the game one minute and waking up the next, wondering what has happened. Actually there are different types of concussions, and at some point in my career I probably experienced all of them.

One of my early games with the Cowboys was against Green Bay in an exhibition. I got knocked out of bounds—and out on my feet— by linebacker Ray Nitschke. Yet I kept functioning. I stayed in for four or five plays but didn't remember any of them. That happened to me several times, again with Dallas in the College All-Star game. I understand it's not abnormal for a player to keep going until a delayed reaction hits him.

The aftermath of the concussion I suffered in the 1979 Pittsburgh game was different in two respects from the others. I had a swollen area on my head for several days which was unusual because of the protection a helmet normally affords. And, for the first time, I lost some feeling in my arm and fingers. It didn't last long, but it had never happened before.

Lying on the field semiconscious, the only fear I ever had was that my neck had been broken. For that reason it was almost automatic that I tried to move my arms and legs just to know that everything was all right. That's what I tried to do in Pittsburgh. At first I couldn't seem to get them to function, but it was because the movement wasn't registering with me in my woozy state. After I got to the bench, the feeling in my arm and fingers returned. But I didn't have any feeling in my face. I remember I kept touching my face, worried by the numbness. It didn't worry me too much, however, because I could move all my limbs. And in a matter of minutes the numbness went away.

Round one with Mel Tom . . .

Even though I ran a lot and took a lot of punishment for it, rarely was I victim of a flagrant foul. In fact, the worst cheap shot I ever took was after passing from the pocket. It happened in 1971 against Philadelphia on the first series of the game. I threw a pass which Bill Bradley intercepted and . . . that's all I remembered for a while.

Not until we saw the game film on Monday was it evident how and why I'd been knocked out. As I stood looking downfield at Bradley, defensive end Mel Tom had come around from behind, pulled me around and delivered a forearm blow to the side of my head. No one saw that during the game, not even officials, and there had been no penalty. But when the film was reviewed by Commissioner Pete Rozelle, he fined Tom $1,000.

This incident led to an example of how my humor often backfired. A bunch of players were sitting around our locker room discussing the incident and I said, ''Boy, I'd like to catch that guy some dark night and use some of my hand-to-hand combat on him.'' That was a joke. Tom was about as big as a freight train, around 6–7, 260 pounds.

Steve Perkins, a local reporter, heard me say that and wrote a story about it. Only Steve wrote it straight, as if I were serious and wanted to go one-on-one with Tom in an alley. And to this day Steve is convinced I really meant it. Honest, I didn't.

So the next time I saw Perkins I said, "Steve, if I really were serious about taking on Tom, why do you think I went out the next morning and bought 100,000 papers with your story in it?"

"I dunno," he said. "Tell me."

"So Mel Tom wouldn't read one."

Foul . . .

Only once during my NFL career was I ever penalized for a personal foul. As you might expect it happened against Washington during a 1975 game that went into overtime.

Again, an interception played a part in what happened. Their great safety Ken Houston picked off my pass. He was on the other side of the field being tackled when out of the corner of my eye I saw cornerback Pat Fischer making a run at me as if he were going to throw a block.

I got my hands out and deflected him to the ground. At the instant I jumped on Fischer an official saw us. He didn't see Fischer trying to hit me late, so I got 15 yards for that. Even worse, Washington won the game 30–24.

How does it look? . . .

I always felt we didn't use some plays during a game only because they had not looked good in practice against our defense. Every year we'd say, "We won't worry about how our defense reacts to this play because they don't react like this team we're going to meet on Sunday." There were cases of certain pass plays I liked but Landry didn't because they didn't work against our guys.

For example, I'd be working on a sideline route. Our cornerbacks are conditioned to hang outside, toward the sideline. I'd throw that pass and there was Benny Barnes waiting for it. I could have thrown it all day and not completed the pass because Benny was not going to let it happen. Yet the cornerbacks we were facing that week may have had an inside tendency and that pass would work against them.

But Tom would see that we weren't doing any good with it in practice and say, "Just not use it," even though we'd agreed not to worry about how it looked against our defense.

"Calvin, . . ."

Calvin Hill and I were rookies together and we remain friends to this day, although he left the Cowboys after the 1974 season to join the World Football League. I remember Calvin with admiration as an athlete because he became one of the truly great running backs in Dallas history. He still ranks No. 2 all-time in career rushing with 5,009 yards. I also recall it was Calvin who welcomed me to the NFL in a way. He missed a block in that rookie scrimmage against Oakland, which resulted in my getting busted up.

One measure of the depth of a friendship is the joking things you can say to each other without offense. Such an incident took place prior to Super Bowl VI while I was being interviewed by a large group of reporters. We'd been going for several minutes when everyone noticed Calvin peeking over the edge of the crowd. He was masquerading as a newsman, making mock notes on an imaginary notepad.

I glanced up and said, "Calvin, this news conference is only for white writers."

The illustrious Walt Garrison . . .

When our family first moved to Dallas, we brought a collie dog with us. Unfortunately, the small apartment we lived in didn't allow pets. Walt Garrison came to our rescue by agreeing to keep the dog on the ranch of his father-in-law, B. F. Phillips. We were delighted until receiving news the dog had either been stolen or run away. It was a crisis in our family, but obviously not with Walt as I learned from this exchange with him one day.

"I got good news and bad news about your dog."

"What's the good news?"

"They found him."

"Terrific, but what's the bad news?"

"He's dead."

Actually no one ever knew what happened to the collie. It just disappeared. Walt was like that, his folksy humor a forerunner of the type which has made Houston Coach Bum Phillips such a delight. On the football field he was a day's work–day's pay player. His competitive instincts were representative of what it meant to play the game full-out, all the time.

Garrison stories abound and a few come quickly to mind. Once the Cowboys front office located Walt at an automobile repair shop where he was having the tires on his car changed. The purpose of the call was to give him a message to telephone a reporter who wanted an interview.

The conversation went like this:

"Walt, where are you?"

"I'm in a phone booth."

"Got a pencil to copy down this number?"

"Nope, but I got a knife. I'll just carve it in the wall."

Walt also wrote the introduction to a book by Cowboys publicist Doug Todd entitled, *How To Talk Country.*

It's a compilation of song verses from country and western music. Walt waxed poetic about the contents, finishing up with, "What I'm trying to say is, this book ain't bad if you ain't used to much."

One of my most memorable experiences with Walt also included Ralph Neely and Danny Reeves. I was a rookie and had been invited out on the town by veteran players. As the evening wore on, I began to worry about missing rookie curfew at 12:30 A.M. Walt, Ralph and Danny said don't worry. Since I was out with them, they said I only had to be back to the dorm for veteran's curfew which was later. Besides, they said, if somehow I wound up getting fined, they'd all pitch in and make up for it.

I did miss rookie curfew. There was a note on my door to report to Coach Landry as soon as I got in, which I did. Sleepy-eyed and standing there in his pajamas, he told me I'd been fined $150.

When I told my buddies about it the next day they said, hey, relax and we'll take care of it. I'm still waiting. Let's see, counting interest on $150 from 1969 that comes to. . . .

X

The Glory Years...
'75–'79 and Beyond

"We all can't be heroes, because someone has to sit on the curb and clap as they go by."—Will Rogers

Judging from the number of people who've asked me about it or claim they saw it, the most famous pass I ever threw in the National Football League was the 50-yard Hail Mary to Drew Pearson in a 1975 playoff against Minnesota.

But nobody seems to remember the mini-Hail Mary from the same game.

I suppose it's natural to focus on the game-winner and that *was* as dramatic a pass as I have ever completed, considering the circumstances. First, because it happened in a playoff game we weren't supposed to win. Second, because from midfield with 32 seconds left in the game and Minnesota laying eight defenders back against a pass, the odds on success were probably about 50–1. Drew caught it anyway and crossed the goal line with 0:26 on the clock to give us a 17–14 victory which had seemed even less possible moments earlier.

That was where mini-Hail Mary saved us. Talk about your bleak situations. We were looking at fourth-and-16 from our own 25 with only 44 seconds left. If the Vikings stopped one more play the game would have been over with us losing 14–10.

Drew and I talked it over in the huddle and I told him, "Go to the corner." Minnesota took a little bit of a chance on that play. Cornerback Nate Wright was playing pretty tight man-to-man and wound up just a step off after Drew faked a post route and broke for the sideline. One of the oddities of that play was that Drew landed out of bounds after making the catch. But it was all legal because Wright hit him when he was in the air and the impetus of Nate's tackle forced Drew over the sideline.

That wasn't the only strange thing about the completion. After Drew came down, a groundskeeper tried to kick him but fortunately missed. The result of the play was a 25-yard gain to the 50 and fresh hope that maybe we could pull off another miracle.

We had played a good game to that point, and that was important to the team's state of mind. Even though the odds were against us we felt something good *could* happen. It did after a first-down pass to Preston Pearson failed. Drew and I got together in the huddle again. "What do you feel comfortable with?" I asked him. He said he thought he could get deep. We had run an in route with success so I said, "Make it look like an in route and break deep." I called a play in which everyone ran what Drew was to fake—the inside route.

As Drew started to go in I pumped the ball in a direction away from him. That kept weak safety Paul Krause out of the play for a split second. After I did that I had a long way to throw the ball, and, frankly, I thought the pass had been underthrown. Drew just made a heckuva catch, although on film even that looked a little shaky because he wound up sort of trapping the ball on his hip at the five-yard line.

Looking back I think the pump-fake helped a lot. Not only did it keep Krause from being involved in breaking up the pass, but it delayed him just long enough so he couldn't tackle Drew and stop the touchdown. The Vikings claimed that Drew pushed off Wright, but I couldn't tell what happened. All I saw was a flash of orange flying through the air, and for an instant I thought a penalty flag had dropped. It turned out to be an orange somebody threw out of the stands.

I never had a more eerie sensation on a football field than during the aftermath of our touchdown. The crowd was so shocked there wasn't a sound from the stands. It was as though all of a sudden we were playing in an empty stadium. The silence, as they say, was deafening.

All sorts of wacky and sad things took place after that. Drew threw the ball high against the Metropolitan Stadium baseball scoreboard behind the end zone. We joked with him later that he'd scored the only ground-rule double touchdown in NFL history.

The Viking fans found their voices as soon as we kicked off. They were screaming at the officials when something happened that I've never seen during a football game and hope never to see again. Some nut threw a bottle out of the stands and hit an official in the forehead. The official went down like he'd been shot, with blood all over his face.

As if that weren't bad enough, driving home from the airport after the game I heard that Fran Tarkington's father had died during the game. I thought, *Oh no,* and prayed it didn't happen because of the shock of that last touchdown pass. His death wasn't related to the play; it was just the last link in an unusual chain of circumstances involved with that game. Still, I felt so bad about Fran's father I couldn't enjoy the victory.

The entire '75 season was out of the ordinary. We were in a state similar to what faced the Cowboys in 1980: people thought Dallas was in decline. What they forgot then—and recently as well—is Tom's coaching ability in times of crisis, and the fact that he keeps a solid nucleus of players, neither too young nor too old. The experience on the roster is usually perfectly balanced.

We still had those ingredients going for us, but, as I mentioned earlier, it was a fantastic draft that proved the key. Bob Breunig, Randy White, Randy Hughes, Thomas Henderson, Herb Scott, Pat Donovan, Burton Lawless and Scott Laidlaw were rookies that summer. They were hitters and hustlers whose enthusiasm infected the whole team. Veterans started thinking, "Hey, we've gotta stay on our toes because these rookies mean business." It was also evident they were going to help us on the field immensely.

Despite these positive signs no one was taking bets that the Cowboys were poised to begin the winningest five-year period in their history. But we were. From '75 to '79 our regular season record was 56–18, a winning percentage of .756. We qualified for the playoffs every season, four times as NFC East champions and once as a wild card team, and we competed in three Super Bowls. But to be honest, a world championship game seemed out of reach in '75.

Among my most dominant memories of that season was an obscure newcomer we had in training camp. He'd written me a letter in the spring asking for advice on how to prepare himself. I thought to myself, "Geez, here's a poor guy who doesn't have a chance in the world." Anyway, I wrote him a long letter. I told him what kind of drills to run, to work on his sprinting, setting up and throwing the ball, and to come to camp with a lot of poise. I advised him not to be intimidated, just work hard.

We had quite a few rookie quarterbacks in camp that year but I was curious to see this guy. I kept looking for him and finally picked him out. Of all things he was a left-hander. Other than Ken Stabler there hadn't been a successful southpaw passer in the NFL since Frankie Albert at San Francisco over 30 years ago. This kid's name was Jim Zorn.

Soon he started getting everyone's attention. He was working hard. He sprinted from drill to drill. He was throwing the ball well. He had a lot of sense, and his release was good. I couldn't believe this was a free agent. I kept thinking, "What's wrong with this guy?" The answer was, "nothing." He just got better and better.

Landry was still intrigued with Clint Longley, who also had ability and had pulled the big upset the year before against Washington. Although Clint still wasn't applying himself, the coaching staff eventually had to make a decision between Longley and Zorn. The league cut down to 43 players, and the choice for Dallas became whether or not to keep only two quarterbacks and sign Preston Pearson who'd been released by Pittsburgh. We went with Preston which was a great move because without him we would have never made it to the Super Bowl. But Zorn got away. He was involved in the last cut, and in the long run that was probably best for everyone. It might have even been best for me.

Los Angeles also had a shot at signing Zorn but missed. Seattle got him, and now Jim ranks among the NLF's best quarterbacks. Since then we've made up for having to let Zorn go by drafting Danny White and Glenn Carano.

Zorn was among the finest group of rookies the Cowboys ever had. They provided an upbeat tempo in training camp, and then the veterans, led by middle linebacker Lee Roy Jordan, took over. Lee Roy had a phenomenal season, the next-to-last in his 14-year career with the Cowboys. Bob Lilly, our Hall of Fame defensive tackle had retired after the '74 season which left the leadership role on defense almost entirely with Lee Roy. He responded magnificently.

This was a happy team internally, unlike the previous year when friction existed between Lee Roy and Calvin. They didn't argue a lot openly. There was just this tension between them. Calvin was the kind of guy who was concerned about everything and harbored grudges against management.

Sometimes he had legitimate gripes and was only expressing himself. I felt like the man in the middle all the time. Lee Roy was my roommate for years. But Calvin and I came up as rookies together, and I considered him a friend as well. Lee Roy always felt Calvin overplayed his grievances and let them affect him more than he should. At times Calvin was prone to see things on a racial basis, although that was never an expressed difference between the two. They were just out of sync in the way they looked at things that happened on the team.

The season of '75 also was the time when Landry

made a major strategic adjustment. The Cowboys would return to the shotgun formation which the club had last used in the early '60s with Eddie LeBaron and Don Meredith. Tom told us about it in the spring a few days before quarterback school. We went to the practice field where he introduced the formation and outlined its concepts.

I liked it from the outset. It was something different. As a running quarterback I liked the idea of a new look, a new situation and feeling more in the center of things. The idea was exciting and the way it was outlined made sense. It shouldn't be a problem for the quarterback to be only five yards deep from the center.

The shotgun was something that gave us a little extra edge over teams that weren't expecting it. Besides, we were coming off a rough year, and the experiment couldn't hurt much. And it certainly *was* an experiment although the theory behind the formation is solid.

Long yardage, third-down situations had become such a problem. Teams were mixing up their defenses so much that our coaches felt, ''Why not give *them* something to worry about?'' I felt comfortable in the spread, as if I had more freedom. I think it's somewhat of an advantage for the quarterback but not an overwhelming one. We did get receivers up close to the line of scrimmage and into the secondary quicker. The defense knew we were going to throw anyway, so why shouldn't I take advantage of being back there looking around instead of getting under the center and then dropping back to the same spot?

On the basis of our success with the shotgun, fans probably wonder why other NFL teams haven't used the formation. I think you're going to see it elsewhere in the league pretty soon because I know of at least two clubs that were strongly considering the shotgun in the 1980 preseason.

I read where Buffalo was working on it and I got a call in the spring from two Minnesota assistants, Jerry Burns and Les Steckel, who were making inquiries.

No technical information changed hands; they know what our plays are from watching film. There's no secret why we think the formation gives us an advantage. I, Tom, everybody involved at one time or another has explained it in the newspapers. What the Vikings' coaches asked me were things like, "Did you feel comfortable with it? . . . Do you think it helped you personally?"

Going to the shotgun is such an obvious alternative; yet coaches in general have too much pride to make drastic changes. I think it's taken them time to realize that my maneuverability as a quarterback wasn't the only reason the formation worked in Dallas. I had to feel comfortable with it or Landry wouldn't have used it. If I hadn't liked the idea then he would have gotten rid of either me or the formation. When Tom uses the shotgun with Danny White, other teams will realize it has advantages for *any* quarterback, not just a scrambler.

I've read that Tom thought 1975 was my greatest season. I never tried to rate them, but it did rank among the best because it was a season when more was expected of me. It wasn't a great year statistically [56.9 completion percentage, 17 TDs, 16 interceptions], but I played well in key games. None was more important than the season opener and NFC Championship, both against the Los Angeles Rams.

We'd also begun exhibition play against the Rams, and they creamed us 35–7. Coming to Texas Stadium to open regular season, they thought they had it made. We played a super game, beating them 18–7, and that gave us confidence for the rest of the year. Once we beat Los Angeles we knew we could beat anyone in our division.

But to get into the Super Bowl we'd have to do it again in the NFC Championship.

That was close to the best playoff [16 of 26, 220 yards, four TDs, one interception] I ever put together and the only time in my career I threw four touchdown passes in a single game. There was a reason for it, too. The Rams were using three different defenses on third down, but they'd wait until we began to shuttle the next play before substituting. By watching their substitutions I could tell what defense they were going to play.

This was happening on almost every third-down situation. I'd get a play and, based on the Rams' substitutions, change it in the huddle. There were also times when the messenger came in without a play. He was just running a dummy route, so to speak. I'd call the play in the huddle or after we were lined up. Preston Pearson caught three touchdown passes, a club record for playoffs, to complete his first year with us as the season-long key on offense.

The success of '75 was as joyful as any I experienced but was followed by a personal downer. Our record was better, 11–3 as compared to 10–4, and we won the NFC East in '76. But below the surface we were in trouble because of an injury to the little finger of my passing hand.

I was going great statistically until the seventh game against Chicago. Early in the second quarter I ran four yards for a touchdown, but just as I reached the end zone Virgil Livers hit me. His helmet struck my right hand which was carrying the ball. I played the rest of the second quarter, but the hand began to hurt. At halftime I mentioned something was wrong with my fingers. X rays were taken and revealed a fracture in the bone where the finger joins the hand.

The only reason I got hurt was that my little finger is such a mess. It's crooked, calcified permanently out of shape from being dislocated so many times. When I make a fist with my right hand the little finger protrudes at an angle. That's why, when Livers's headgear hit my hand, the finger was sticking out and caught the brunt of the blow.

Maybe I'd have gotten by with the injury, but against Washington the next week somebody stepped on the fracture. I couldn't pass effectively the rest of the year.

As I mentioned before I was so frustrated by a first-round playoff loss to the Rams, I went to Landry to suggest a trade. I felt personally responsible for the team getting beat 14–12. And all because of that little finger of mine.

On other occasions I've had great fun when someone noticed its zig-zag shape. Everyone always stares in disbelief and asks what happened. I've used a variety of explanations. Once I told a lady on an airplane I was a professional boxer. Another time I said it was because I'd caught shrapnel in my finger charging a machine-gun nest in Vietnam.

The truth is my problem with that finger began in the Naval Academy. I dislocated it there for the first time. A splint should have been applied to such an injury, but that was my freshman year and I was hyped up about playing so I asked to continue. I got a shot of novocaine to deaden the pain and kept going. The dislocations started then and many more followed. They became so routine that either a trainer or I would just yank the finger back into place.

Then came a game in the Astrodome in which I jammed the finger against the turf and suffered what was to be a significant dislocation. I pulled it back into place and took a shot of cortisone in hopes of healing the damage. Only this time the finger locked. It wouldn't snap back into its original form. Calcium gradually collected around the middle joint to freeze the finger into what amounted to a permanent dislocation. The best way I can describe what it looks like is this: the index, middle and ring fingers of my right hand are going north and south; my little finger is headed almost east and west.

The team as a whole was headed toward a great season in '77. The fruits of that marvelous draft in '75 were still paying off, and we were far advanced with the shotgun formation by then. Something else began to pay dividends at this point—strength coach Bob Ward's offseason conditioning program.

Ward came to the Cowboys in the spring of '75 to expand a program begun by the late Alvin Roy. I don't think it was entirely a coincidence that the glory years began at the same time. Ward's system, a combination of running, aerobics and weight-lifting, accomplished three objectives for us. It helped players avoid injuries, reduced their recuperative time after they were hurt and gave everyone confidence our conditioning was superior to the opposition when the season began.

Increased confidence is a definite mental advantage. You know you've worked hard. You know you're physically fit, and what emerges from those thoughts is the belief you can accomplish more. I think Bob's program helped us during the fourth quarter of tough, tight games, because I believe the old theory that fatigue makes cowards of us all. If you're not as tired as the other guy in the fourth quarter you'll play better. Our success in the last period through the last five years has been a tribute to Ward's conditioning process.

What the Cowboys needed in '77 was a catalyst for our running game. The few injuries we experienced had been concentrated in the backfield. Preston hurt his knee in training camp and Robert Newhouse, our starting fullback, tore muscles in his stomach the year before. The '77 draft was the answer to our prayers because that's when Tony Dorsett came to Dallas. Of all the developments over the last three years his addition has had the most positive impact.

I know people have been down on Dorsett at times, but look what he's done over the last three seasons: fantastically, more than 1,000 yards rushing every season. I think Tony could get more out of his abilities simply because they are so enormous, but I have no complaints about him. I think he's tremendous.

He has come on as a pass receiver. He's improved in that area. If I have a criticism it's that Tony doesn't seem to realize what unbelievable potential he has as a receiver. His hands are good and with that speed he is dynamite in an open field. But it was as a runner that Tony gave us that spark we needed in '77. Now we had a complete team, in my opinion the best Dallas team during my career.

Because of a series of incidents during the following years—breaking curfew, oversleeping a Saturday practice, a barroom fight—questions have arisen about Tony's personality. All I can say is I liked him. He came out of college a Heisman Trophy winner, an instant millionaire, and was king of the hill. Give a young guy that much and sometimes it ruins him. Tony has been irresponsible in the past, but he is a caring guy. He does a lot of good things people don't see or read about. All things considered, he's probably handled his situation pretty well. Perhaps not perfectly, but better than a lot of guys.

Tony has the usual people trying to take advantage of him, some hangers-on who are more hindrance than help. I see him as a nice person who is particularly fond of and good with children. He's smart and likeable, and he never caused any internal problems that I knew about.

Coming in with all that fanfare in '77 he adjusted

well. He didn't cause any ripples except when Landry fined him for being late to meetings and practices and missing curfew in training camp. I think that was just immaturity on Tony's part, and that he'll grow out of it. Nobody on the team felt any animosity toward him.

Dorsett's best years are still to come, in my view. His potential is unlimited because on any play he's capable of going all the way. Last season it didn't happen, but that wasn't all Tony's fault. We had a lot of injuries at fullback again, and a tailback's No. 1 blocker is the fullback. The Cowboys moved young Ron Springs to fullback, which could be the key to the whole offensive picture. If Springs comes through, or Newhouse stays healthy and takes over, then you're going to see Dorsett break his club record for rushing by a bunch.

Just one more thought about Tony. I was grateful the Cowboys drafted him. He made me a better quarterback the last three years I played.

The same is true for Preston Pearson. Here was a guy who came to us from Pittsburgh without a reputation as a receiver. He turned out to be fantastic at catching the ball and was one of the best third-down targets I ever had. Preston's biggest assets are his moves and his knowledge of defenses. His hands are good, but it's the moves which get him open.

By 1978 when Tony Hill emerged as a top-flight threat, I thought we had the best receivers in football, and still do: Hill, Preston, Drew Pearson, Butch Johnson, Billy Joe DuPree and Jay Saldi. I was on a consistent streak and all those ingredients gave us a powerful offense. Our defense was just as outstanding and so were the results—a 15–2 record through regular season and a win in Super Bowl XII against Denver.

So why, with all these weapons, were we 6–4 late in

the '78 schedule? I think it was the Super Bowl syndrome, just not giving it everything you've got. We were inconsistent, tentative, as if waiting for the other guy to do something to get us out of the slump. One week the offense had trouble. Next week it was defense. But the biggest problem was turnovers.

I was throwing more interceptions than I had in years. Dorsett was fumbling too much. Our defense wasn't forcing any turnovers. What turned the season around was rediscovering our old aggressive style of play. All of a sudden we flip-flopped. Offensive errors went down. I probably threw only one or two interceptions the rest of the season. If there was a stray football anywhere our defense was jumping on it. Off we went to win eight straight before losing to Pittsburgh in Super Bowl XIII.

We expected to field the same team in '79 but older, wiser, better. Everything was in place for another Super Bowl run, but it soon began falling apart. Defensive end Ed (Too Tall) Jones stunned everyone by retiring to become a heavyweight boxer. Strong safety Charlie Waters, our defensive quarterback, tore up his knee in a preseason game. Over at strongside linebacker Thomas Henderson's head had welled out of shape.

All of a sudden the left side of our defense was in trouble. I'll tell you why that hurts so much. Most offensive teams are right-handed. That is, the tight end lines up on the right which gives that side one more blocker. That's the direction offenses run a greater percentage of the time. To counter it the defense puts its strong safety to that side and stations the strongside linebacker over the tight end.

Instead of playing left end Too Tall was beating up on those 5–8, 260-pounders in the ring. Waters was gone, and although Randy Hughes replaced him brilliantly in a physical sense, no one could take up Charlie's leadership role. Then there was Henderson waving to people on TV and a problem at left tackle when Larry Cole, who's a natural at that position, was forced into a switch to end where he's less effective. As hard as the club tried—we even gave up our first two draft choices in 1980 at midseason to get defensive end John Dutton from Baltimore—the Cowboys were vulnerable on the left side of our defense.

We had no internal problems except for the Henderson situation which sort of pulled the rest of the team together. We worked hard and tried. We played as tough as we could. Even Landry didn't have any major complaints about the team's attitude. The fact is we just weren't any better than our 11–5 record and we had to win four games in the last two minutes to get that.

Offensively, we had a pretty good season. Drew and Tony Hill each went over 1,000 yards in receiving. Dorsett ran hard once he got over a fractured toe which wiped out his preseason. The problem was at fullback where Newhouse and Laidlaw were hurt.

Of all the people who were injured or retired or weren't playing well, Waters's absence was the most damaging because it affected so many other players. Hughes didn't get the credit he deserved because Charlie's shadow overhung the position all year. But it went deeper than that.

Charlie directed the defense. He was the one who told Henderson where to go and what to do. He was the stabilizer. I don't imagine anyone missed Charlie more than Cliff Harris at free safety. Cliff and Charlie not only were close personally but over the years had developed an almost psychic understanding of how they would react to any situation. They didn't have to say anything, call a signal or even point. They simply moved in concert with the instincts of guys who knew each other inside-out as athletes. It was beautiful to watch.

Somewhat surprisingly this was Cliff's last season. In '79 he announced a retirement at age 31 and for him the finish was bittersweet. He took a lot of criticism all year long and yet was named to the Pro Bowl.

Looking back through all the years I played and at all the weak safeties I ever saw, Cliff was the best. He was in on *all* the plays. He made tackles. He defended passes. He caused fumbles and, with his reckless style, intimidated receivers into dropping passes. Cliff was a dynamo. When you look at other weak safeties you see they have their strengths here and there. But most of them aren't tacklers. Cliff was like a linebacker for us.

What happened last season was that other people weren't making their plays, and Cliff faced more last-man tackling situations than ever. He missed some, which could happen to anybody, but they came at the wrong time and he was maligned for it.

But it was losing Charlie which I think hurt Cliff more than anything. The responsibility of directing the secondary fell to Cliff and he's not the type for it. He'd rather just go out there, play at 100 percent and call it a day. With Charlie gone he was expected to tell other players what to do, and he didn't like that role. Believe me, Cliff Harris can still play, and he's still the best weak safety I ever saw.

Nor do receivers come any better than Drew Pearson. Drew is a winner. He has instincts and intangibles that don't show up on anyone's computer. When Drew came to Dallas as a free agent in the spring of 1973 I said to myself, "Hey, we've got something here." He had a feel for what he was doing. Even in those days Drew ran his routes precisely. His specialty, making the catch in heavy traffic, would come through later. Back then he was just out there running. His times weren't the fastest, but his speed was deceptive and he caught *everything*.

Drew got to start midway through the '73 season when Otto Stowe hurt his ankle. He's been starting ever since. I think if you look at Drew's career from that moment forward in the light of consistency and number of receptions, he's been the best receiver in the NFL. Lynn Swann and John Stallworth of Pittsburgh you can lump together. Like John Jefferson of San Diego, Stallworth hasn't played enough seasons to rank with Drew. Swann has been in and out. Game in and game out, year in and year out, Drew has been the best.

He will catch the ball in a crowd. He is tough. He will go for the ball anywhere on the field which is why he's made so many big plays. Drew has a great feel for adjustments on his routes. When he rolls into a hole 17–20 yards deep, he knows exactly who the people are in front of him and where the people are in back of him. That's why we hit that pass so many times. I had great confidence he would be in the right spot and knew he'd do everything possible to get to the ball. Drew was very special to me. There was good chemistry between us. I always felt if I threw the ball out there he'd make the play, which is the highest compliment a quarterback can pay a receiver.

The guy who helped Drew in recent seasons is Tony Hill. Tony relieved some of the defensive pressure and is on his way to becoming one of the great NFL receivers. Tony is a big-play athlete, the kind who can turn a mediocre pass play into a touchdown. He's faster than Drew, runs with long, lanky strides and goes for the ball well.

You can't load up on either one of them. One other thing about Tony. He's open *all* the time, on every play. At least that's what he always told me in the huddle.

I was blessed to have tremendous receivers during my career. Golden Richards was another good one. Butch Johnson, who could start for almost any other team in the league, always made the most of his playing opportunities. He caught touchdown passes in two Super Bowls, once with a broken thumb, and scored the winning touchdown in a playoff-clinching victory over Philadelphia last season. There have been others, such as Billy Joe DuPree, as dependable a tight end as ever played. My first professional touchdown pass covered 75 yards and went to Lance Rentzel, and my last in regular season went to Hill. I finished my playing days in debt to them all.

The way I see it the glory years for the Cowboys haven't ended. I think Dallas will be stronger in 1980 than we were the season before. The areas which needed to be shored up were on defense, and I saw at least three major developments in preseason that were encouraging. First, Too Tall gave up boxing and came back to play left end, which meant John Dutton might wind up playing left tackle. Second, Waters returned in excellent shape at strong safety, and that freed Hughes to replace Harris at the weakside spot. Third, Tom was going to concentrate his coaching talent on defense, and wherever he focuses his attention, performance gets better almost automatically.

When Tom decided to work with the defense he surrendered play-calling duty to Danny Reeves, the offensive coordinator, at least through preseason. If the system was successful, I assume it would continue during regular season. Landry and Reeves will call similar plays, I believe. I don't look for a big change if Danny calls them all year.

Dan is Landry-trained and a great offensive mind. Whatever the final decision is, the door has been opened for Reeves to share the play-calling or someday call plays himself.

I think in one respect the play-calling situation will improve if Reeves handles it because he'll work with quarterbacks all week. Because of his other responsibilities, Landry couldn't maintain such close contact with us. Therefore, with Reeves communications should be better between the play-caller and quarterback.

As for my being gone I don't think they'll miss a beat with Danny White. He is a winner and so is backup Glenn Carano. Look at their playing history. Everywhere they've been, their teams have won. What the Cowboys will have to do is develop confidence in Danny's ability to pull them out of a tight spot. That may be the only place they'll miss me because we did build a reputation for last-minute comebacks. In time, which is the only way it happens, the Cowboys will feel this way about Danny because he can do it.

White is very mature and, I believe, will reach a high performance level very soon, not only because of his great ability but through application of an excellent football mind. Danny's future is unlimited. I think he will go on to establish himself as one of the NFL's superior quarterbacks.

So where does that leave Glenn? He, too, has great talent. Either Glenn will seize upon a break if something should happen to Danny or he will challenge White on merit. If Glenn is frustrated both ways for too many more years, he'll ask to move on. Any player with pride, ego and self-confidence would have to do the same because he must know for himself whether he is No. 1 material.

I empathized with Danny during the years he played

behind me. I never forgot the hollowness of being No. 2 to Craig. Now Carano feels as I did and as Danny did before him. That's the nature of the sport to every player. He's either competing to earn a job or to protect one. While the strain on individuals never eases, sometimes the burden of expectation is removed in a collective sense. For instance, there was less pressure than usual on the Cowboys in 1980, similar to '75 when people said if we won our division it would be a great season. With the exception of '75, it was always Super Bowl or bust for Dallas all the years I was active. Although this may not be one of the great Dallas teams of the '80s, I still think the Cowboys and Los Angeles will be the cream of the National Conference.

Perhaps we were fortunate to accomplish what we did in '79. But I don't see anybody who's stronger than the Cowboys in the NFC East in 1980. Sure, other teams are getting better. Philadelphia is coming into its own. Yet when I look at Philadelphia man-for-man against Dallas, I am still going to bet on the Cowboys.

XI

A Game Apart...
Cowboys 35,
Redskins 34

"I went through that film trying to find out what we did wrong so it wouldn't happen again. My final conclusion was that Roger pulled off two or three plays that made the difference with sheer athletic ability." —Jack Pardee, Washington Redskins coach

Prior to December 16, 1979, I had played football for 30 years, from age seven to 37, and felt I'd already competed in the most thrilling game of my career somewhere along the way.

As an adolescent I thought nothing could top the excitement of helping win a city co-championship for Purcell High School. In my early 20s Navy versus Army represented the ultimate. As a mature adult in my 30s I was convinced no game could stimulate like an NFL playoff or Super Bowl.

But on that chilly December afternoon in Texas Stadium I played in a game like no other. In the tradition of the Dallas–Washington series it was expected to be a great game but in my opinion it wasn't. It was better than that, absolutely the most thrilling 60 minutes I ever spent on a football field.

There is one thing to keep in mind about *any* Cowboys-Redskins game. To the players the least it can be is special. Our rivalry is long and unfriendly, spiced with personal feuds that at times have included coaching staffs and even management. For the last 10 years the twice-annual series usually determined the division championship or lesser playoff spots. Hostile feelings naturally escalate under those conditions.

Such was the case as we prepared to meet the Redskins in the last game of regular season. Not only was the NFC East title at stake but the customary feud had flamed. During an earlier game at RFK Stadium the Redskins had stopped the clock with nine seconds left to play in order to kick a field goal. Leading 31–20 they wanted to beat us 34–20 and what was worse, they did. Ever since then we'd been thirsting to get even for what we considered flagrant insult.

The playoff situation for both teams was very odd. Each had a 10–5 record but through a tie-breaker quirk ours was better than theirs. We were assured of no worse than a wild card spot on the basis of a better record than Washington's against National Conference teams. But we didn't want it. That would mean returning to icy Veterans Stadium in Philadelphia where we'd won a tough 24–17 game the previous week. The obvious preference was to beat Washington, win the division outright and accept the benefits—a first-round bye while wild card teams played and the home field site for our first playoff game the following weekend.

Washington was in an unusual position. The Redskins didn't have anything cinched unless they beat us, but it also looked possible for them to lose and still make the playoffs. That would be determined by the point-differential tie-breaker between Washington and Chicago. If an NFC wild card berth was to be decided this way the Redskins were in good shape. They had a 33-point lead over the Bears who were playing St. Louis at home in a game that started earlier than ours. Midway through the third quarter at Texas Stadium, the Chicago–St. Louis final would be in and Washington would know whether the point-differential was a playoff factor. It was with this eventuality in mind that Redskins coach Jack Pardee had sent in Mark Moseley to kick that last-second, 45-yard field goal in the first game. I remember standing on the sidelines watching the clock tick down and then hearing the Redskins hollering, "Time out!" I looked across the field and saw that one of the main guys running up and down was my old nemesis Diron Talbert. I couldn't believe what they were doing. I didn't understand why they were doing it, and it made me furious.

We were getting beat 31–20. I'd thrown a couple of interceptions. One of them happened when we had a halfway chance to come back in the fourth quarter. I threw a pass to Drew Pearson over the middle, somebody hit him from behind to knock the ball loose and one of their linebackers dived to catch it. Then right before the half we'd been on their goal line and failed to score when they came with a strong safety blitz which forced me to fumble.

All those frustrations came out seeing them kick that field goal. I thought it was too much. I thought they were rubbing it in.

Looking back, kicking the field goal probably wasn't as bad a move as we thought because of the point-differential tie-breaker. Pardee defended his strategy as necessary padding in case a playoff spot might hinge on points. And by golly it did. But back in November that appeared such a long-shot possibility that I thought they wanted to kick the field goal just to rub our noses in it. Our locker room was filled with players talking about the field goal and how they literally had spit in our faces. That would have a big impact on us because it simmered in the back of everyone's mind for a month. Regardless of Washington's motivation for sending out Moseley, his kick dominated our thoughts toward the Redskins before the second game.

Landry didn't harp on that issue. He probably knew it wasn't necessary. We were now resurrected from the team which had lost three games—to Philadelphia, Washington and Houston—within the space of 10 days in November. We'd won two straight against the Eagles and New York Giants and played well, so our confidence was up.

There were some negative aspects, however. Tony Dorsett was hurt and not expected to play. Rookie Ron Springs started for Tony, who had suffered a shoulder bruise against the Eagles. Drew still limped with a sore knee he twisted under bizarre circumstances. He landed awkwardly while spiking one of his three touchdown catches in the Giants game. Drew tried to play, and made one big catch for 20 yards early but obviously was handicapped. Another starter had gone down on defense against the Eagles. Strong safety Randy Hughes was disabled by a shoulder separation and Dennis Thurman, a second-year pro, would make his first start in Randy's place.

Other than that we were a healthy, rejuvenated team at kickoff. Mentally, the Cowboys could not have been more ready to play. Moseley's field goal now was working *for* us psychologically. We were committed to play tough; determined to give maximum effort for 60 minutes no matter what happened. I think that attitude kept us from falling completely apart early in the game. As it was we gave a pretty good imitation of coming unraveled because Washington jumped to a 17–0 lead two minutes deep in the second quarter.

That score reminds me of why this also was the most unusual game I ever played. The scoring pattern was so strange, all of the points coming in consecutive spurts. Washington scored the first 17, Dallas the next 21, Washington the following 17 and Dallas the final 14. I was never involved in a game with so many dramatic scoring shifts.

Even *after* the clock showed 0:00 there was a question whether one more might occur. The Redskins reached our 40-yard line when the final gun sounded but argued they had called time out with one second left. If so, Moseley would get a chance to try a game-winning, 57-yard field goal. After a brief conference officials denied Washington's appeal. They determined that time had run out and the game officially ended as it had begun—in controversy over a field goal. Later I'll explain the ironic reason the Redskins weren't able to save at least one precious second on the clock.

The way the game began no one dreamed the difference might be the time it takes to blink your eye. In fact, at the outset we played offensively as if our eyes were closed.

Our first two possessions ended in fumbles the Redskins used to build a 10–0 lead. As bad as that was, only in retrospect do I see how it could have been fatal without a key defensive play.

Before Moseley kicked a 24-yard field goal courtesy of the first turnover, Washington was at our three-yard line on third down. Quarterback Joe Thiesmann faded to pass but was trapped for a four-yard loss. Had he hit a touchdown then our fourth quarter rally would have been futile. This play was forgotten amid the chaotic finish but it deserves attention. The guy who made the sack was defensive tackle Larry (Bubba) Cole. Early and late Bubba would save us, because with two minutes left to play he did it again.

Not until Washington led 17–0 did we get untracked. I don't suppose it would have made much difference had we known that no Dallas team had ever come back to win after trailing by 17 points. The fact emerged after the game when somebody reviewed 20 years of records. At this point Washington not only had our attention but had us by the throat. Finally, late in the second quarter we put together a 70-yard scoring drive that began the first of two major comebacks we would stage.

The early rally continued later in the period, almost too late since we beat the halftime gun by only nine seconds on my touchdown pass to Preston Pearson. It was this play which provided us with the biggest lift of the first half and, frankly, we had no business completing it. The situation itself was not what you'd call hopeful: third-and-20 from the Washington 26. Tactically we were playing a forced hand that called for a pass and probably a deep one at that. The Redskins correctly dropped into a defense we didn't want to see so the odds were in a double-stack against us.

The play was designed to get Preston man-on-man with a linebacker, and behind him. But safety Mark Murphy slid over either to take Preston himself or help out. Either way, it was the coverage we hoped they wouldn't play. Preston made a good move (as he always does) and I saw he had Murphy by a step so I let it go. In all honesty it was a perfect pass and equally perfect catch although the knowledge that their defense *should* stop the completion bothered me. But it didn't and we left the field behind only 17–14.

We were really upbeat at halftime in the locker room. We were back in the game now and playing well. Their lead had been cut from 17 points to 3. Further, we would receive the second-half kickoff, and all we talked about was taking it and getting some points.

Landry was calm as usual during halftime. Most of what he said was technical stuff about the defenses they were using. At the end of his talk he repeated one of his frequent themes: "It's how you play the third quarter that will decide who wins." Landry believes how you begin the third quarter determines the tempo of the second half. Our performance then will dictate whether we're in a position to win the game in the fourth period. I guess you'd have to say he was right because we won the third quarter 7–0. We came out and took it right to the Redskins on a 52-yard scoring drive which fullback Robert Newhouse ended with a two-yard plunge.

The game's momentum had turned completely. We'd run off 21 straight points to lead for the first time 21–17. A few minutes later it was evident the Redskins were in more trouble than anyone thought possible. The final score from Chicago flashed on the scoreboard: Bears 42, Cardinals 6.

That meant Washington's 33-point tie-breaker advantage over Chicago had vanished. If the Redskins didn't beat us and win the NFC East they were out of the playoffs entirely. This twist added more pressure to a game that really didn't need it.

By now we were getting great play from Preston, Ron Springs and Tony Hill in particular. Springs finished with 75 yards rushing and caught six passes for another 58. Tony went eight-for-113 receiving and Preston five-for-108.

This also would be my second-best passing day as a pro. [Staubach completed 24 of 42 for 336 yards, only three yards short of his 1976 club record against Baltimore. With three touchdown passes he finished the season at a club record total of 27 and won his fourth NFL passing championship.] I mention it for the purpose of saying one more thing about my passing. I darn near threw the game away early in the fourth quarter.

We were still ahead 21–20 when I tried to connect with tight end Jay Saldi on a medium-range pass over the middle. Instead, it hit Murphy right in the jersey numbers and he returned the interception 13 yards to our 25. Two plays later Washington scored to regain the lead 27–21.

I was throwing to a spot. There is no other way to describe the pass except to say it was a bad one. Jay didn't have much of a chance to get to it because he'd been bumped to the outside by one of their defensive backs. But I thought if he got around the cornerback and cut in front of Murphy he'd have a chance. Jay never reached the intended hole and Murphy was just standing there.

I threw on anticipation, a very poor play on my part. It was one of those things you simply can't believe you did. I came to the sidelines and told Landry, "I blew it." It was a huge mistake. No sooner had I let the ball go than I saw Murphy.

That turnover fired up Washington. Next time the Redskins got possession fullback John Riggins ran 66 yards for a TD right past our bench. He didn't say hello and to us it looked like goodbye to the game. With 6:54 left, Washington had us down 34–21.

With each passing minute our situation turned from gloomy to near lights out. With four minutes to go Washington not only still led by 13 points but had the ball. All we could do was pray for a break, a turnover, and then some big plays to take advantage of it. We weren't the people's choice to pull it off either, because fans began leaving Texas Stadium by the thousands.

Our break came when Clarence Harmon fumbled and defensive tackle Randy White was in position to recover on our 41-yard line. Randy admitted later there was more luck than skill involved in coming up with the ball. In fact, the ball came to him. "Actually I got blocked," he said. "I was on the ground and the ball fell out of his hands. I didn't have to move to get it."

Here was the key part of the game. The Redskins had been playing so well on defense. They'd made traps, forced errors. All they had to do was play *one* more series of good defense and they would win. Instead, we made the plays.

We hit a hook pattern to Butch Johnson for 14 yards, then Hill in the middle for 19. Springs got loose man-for-man on a linebacker and beat him deep for a 26-yard TD. We connected on three plays in a row—good throws, good protection and good routes. Even behind 34–28 we were like a new team with 2:20 remaining in the game.

Washington reached another crisis, this time offensively, at the two-minute warning. The Redskins had third-and-two from their 33-yard line. If they made a first down our chance of winning would slip from reasonable to remote. We'd have to spend our last two time outs stopping the clock. Then if we forced a punt our offense probably would face an 80-yard drive without being able to stop the clock except by an incompleted pass.

It's in these situations every team needs a Bubba Cole. It was our fortune to have him on this day. Theismann handed to Riggins who swung wide right, exactly the move he'd made on that earlier 66-yard scoring run. On 21 previous carries Riggins had gained a career-high 153 yards so the Redskins liked his chances of picking up two more.

But Cole knifed into the Redskins' backfield and tackled Riggins for a two-yard loss. Bubba explained the play later with typical deadpan: "Riggins showed some indecision, and I had more speed than I thought."

Washington punted and, thanks to Cole, we not only had a good chance to win but plenty of time to do it. The atmosphere in our huddle was, "We don't have to rush." We took possession on our 25 with 1:46 on the clock and those two vital time outs Cole had saved by stopping Riggins.

A poised, experienced, offensive team could not ask for more under the circumstances. Under these conditions the fans usually develop a hurry-up sweat whereas on the field there's a different outlook. For us what was left to play represented a virtual eternity of time. We just needed to avoid the psychological damage of making a mistake. If we made one it was all over.

I'll remember the first play of that series almost as long as the last because I sort of made it up. Instead of having Hill run an inside route where he'd caught so many passes I told him, "Act like you're going in and break to the outside.'' I thought Washington would be in a defense that would make it tough to cover that route. I was startled to discover they weren't. I threw a pass that somehow sailed between two defenders. How it did I'm still not sure because the ball wobbled all the way. It became a great pass only because it reached Hill who helped by making a great adjustment to be in the right place.

The fact was we free-lanced our way 20 yards upfield with that one. Then Preston worked free for completions of 22 and 25 yards to put us on Washington's eight-yard line. From there I threw an incompletion before Landry called for a change in formations. Up to this point I'd been passing from the shotgun but here Tom went with a play we timed better if I took a direct snap from center John Fitzgerald.

The play was the same we'd used on the goal line in the first game against Washington. It had ended in the disaster I mentioned earlier where I was blitzed, trapped and fumbled. This time it worked although not the way it was diagramed.

I knew the only way they could stop us was to foul up the play with another blitz. We'd used all our time outs so if I got trapped outside the 10-yard line we'd be in a must-rush situation. As matters stood we had 45 seconds to work with and four point blank shots at Washington's end zone—if we didn't make a critical mistake.

In the huddle I told Hill, ''Be alert, 'cause if they blitz I'm coming to you.'' I think if I hadn't mentioned that Tony wouldn't have been looking for the ball because tight end Billy Joe DuPree was the hot receiver. The Redskins did blitz and frankly I never looked for DuPree. Instead I lobbed a semi-Alley Oop pass toward the end zone corner where Hill had gotten behind cornerback Lemar Parrish.

Tony ran under it to make a touchdown catch with 39 seconds left. "It was a perfect play," Parrish said later. "Anything else I could have covered."

Even before Rafael Septien's extra point put us ahead 35–34 there was bedlam in the stands and on the field. What had happened was so unbelievable I ran around jumping into the air. According to a picture in the paper the next day I jumped into the arms of Springs. I don't remember doing that because of the excitement. I don't remember half the things I did that day.

We almost began celebrating too early. To their credit the Redskins didn't fold. They barged right back after the kickoff to threaten when one of our rookies, cornerback Aaron Mitchell, committed a senseless pass interference foul at midfield. There were five seconds on the clock when Washington snapped the ball for their final play, a nine-yard pass from Theismann to tight end Don Warren.

Warren caught the ball going down and it was at that point more inexperience in our secondary showed up. Somebody hit Warren immediately. What they should have done was let him alone for a second or two, long enough for the clock to run down without any question. Warren couldn't have scored or even gotten out of bounds. No one should have touched him.

Theismann argued that the referee's whistle had blown with one second to play. It's possible that actually happened. The referee has to be watching the quarterback for a time-out signal and also where the receiver went down to be sure the play is dead. By the time he's seen everything a couple of seconds will elapse. You just don't call time out and get the clock stopped immediately.

In fact, the reason Washington didn't have time left for Moseley to try a game-winning field goal was that it took officials at least five seconds to stop the clock on one of *our* time outs. It happened on the completion to Preston at Washington's eight-yard line, the catch which set up Hill's game-winner.

I saw the TV replay. It showed me calling for a time out—the announcers even mention it—and you can see the clock ticking down. At least five seconds drifted away before the officials got the clock stopped.

Do you realize what that means? If my time-out signal had been acknowledged as soon as I made it then Washington would have had time for Moseley to try a final field goal. Never mind that 57 yards sounds so far. Moseley is a sensational kicker, best in the NFL in my opinion. Sure it would have been an abnormal field goal considering the distance and pressure, but Moseley just might have kicked it. Because of all the things that already had happened in the game I wouldn't have bet against him.

After officials waved off Washingtons argument about the clock we were finally, officially, 35–34 winners. The Redskins seemed torn between being mad at us, the officials and St. Louis. "How can they call themselves professionals?" Redskins center Bob Kuziel stormed at the Cardinals. "Did they have a U-Haul backed up to their locker room or what?"

Theismann explained that the referee beside him had whistled the last play dead with one second left. "But the official at the line [of scrimmage] said the game was over. The game never should have boiled down to that play," he said. "We let it out of our hands. But the call on that last play was wrong."

I read where Terry Hermerling, one of their offensive tackles, believed Washington had been victim of a homer call. "We had one second on the clock! One second!" he shouted. "But do you expect them to be fair in their own stadium? Don't expect it when you come to Dallas. We should have had that chance."

Pardee was ashen, and who could blame him? His team had lost the game, the NFC East title and along with it their playoff spot to Chicago. The margin on the point-differential tie-breaker was a mere four points. Losing to us by one point, said Pardee, took the Redskins from "being division champs to the outhouse."

It had taken a double-rally to do the job. First we came back from being behind 17–0. In the last four minutes we'd rallied after trailing 34–21.

"We were out of it . . . then we were in it . . . out of it again . . . then back in," I told reporters afterwards. "I've never played in a game like this before. I can't remember when I've ever been so excited. This beats them all."

Cowboys exec Tex Schramm thought so, too. He'd seen every game the team played over 20 years and was asked to compare this one with the three best winning rallies from the past. Those were the Hail Mary playoff in 1975 against Minnesota; the '72 playoff in San Francisco where we scored 14 points in the final 2:02 to win 30–28; Clint Longley's spree that beat Washington 24–23 in '74.

"It's the greatest comeback ever," Schramm said. "It's greater than the '72 playoff because that all happened at the end of the game. We came back twice this time. We had a double chance to cave in."

Even Drew Pearson, who caught my 50-yard pass against the Vikings, agreed. "This puts Hail Mary in second place," he said.

I guess Fran O'Connor, a Washington assistant coach, put the game in perspective as well as anyone. "If a better football game has been played in the last 10 years I want to hear about it," he said.

Judging from a postseason poll taken by the NFL to determine the best games of the 1970s, O'Connor was right. Nine of the Top Ten spots were filled by playoff games and Super Bowls. Only one regular season game was included on the Best of the Decade list, which only confirmed what I already knew: On December 16, 1979, Dallas and Washington played a game apart.

XII
The Rest of My Life

"I can do all things through Christ which strengtheneth me."—Philippians 4:13

As long as I live I will miss playing football. I don't say that sadly because I always was aware that leaving the game was inevitable and someday my time would come. I don't say it to gain sympathy or to imply that I can't make the adjustment to becoming a full-time civilian. I'm not the type who lives in the past and must feed on what-used-to-be to maintain self-esteem.

I say it because that's the way it's going to be, and I believe the emotion is quite natural.

What I'll miss is the competition on Sunday. There is no greater ecstasy in athletics than the thrill of victory. Nor is there a substitute for those moments. You prepare all week for a game, play well and win, and afterwards there's a feeling you can lick the world.

The sharing of that sensation was special to me. With teammates it was in the locker room and during the flight back to Dallas when we replayed and relived the game. With Marianne it was when we drove home and she could see there was a glow about me. She felt good because I was happy, and usually we'd have a get-together of friends at our house. There were many of those moments and I got used to them. They were fun, a part of my life, but now they are gone. Nothing will ever replace them.

There will be other good times and get-togethers. There will be occasions when I may close a big real estate deal. Those will be happy, satisfying experiences, but they won't match the emotional high of victory on the football field. Those stand apart.

Winning in Dallas carried an extra dimension because each victory represented a step toward reaching the Super Bowl. Except in 1974, in all the years I played with the Cowboys reaching the Super Bowl was a reasonable goal. Probably most Dallas players take that for granted, never stopping to realize the uniqueness of such an opportunity season after season. It's awesome to know our ultimate objective was within reach *every* year. I won't have that chance anymore and I'll miss it.

There are aspects of football I am happy to leave behind. The idea of being treated a little special, of being the object of attention and publicity never appealed to me. It may be an ego stroke for someone else to be surrounded by people because of his athletic ability, but I was never comfortable with it. I won't miss being a public figure at all.

For that reason I almost didn't take the CBS-TV announcing job. I considered the negative factors: returning to the limelight, becoming a celebrity of sorts and the travel. The first proposal from CBS was for me to work the entire NFL schedule and also be involved in other network sports programs. I told them I had no interest in that but would like to do six or eight games. We reached a compromise of eight games, and Marianne agreed to go with me to all of them.

Having her with me was one reason I accepted. Another was to remain involved with football to help ease my withdrawal symptoms from the game. The challenge also intrigues me. I signed a one-year contract, and if I do well then television could always be something to fall back on in the future. I don't want them paying me if my work isn't good, though. At the outset I'm being paid a salary in line with the best of their other color analysts.

I've never had a desire to remain in football in any other capacity, such as coaching. I would enjoy coaching from the standpoint of being on the field with the athletes, but nothing else about the job appeals to me. Coaches have to watch film until it comes out their ears. There's also a lot of detail work behind the scenes that doesn't interest me. I have even less interest in college coaching because of the pressures of the recruiting situation, which I find distasteful and demeaning.

As for politics, I have no ambitions in that field either as of today. I hate to say never because it's not smart to slam doors and lock them. Who can say for sure? Two or three years from now, as a concerned citizen, this might be a possibility. But for now, absolutely not. One reason I retired from football was to spend time with my family. If you're in politics you are even more of a public figure and your family becomes secondary. That is exactly what I don't want at the moment.

Nor do I feel qualified to be a politician. I'm deeply

concerned about the direction this country is headed, and in certain areas I believe I'm qualified to speak out. Now that football is behind me I will. I can play an active political role at the grass-roots level, and I won't mind stumping for candidates I favor or letting people know where I stand on issues. But at this time I do not feel my background is sufficiently broad to be a candidate.

My immediate focus is on the commercial real estate business and the company I co-own with Robert Holloway. I've been fortunate to have a partner who kept the company growing and prospering while I was playing football. Robert's done a super job and I'm looking forward to future challenges with him on a full-time basis.

I like challenges, and the business world is full of them. Sales is a constant challenge. On the football field you're selling physical ability. In real estate you're selling a product through mental ability. In either case you have to prove yourself through competition, and I've always liked tests of skill.

Beyond business plans and charitable work that I will continue, my future does not include a dramatic change at this time. Most of all I want to relax, to exhale in a way, snuggle up to my kids, be as much of a full-time husband to Marianne as I can and enjoy the comforts of a lifestyle that isn't dominated by football six to eight months each year.

I reflect on my life and athletic career with few regrets.

There was a big to-do in the media when I retired about my never having been named All-Pro. That was something that never bothered me in any way, shape or form. In fact, I'm not sure what it would mean to be All-Pro because I've received almost every award possible from Most Valuable Player to the Bert Bell Award to

Quarterback of the Year from magazines. I've had more awards than I deserve.

Apparently the All-Pro team everyone referred to was the one selected by pro football writers. It's true I never was selected to that team but in a way it's understandable. I had a lot of consistent but not what you'd call spectacular seasons. In 1971, the first year we won the Super Bowl, Bob Griese had a phenomenal season. I thought I played well last year but Dan Fouts of San Diego was sensational. It just seemed when I had an outstanding season another quarterback hit a higher peak.

I'm honest enough to admit that it would have bothered me to have played eleven years and not been recognized in some way. But the All-Pro thing never upset me in the slightest. I am embarrassed by being recognized too much anyway.

Am I proud of *any* personal accomplishments? Yes, two in particular. The first was, I hope, in maintaining a visible balance in my life: proving it's possible to be successful in athletics without being the stereotyped athlete. It's been important to me to compete in a tough, physical game—a game surrounded by flattery and publicity which can change a person—and emerge as an everyday guy. I think I've been able to participate in this arena without being altered from the person I was at the beginning.

Second, I did produce on a consistent basis. If you review my entire athletic career you'll see a consistent pattern to the way I played and went after my objectives. There were downers and extremely high points, but the overall medium has been above average. To me that is the criterion for judging any athlete—how long and how well he performed at a winning level.

I've been fortunate, too. I entered the Naval Academy during a period when there were great athletes on our teams. I was surrounded by excellent talent in Dallas as well. So whatever I did it wasn't alone.

The regrets I have are personal and deep. My parents were not able to follow my athletic career to its conclusion or even to see all their grandchildren. I'm not one to dwell on the past except when the memories concern them.

Going to my games was a big part of their lives, from Pee Wee leagues through all the Army-Navy games. But I was never able to share a successful NFL season with my father. By the time I joined the Cowboys his health was deteriorating. He died in the spring prior to my second year in Dallas. Of his grandchildren he only got to know our firstborn, Jennifer, who was a baby when I was in Vietnam. He had a fantastic time playing with her which was characteristic of my father.

He liked people. He made people first in his life. Dad may not have been overly ambitious but he was a good man. He was the type you could say you were proud to know. I was proud to be his son and saw things in him that have had a lifelong influence on me.

People liked and respected my father for the person he was and no other reason. That's a supreme compliment for anyone. They weren't drawn to him because he had money. He didn't. They didn't like him because he had power. He had none. Those relationships are hard to find nowadays. Too often people like each other because there is money, power or influence involved. But not with my father. He was loved because he was good.

My mother was very, very special, a strong Christian woman who lived her faith. I like to remember her as she appeared in January, 1972, during a luncheon in New Orleans when I received the MVP award for Super Bowl VI. She was more than 60 years old on that day and looked much younger and so happy. Most of all she looked healthy which, tragically, was not the case.

We first noticed something was wrong when mother visited us that summer. Marianne was worried because she wasn't eating properly. It was obvious to everyone she wasn't feeling well. She went home to Cincinnati and was examined by several doctors who believed she probably had gall bladder problems. Exploratory surgery, however, revealed the worst: terminal cancer.

At first, mother wasn't told of the severity of her condition. We talked her into coming to Dallas simply to recuperate from the operation in our home. She arrived about the same time I left for training camp and not long afterwards was examined by Dr. Dale Rank, a surgeon friend of mine. He recommended she be told the true state of the disease.

I flew back to Dallas to be with her but arrived after she had entered Dr. Rank's office. She didn't know I was there. Therefore, it was a double shock for mother as she left Dr. Rank. She knew she was dying. She knew I knew because I was there. We both broke down crying and hugged each other.

I said my mother was special and from that moment on she was even more so. With the courage that would mark her final days she dried her tears before we had driven home and acted as if nothing were wrong. Cancer would waste her body but it never conquered her spirit.

During this grief-stricken period I was reminded of how my life was blessed by the presence of two remarkable women. One was my mother who typically worried that her illness might be upsetting to others. As she told Honey Rank, wife of Dr. Rank who became so close to her: "Oh, Honey, can you see the agony on Roger's face? I hate this so much. It's hard to watch someone you love suffer. You'd so much rather have the suffering yourself.''

The other woman is Marianne, whose love, patience and understanding stabilized everyone. Marianne's background as a registered nurse allowed us to care for mother in our home until she became critical. Marianne did everything—administered shots, turned mother in her bed when she was unable to move and saw to all her needs. Think of what it was like for her. She was mother to three children, wife to a husband and nurse to a terminally ill patient all at the same time.

Mother knew she had no hope of recovery but only occasionally said something that indicated an awareness that the end was near. Once she told Honey, ''The pain can really wear a person down.'' More often she spoke in terms of accepting what was happening to her. ''You know, I feel so peaceful,'' she said one day. ''God is very near.''

Faith sustained her during hours and days when pain must have been agonizing. So did her Irish sense of humor. Illness never subdued that, either.

''I'm not afraid of dying but I do hate to leave Roger, Marianne and the girls,'' she told Honey. ''If I only had three weeks left I'd want to enjoy it with them . . . and I'd much rather go from the bridge table than from this bed.''

By Thanksgiving it was obvious her remaining time was short. That thought overwhelmed me one day when I was visiting her in the hospital. The nearness of her death made me burst out crying in front of her. She motioned me toward her and that once strong, vibrant voice, now reduced to a husky whisper, said words I'll never forget.

''Please don't do that,'' she said. ''I'll be fine. Look at it this way. You'll always have a friend in heaven.''

I learned a lot about love from her. I don't believe there is enough love in the world today. Most of the love I see is not the giving kind of love. It's extended because someone expects something in return. I'm frequently distressed by the way people react to and use each other.

It seems to me we are prone to self-interest and self-congratulation. Too many people orient the world around themselves. They are the center and everything revolves around them. If they are happy, they think everyone else should feel the same way. What none of us does often enough is wear the other man's shoes, shoulder his burden for awhile.

As an athlete riding an emotional high after a game, I was frequently returned to the realities of the world by flipping on a TV news program. It was always depressing to see all the negative things going on while I was feeling so good. Quickly the game I'd played was brought into perspective. To the person starving to death, to the person struck by a car or involved in a shooting, football was of no consequence.

It was a big deal to me, though. Football was my profession, the means by which I supported my family. Therefore it *was* important to me because, within my set of values, if I believed this was worth my time, then it was worth my total dedication. But I also understood that to millions of people, and in the grand scheme of things, what I did bordered on the trivial.

Still, it's been an odd feeling to encounter people who say, "We're going to miss you," as if I were going somewhere. They equate me with a function—an NFL quarterback—instead of seeing me as the same person who is merely taking on a different function. I've seen athletes who never got past being football players, who never went into anything else. When they stopped being football players they became ex-football players. The function had taken over the person.

I was always aware of maintaining control over my function. Perhaps I flatter myself, but I don't believe I was dramatically altered as a human being by a successful NFL career. My values are the same. I still practice my Christian faith through the Catholic Church. I believe more than ever that Jesus Christ is the Son of God, that He died for our sins and rose from the dead to give us salvation.

There have been challenges on and off the football field, and my ability to handle them has been dependent upon keeping everything in perspective. Especially do I keep my life in perspective in relation to what my Christian faith means—the ability to have a temporal life as well as everlasting life.

Epilogue

I witnessed and reported every game Roger Staubach played in the National Football League and spent many hours in his home compiling material for this book. I think that background entitles me to express a personal opinion about him, as a man and an athlete. However, as I seek, not a eulogy for Roger, but a summing up of my perceptions, I am struck by words others have said before me.

It was his secretary, Roz Cole, who captured the essence of Roger the man when she observed, ''It's nice to say he's exactly the same as his image.'' I found that to be true. I expected it to be that way and it was.

Roger revealed perhaps 75 percent of himself in this book in terms of things he does for others. He would not allow publication of many charitable deeds. Some of them simply involved loaning money to former Dallas players now down on their luck. You would recognize all the names. By saying he loaned them money, I mean he gave it to them with scant prospect of being repaid and, most likely, no prospect at all. There were other involvements with people he preferred to withhold from public knowledge, and I mention this only for the purpose of noting that his story remains incomplete in an uplifting way.

Roz saw Roger through a different prism—she saw the businessman's side of his life—but his portrait is the same everywhere. For those who competed with him, those who opposed him, and for railbirds like myself, he is as Roz said.

Cliff Harris, the retired Cowboys' safety, once made the same point from a different angle. "The Cowboys have been conceived as 'America's Team,' " he said. "They were the clean-cut team. It's because of Roger. They developed *his* image because that's what he was—Captain America."

Roger always wrinkled his nose in distaste over the Captain America tag. Knowing this, I needled him one day when we were discussing book titles. With a straight face, I said, "Listen, here's one I really like. How about *Roger Staubach: Goodbye Captain America?*" His reply was to frown and say, "Geez, you gotta be kidding." Which proved, in case you ever wondered, that he actually does use words like *geez* and, upon sizing up the immense turnout for his retirement press conference, "Holy cow!"

It was Marianne who isolated the "why" behind Roger's athletic greatness. She did so by saying, "It took me a long time to realize that for him to survive he has to be competing most of the time." Competing in the final two minutes of football games was what her husand did best. In my view the number of games he won coming from behind in the fourth quarter (23), or in the final two minutes or overtime (14), will be the hallmark statistic of his career.

To me, Roger actually appeared transformed by a comeback crisis. He could play a quite ordinary game until those moments arrived. Then he became something else, almost somebody else compared to previous performance. It may not sound reasonable but I always had the impression he simply willed himself to succeed by refusing to lose.

You see that only in the great ones. They control. They dominate. They exude a vibrancy and reek with confidence. Roger was all that plus the most stubborn loser I ever saw at quarterback. I believe that because he resisted losing with such ferocity, because he fought it and wrestled it and never allowed himself to believe he *could* lose, he defeated defeat itself when it shouldn't have been possible. This was where he separated himself and made of himself something special.

Finally, it was Bob Ryan, editor and chief of NFL Films, Inc., who supplied the fitting goodbye. He did so at the conclusion of a career highlight film of Roger, the first NFL Films ever compiled on an individual player.

As the film ends Roger is seen in uniform running toward the camera. Closer and closer he comes until his helmeted face dissolves into an out-of-focus blur which remains frozen on the screen. The visual impact is enormous, as if we have seen the last of a rare athlete. Such was Ryan's purpose, for these are his accompanying voice-over words:

"For everyone touched by Roger Staubach, say a

fond farewell. For you and the game of football will be diminished by his absence.''

I couldn't say it any better and, in fact, won't try.

Frank Luksa
August, 1980

Appendix

NFL Quarterback Rankings

	Rank-Player	Yrs.	Att.	Comp.	Yds.	TD	Int.	Rating Points
1.	Roger Staubach	11	2958	1685	22,700	153	109	83.5
2.	Sonny Jurgensen	18	4262	2433	32,224	255	189	82.8
3.	Len Dawson	19	3741	2136	28,711	239	183	82.6
4.	Fran Tarkenton	18	6467	3686	47,003	342	266	80.5
5t.	Bert Jones	7	1592	890	11,435	78	56	80.3
5t.	Bart Starr	16	3149	1808	24,718	152	138	80.3
7.	Ken Stabler	10	2481	1486	19,078	150	143	79.9
8.	Ken Anderson	9	2785	1570	20,030	125	101	79.1
9.	John Unitas	18	5186	2830	40,239	290	253	78.2
10.	Otto Graham*	6	1565	872	13,499	88	94	78.1
11.	Frank Ryan	13	2133	1090	16,042	149	111	77.7
12.	Bob Griese	13	3329	1865	24,302	186	168	77.0
13.	N. Van Brocklin	12	2895	1553	23,611	173	178	75.3
14.	Sid Luckman	12	1744	904	14,686	137	132	75.0
15.	Don Meredith	9	2308	1170	17,199	135	111	74.7
16.	Roman Gabriel	16	4498	2366	29,444	201	149	74.5
17.	Y. A. Tittle	17	4395	2427	33,070	242	248	74.4
18.	Earl Morrall	21	2689	1379	20,809	161	148	74.2
19.	Greg Landry	12	2204	1227	15,383	95	96	73.6
20.	Daryle Lamonica	12	2601	1288	19,154	164	138	72.9

*Does not include Graham's records in the All-America Football Conference. If those figures are included, Graham becomes the all-time leader with a rating of 86.8.

Staubach's Records

COWBOYS RECORDS
Game
Most Passes Attempted: 49 vs. Philadelphia, Oct. 1975

Most Yards Lost Attempting to Pass: 63 vs. St. Louis, Sept. 21, 1969

Season
Most Passes Attempted: 461, 1979

Most Completions: 267, 1979

Most Yards Gained: 3,586, 1979

Most Touchdowns: 27, 1979

Best Percentage: 62.6, 1973

Best Average Gain per Attempt: 8.9, 1971

Career
Most Attempts: 2,958

Most Completions: 1,685

Most Yards: 22,700

Best Percentage: 57.0

Most Touchdowns: 153

Miscellaneous
Most Consecutive Passes Completed: 12, last 11 vs. Baltimore, Sept. 4, 1978 and first one vs. NY Giants, Sept. 10, 1978.

TEAM PLAYOFF RECORDS
Game
Most Pass Attempts: 37 vs. Los Angeles, Dec. 19, 1976

Most Pass Completions: 17 vs. Minnesota, Dec. 28, 1975; vs. Denver, Jan. 15, 1978; vs. Pittsburgh, Jan. 21, 1979

Most Yards Gained Passing: 246 vs. Minnesota, Dec. 28, 1975

Most Touchdown Passes: 4 vs. Los Angeles, Jan. 4, 1976

Most Passes Had Intercepted: 4 vs. Minnesota, Dec. 30, 1973

Most Yards Lost Attempting to Pass: 52 vs. Pittsburgh, Jan. 21, 1979

Most Quarterback Sacks: 7 vs. Los Angeles, Dec. 23, 1972; vs. Pittsburgh, Jan. 18, 1976.

Staubach's Comebacks

1971
Dallas 16, St. Louis 13—The Cowboys score ten fourth-quarter points, on a touchdown pass and a 26-yard field goal with 1:53 remaining to nip the Cardinals. Dallas trailed 10–6 after three quarters.

Dallas 28, Los Angeles 21—Winning TD came with 11:36 to play. After three quarters the game was tied 21–21.

1973
Dallas 20, Chicago 17—Field goal with 1:26 left to overcome 17–17 deadlock; Dallas led 17–10 after three quarters, but Bears scored fourth quarter TD to tie the game.

1974
Dallas 31, Philadelphia 24—Staubach one-yard run with 9:34 left; after three quarters game was tied at 24.

Dallas 17, St. Louis 14—Dallas scored ten fourth-quarter points. Winning 20-yard FG came with four seconds to play; St. Louis led 14–7 after three quarters.

1975
Dallas 37, St. Louis 31 (OT)—Touchdown pass 7:53 into overtime; St. Louis scored ten fourth-quarter points to tie game at 31–31. Dallas led after three quarters 28–21.

Dallas 13, NY Giants 7—Touchdown pass with 9:37 left; Cowboys trailed 7–6 after three quarters.

Dallas 20, Philadelphia 17—Ten points in final 64 seconds on a 21-yard pass play to Drew Pearson and then a Tony Fritsch FG with one second to play. Cowboys trailed 14–10 after three quarters.

1976

Dallas 30, Baltimore 27—Two field goals and touchdown pass in fourth quarter; final FG with three seconds to play; 17–17 after three quarters.

Dallas 9, New York Giants 3—Two fourth-quarter field goals, final coming with 7:34 to play; game tied 3–3 after three quarters.

1977

Dallas 16, Minnesota 10 (OT)—Staubach 4-yard run 6:14 into overtime.

Dallas 30, St. Louis 24—Two fourth-quarter TDs, winning TD coming with 6:53 to play; Cowboys trailed 24–16 after three quarters.

Dallas 16, Philadelphia 10—Ten fourth-quarter points on a blocked punt for a TD and a FG with 7:49 to play. Dallas trailed 7–6 after three quarters.

Dallas 14, Washington 7—Dorsett touchdown run with 10:08 to play; game tied at 7–7 after three quarters.

1978

Dallas 21, St. Louis 12—14 fourth-quarter points; final TD coming with 7:59 to play on pass from Newhouse. After three quarters, St. Louis led 12–7.

Dallas 24, St. Louis 21 (OT)—Field goal 3:28 into overtime.

Dallas 17, New England 10—TD pass with 12 minutes to play; Staubach

to Dupree. 10–10 going into fourth quarter.

1979

Dallas 22, St. Louis 21—Field goal with 1:16 left from 27 yards; Cowboys trailed 14–13 after three quarters.

Dallas 24, Chicago 20—Touchdown pass with 1:53 left to play. Cowboys trailed 20–17 midway through fourth quarter.

Dallas 16, NY Giants 14—Ten points in final 2:24 on a 32-yard TD pass to Drew Pearson and a 22-yard FG by Septien with three seconds to play; Cowboys trailed 7–6 after three quarters.

Dallas 35, Washington 34—Cowboys trailed 34–21 with 3:49 to play. Two touchdowns in final 2:20. A 59-yard, 3-play drive, capped by a 26-yard TD to Ron Springs and a 75-yard, 7-play drive, with an 8-yard strike to Tony Hill for winning TD with 39 seconds to play.

PLAYOFFS
Jan. 2, 1972

Dallas 30, San Francisco 28—17 fourth-quarter points on a FG and two Staubach TD passes; final 14 points coming in final 90 seconds of the game; Dallas trailed 28–13 after three quarters.

Dec. 28, 1973

Dallas 17, Minnesota 14—Touchdown pass, Staubach to Drew Pearson covering 50 yards with 24 seconds to play. Game tied 7–7 after three quarters.

ROGER THOMAS STAUBACH

Name pronounced STAH-bock.
Born February 5, 1942, at Cincinnati, O.
Height, 6.03. Weight 202.
High School—Cincinnati O., Purcell.

Attended New Mexico Military Institute and graduated from United States Naval Academy in 1965.
Heisman Trophy winner, 1963.
Named quarterback on The Sporting News College All-America Team, 1963.
Named The Sporting News College Player of the year, 1963.
Selected (as future choice) by Dallas in 10th round of 1964 NFL draft.
In military service, 1965 through 1968.
Named to The Sporting News NFC All-Star Team, 1971, 1976, 1977, and 1979.
Named by The Sporting News as NFC Player of the Year, 1971.
Led NFL in passing with 94.6 rating points in 1973 and with 84.9 rating points in 1978 and with 92.4 rating points in 1979.

| | | | | PASSING | | | | | RUSHING | | | | TOTAL | | |
Year Club	G.	Att.	Comp.	Pct.	Gain	T.P.	-PI.	Avg.	Att.	Yds.	Avg.	T.D.	T.D.	Pts.	F
1969—Dallas NFL	6	47	23	48.9	421	1	2	8.96	15	60	4.0	1	1	6	2
1970—Dallas NFL	8	82	44	53.7	542	2	8	6.61	27	221	8.2	0	0	0	4
1971—Dallas NFL	13	211	126	59.7	1882	15	4	8.92	41	343	8.4	2	2	12	6
1972—Dallas NFL	4	20	9	45.0	98	0	2	4.90	6	45	7.5	0	0	0	1
1973—Dallas NFL	14	286	179	62.6	2428	23	15	8.49	46	250	5.4	3	3	18	5
1974—Dallas NFL	14	360	190	52.8	2552	11	15	7.09	47	320	6.8	3	3	18	7
1975—Dallas NFL	13	348	198	56.9	2666	17	16	7.66	55	316	5.7	4	4	24	5
1976—Dallas NFL	14	369	208	56.4	2715	14	11	7.36	43	184	4.3	3	3	18	4
1977—Dallas NFL	14	361	210	58.2	2620	18	9	7.26	51	171	3.4	3	3	18	8
1978—Dallas NFL	15	413	231	55.9	3190	25	16	7.72	42	182	4.3	1	1	6	5
1979—Dallas NFL	16	461	267	57.9	3586	27	11	7.78	37	172	4.6	0	0	0	8
Pro Totals—11 Years	141	2958	1685	57.0	22,700	153	109	7.67	410	2264	5.5	20	20	120	55

Quarterback Rating Points: 1969 (69.3), 1970 (42.8), 1971 (104.8), 1972 (20.4), 1973 (94.6), 1975 (78.6), 1976 (79.9), 1977 (87.1), 1978 (84.9), 1979 (92.4), Total 83.5.

Additional pro statistics: Recovered one fumble, 1969 and 1970; recovered one fumble and fumbled six times for minus 10 yards, 1971; recovered one fumble, 1973; caught one pass for minus 13 yards, recovered two fumbles and fumbled seven times for minus four yards, 1974; recovered one fumble and fumbled five times for minus two yards, 1975; recovered one fumble, 1976; fumbled eight times for minus two yards and recovered three fumbles, 1977; recovered two fumbles and fumbled five times for minus five yards, 1978, recovered six fumbles 1979.

Played in NFC Championship Game following 1970 through 1973, 1975, 1977 and 1978 seasons.
Played in NFL Championship Game following 1971, 1975, 1977 and 1978 seasons.
Member of Dallas Cowboys for NFL Championship Game following 1979 season; did not play.
Played in Pro Bowl (NFL All-Star Game) following 1971, 1976, 1978 and 1979.
Named to play in Pro Bowl following 1977 season, replaced due to injury.

OUTSTANDING READING FROM WARNER BOOKS

HOW TO PROSPER DURING THE COMING BAD YEARS
by Howard J. Ruff (K96-952, $3.50)
Will you survive this round of inflation? You will if you listen to Ruff. Now he tells you what you must do to keep your money intact, be sure of making intelligent investments. "I recommend this book to everyone," said the *Dow Theory Letter.*

NEW PROFITS FROM THE MONETARY CRISIS
by Harry Browne (K36-021, $3.50)
In 1970, Harry Browne advised buying gold when it was $35 and silver when it was $1.65. Remember how right he was in "How You Can Profit From The Coming Devaluation"? The hold and sell market is over. The hard money boom is behind us. Now you need Harry Browne's advice on a strategy to make NEW PROFITS FROM THE MONETARY CRISIS.

THE CULTURE OF NARCISSISM
by Christopher Lasch (S93-264, $2.95)
Have we fallen in love with ourselves? Have we bargained away our future for self-gratification now? With an unsentimental eye, Christopher Lasch examines our society and our values and discovers that we are in thrall in a new enchantment—self-involvement. We live today in THE CULTURE OF NARCISSISM.

FIGHTING BACK
by Rocky Bleier & Terry O'Neil (S95-704, $2.75)
It's the remarkable true story of one man's triumphant return from battlefield injury in Vietnam to Superbowl victory. A story of hardship, dedication to a purpose and a dream fulfilled.

MONEYLOVE
by Jerry Gillies (J91-009, $2.50)
Want to get rich? Don't save your money—spend it! Your key to personal prosperity '70s style can be found in a revolutionary new system called MONEYLOVE. The book that shows you how to get the money you deserve for whatever you want!

FUN & GAMES FROM WARNER BOOKS

THE AMAZIN' BILL MAZER'S BASEBALL TRIVIA BOOK
by Bill Mazer and Stan Fischler   (S91-784, $2.50)
Bill Mazer is the sportscaster that nobody can beat. Now he makes
you an expert too. The record makers and breakers; blasts from baseball's past; game anecdotes and player stories you won't want to
miss; and little-known facts and figures. Bill Mazer has the facts and
gives them to you in amusing anecdotes, quickie quizzes, and question and answer stumpers.

HIGH & INSIDE
The Complete Guide to Baseball Slang
by Joseph McBride   (S91-939, $2.50)
This book answers the question "Why do they call it...?" for over
1000 baseball terms and nicknames. Loaded with definitions and
origins plus a dictionary of nicknames with the background of each.
And baseball one-liners that have been quoted often with their
courses and stories.

THE COMPLETE UNABRIDGED SUPER TRIVIA ENCYCLOPEDIA
by Fred L. Worth   (V96-905, $3.50)
Xavier Cugat's theme song? The bestseller of 1929? Miss Hungary of
1936? Here's more than 800 pages of pure entertainment for collec-
tors, gamblers, crossword puzzle addicts and those who want to
stroll down memory lane. It asks every question, answers it correctly,
solves every argument.

CELEBRITY TRIVIA
by Edward Lucaire   (V95-479, $2.75)
Crammed with gossip galore, this book was written with the name-
dropper in all of us in mind. It's loaded with public and private
memorabilia on actors, writers, rock stars, tyrants—and the scan-
dalous facts they probably wouldn't want you to know. From
Napoleon to Alice Cooper, anyone who has caught the public eye is
fair game.

HOLLYWOOD TRIVIA
by David P. Strauss & Fred L. Worth   (V95-492, $2.75)
Spotlighting the characters that made Hollywood happen, here are
thousands of film facts that will delight and surprise you. Who was
buried wearing vampire gear? Who stood on a box to appear taller
than his leading lady? Why couldn't Clark Gable secure the leading
role in *Little Caesar?* Almost 400 pages of fact and history.

BEST-SELLING BOOKS
ON BUSINESS AND FINANCE
FROM WARNER

HOW TO SELL ANYTHING TO ANYBODY
by Joe Girard with Stanley Brown   (K95-810, $2.75)
The World's Greatest Salesman tells: How he became a winner, the winning attitudes that put him on top after a 35-year losing streak, and how anyone can get anything he wants with the application of his honest, down-to-earth principles.

DRESS FOR SUCCESS
by John T. Molloy   (K93-706, $2.95)
DRESS FOR SUCCESS explains how what you wear affects the people who see you, what messages your clothes send about you, and how you can change your wardrobe to project a winning image. Illustrated with more than 70 drawings and diagrams.

WORKING SMART:
How to Accomplish More in Half the Time
by Michael LeBoeuf   (K33-147, $2.95)
Mr. LeBoeuf applies his knowledge as a professor of Management, Organizational Behavior and Communication to helping people understand how to: increase effective use of time and energy, set goals and priorities, and eliminate anxiety and anger by being able to cope with everyday activities.

GETTING ORGANIZED: Time and Paperwork
by Stephanie Winston   (J97-564, $2.50)
Extremely practical guidelines for simplifying and arranging one's time and demands made upon it. Ms. Winston provides checklists and charts to help teach anyone to use time to its maximum advantage and keep paperwork to a minimum.

OFFICE POLITICS: Seizing Power, Wielding Clout
by Marilyn Moats Kennedy   (K93-718, $2.95)
Ms. Kennedy leads a crash course in the mastery of office politics: how to get to the top and how to stay there, how to recruit friends "upstairs" and how to use them. She advocates office politics, not as dirty backstabbing, but the way to get things done.

BOOKS OF INSPIRATION FROM WARNER BOOKS

THE HOLY SPIRIT
by Billy Graham (P95-038, $2.75)
The world-famous evangelist answers many of your questions about the work of the Holy Spirit and shows how you can experience His reality and power in every day of your life. "In the midst of the world's dark hour this is an urgent appeal for twentieth-century Christians to be Spirit-filled, Spirit-led, and Spirit-empowered."—*The Alliance Witness*

HOW TO BE BORN AGAIN
by Billy Graham (P92-037, $2.25)
At last, the most famous evangelist of our time gives you the step-by-step primer for personal salvation and continuing growth. In simple, direct, and dynamic language, he shows you how to quickly release and realize the new power of God's will.

FAITH, HOPE & HILARITY
by Dick Van Dyke (P84-970, $1.75)
When the famous comedian taught Sunday School he found that his little pupils said the funniest and the most perceptive things he ever heard. Here are his best, plus the most hilarious ones sent to him from Sunday School teachers across America.

MS READ-a-thon—
a simple way to start youngsters reading

Boys and girls between 6 and 14 can join the MS READ-a-thon and help find a cure for Multiple Sclerosis by reading books. And they get two rewards — the enjoyment of reading, and the great feeling that comes from helping others.

Parents and educators: For complete information call your local MS chapter. Or mail the coupon below.

Kids can help, too!